LOCAL HISTORY
AND
GENEALOGY ABSTRACTS
FROM

FAIRMOUNT NEWS

FAIRMOUNT, INDIANA

1901–1905

Ralph D. Kirkpatrick

HERITAGE BOOKS
2012

HERITAGE BOOKS
AN IMPRINT OF HERITAGE BOOKS, INC.

Books, CDs, and more—Worldwide

For our listing of thousands of titles see our website at
www.HeritageBooks.com

Published 2012 by
HERITAGE BOOKS, INC.
Publishing Division
100 Railroad Ave. #104
Westminster, Maryland 21157

Copyright © 1998 Ralph D. Kirkpatrick

All rights reserved. No part of this book may be reproduced or transmitted in any form or by any means, electronic or mechanical, including photocopying, recording or by any information storage and retrieval system without written permission from the author, except for the inclusion of brief quotations in a review.

International Standard Book Numbers
Paperbound: 978-0-7884-0860-1
Clothbound: 978-0-7884-8994-5

FOREWORD

The town of Fairmount located on Back Creek in Fairmount Township, Grant County, Indiana was established and named by Quakers in the mid-nineteenth century. The town was named for the beautiful 'Fairmount Park' in the Quaker City of Philadelphia, Pennsylvania. The Civil War claimed the attention of the community and also claimed the lives of several who died in the northern army. Growth of the town and its population following the war was slow but quickened with the coming of the railroads. Natural gas discoveries and gas exploitation dominated the 1890's. Factories, particularly glass factories, were built to utilize the gas. The first years of the twentieth century saw further development of the institutions that gave added meaning to the lives of Grant County citizens. Churches and educational facilities, as well as industrial and commercial enterprises were all enhanced by technological advances that made possible the electric lights, telephones, and automobiles that now appear on the scene. The Spanish-American War and the War in the Philippines caused hardly a ripple in the community even though several local men served in the military during these conflicts.

Newspapers chronicled the births, marriages and deaths in the community. The movements of persons to the West or to other places were also noted. All existing Fairmount newspapers published 1901 through 1905 were gleaned for the following abstracts.

Ralph D. Kirkpatrick, Ph.D.
Osage Farm

Abbreviations and conventions used:
anniv - anniversary
att - attends or attended
b - born in or date of birth
bldg. - building
bur - buried at
ca - circa; about
Cem - Cemetery
Ch. - Church
Coll - College
Co. - County (county name not followed by a state name is an Indiana county)
CW - Civil War
d - died on
dec - deceased
dt - daughter of
f - former or formerly
FFA - Fairmount Friends Academy
Fmt. - Fairmount
GAR - Grand Army of the Republic, Civil War veterans organization
grad - graduate or graduate of
HS - High School
m - married
mbr - member of
M.E. - Methodist Episcopal Church
Mgr. - manager
MH - Meetinghouse; building used for religious services
mi. - mile or miles
M/M - Mr. and Mrs.
M.P. - Methodist Protestant Church
(Name) - maiden name of married woman or widow
'Name' - nickname
Name - name this person was known by or 'went by'
[Name or other data] - explanatory data not from Fairmount News
prop. - proprietor
RC - Roman Catholic

RR - railroad
s - son of
Sch - School
serv - served in
SS - Sunday School
tchr - teacher
Twp. - Township
U.B. - United Brethren Church
Univ - University
vet - veteran _or_ veteran of
WCTU - Women's Christian Temperance Union
wk. - week
W.M. - Wesleyan Methodist Church
yr. - year _or_ years

LOCAL HISTORY AND GENEALOGICAL ABSTRACTS FROM THE FAIRMOUNT NEWS 1901-1905

ABBOTT, S.B. - sold his barber shop for more than $500, gave the money to his wife for safe keeping; taking the money, she left him a note telling him she was gone for good; he thinks she may be in Illinois (3/18/01)

ABEL, Josephine - 1904-05 Fmt. HS tchr (9/2/04)

ADAMS, Edwin - s M/M John Adams of near Hackleman; FFA student; d 6 Jan 1904, bur Park Cem (1/8/04; 1/12/04)

ADDISON, Clysta 'Lesta' - is assaulted by Robert F. Kirkman (6/13/01); see Earl UNDERWOOD

ALBERTSON, __ - age 5 months; child of M/M James Albertson; d 24 May 1902 (5/27/02)

ALE, Mrs. Samuel C. - of Alexandria, VA; dt Mrs. Sarah Ink (10/20/03)

ALEXANDER, Elijah - serv Pvt., Co. I, 130th Ind. Inf. during CW (5/27/04; 5/26/05)

ALLEN, __ - infant of M/M Newton Allen; d recently (11/8/04)

ALLEN, Mary E. - Mary E. (Allen) SCOTT

ALLEN, Newt - paid $151 for tabernacle built for/used by Billy Sunday revival; will take down for lumber (4/8/02), beginning next wk.; lumber will be used to build 2 new houses in S part of Fmt. (5/2/02)

ALLRED, Miss Cora - of 2.5 mi. NE of Fmt.; d 29 Apr 1902, funeral to be in Back Creek Friends MH (4/29/02)

ALLRED, David E. - Fmt. painter and wallpaper hanger; d 22 Jan 1901, bur Park Cem (1/24/01)

ALLRED, Mrs. Ella - see Willis McCOY

ALLRED, George N. - elected Quartermaster, Beeson GAR Post 386 (1/24/02); serv Corp., Co. K, 130th Ind. Inf. during CW (5/27/04; 5/26/05)

ALLRED, Oscar - s Charles Allred (11/17/05)

ANDERSON, Miss Flossie - employee, Miller & Haas Store (1/6/02)

ANDERSON, Florence - see Glenn VanARSDALL

APPLE, Ray - age 19; s Frank Apple; employee, Fmt. Glass Works; 1 Oct 1904 killed in street car accident, bur Oaklandon (10/4/04)

ARK/ARC, __ - see Will STIBBS

ARMFIELD, William E. - employee, Fmt. Glass Works; 6 Jul 1904 m Almeda, dt M/M Eli Felton; will live in Fmt. (7/8/04)

ARMSTRONG, Vannessa - 23 Oct 1905 is given party for her 12th birthday (10/27/05)

ARMSTRONG, Mrs. William - age 26; d 4 Sep 1904, bur Glasgow, KY; colored (9/6/04)

ARNETT, Achsah T. - see Achsah T. McCOY

ARNETT, Annis - see James SCOTT

ARNETT, Daisy - of Hackleman is given party for her 15th birthday 20 Oct 1901 (10/24/01)

ARNETT, Iva - 1901 Fmt. Twp. Dist. # 6 Sch grad (5/30/01)

ARNETT, Lindley - m; age 71; serv CW; d 10 Sep 1903, bur Back Creek Friends Cem (9/15/03; 6/6/05)

ARNETT, Mrs. Phil - of Fmt.; dt Mrs. Winnie Brewer (9/12/05)

ARNETT, Thurza - see Thurza (Arnett) HOWELL

ARNOLD, Rev. __ - pastor, Jonesboro M.E. Ch. (2/12/04)

ASKRAN, __ - see Mrs. Schuyler SMITHSON

ASKRAN, John - age 75; d 1 Dec 1904, bur Summitville Cem (12/6/04)

ASPY, Rev. Lotus - f Fmt. Baptist Ch. pastor; now pastor, Gas City Baptist Ch. (2/9/04)

ATKINSON, Elsworth - of Fmt.; s Mrs. Hulda Jane Atkinson (12/26/05)

ATKINSON, Mrs. Hulda Jane - came to Fmt. ca 1890; age 71; d 21 Dec 1905, bur Mt. Pisgah Cem, Alexandria (12/26/05)

ATKINSON, Mrs. Lizzie - see Al SHIELDS

ATKINSON, William - of Back Creek Friends area; father recently d at Osgood (7/12/04)

AULT, __ - b 27 Dec 1903; dt M/M Emory Ault (12/29/03)

BACK CREEK - Fmt. sewers under Main St. then down Harrison St. will empty directly into the creek (5/27/01); new foot bridge is built over creek at 2nd St. (10/28/04); sewer is to be placed in bottom of creek bed from 300' N of 8th St. to where the Harrison St. storm sewer enters the channel (7/11/05); fall in creek bed is less than 1" per 100' so bed is not suitable for sanitary sewer (7/21/05)

BACK CREEK FRIENDS CEMETERY - Neal McMasters bur (8/1/01); William SCOTT bur (9/30/01; 10/3/01); Samuel H. Pierce bur (4/1/02); Nathan Little bur (7/22/02); Lindley Arnett bur (9/15/03; 6/6/05); Thomas Newby bur (12/11/03); John Brooks bur (3/15/04); child of Al. Underwood bur (3/22/04); Leota Wheeler bur (5/10/04); Will Davis bur (9/27/04); child of M/M John McCorkle bur (2/10/05); Malinda Kirk bur (3/17/05); Mrs. Laura Foust bur (4/25/05; 4/28/05); Samuel Felton bur (5/5/05); Joseph Whybrew, CW vet, bur here during CW (6/6/05); Effie Little bur (9/15/05; 9/19/05)

BACON, Mrs. Lizzie - of Gas City; recently dec (8/22/01)

BAKER, __ - see Mrs. Willard ELKINS

BAKER, E.L. - Hartford City druggist; 2 Jun 1901 m Frances Wilson, dt M/M John H. Wilson of Fmt.; lives in Hartford City (1/30/02); files bankruptcy due to expenses of his wife's illness (8/14/03)

BAKER, John S. - contracts to build new Fmt. HS bldg. (7/25/01); Supt. of Construction for C.I.&E. RR, completed Fowlerton depot (1/30/02); drew up plans for new Fmt. Odd Fellows Hall (7/25/02); a Director, Fmt. Fair Assoc. (1/12/04); contracts to build new brick Masonic Temple on N. Main St. (6/10/04)

BAKER, Mary (HIATT) - of Fmt.; dt Cuthbert and Clementina (Mendenhall) Hiatt (3/7/02); wife of John Baker; age 47; d 5 May 1905, bur Park Cem (5/9/05)

BALDWIN, Cyrus - 27 Oct 1904 m Elizabeth, dt Dr. Clotilde Pretlow; to live in Whittier, CA (11/4/04)

BALDWIN, David A. - Supt., Winslow Glass Factory, Matthews (8/7/03); m; his dt is Mary Baldwin; he is now working in new Winslow Glass Factory, Columbus, OH (9/19/05)

BALDWIN, Daniel - from NC to Fmt. area as an early settler (1/13/05)

BALDWIN, Elizabeth 'Lib'(COLEMAN) - b Belmont Co., OH 7 Apr 1825; dt Thomas and Mary (Bates) Coleman; had 10 brothers and sisters; 4 Apr 1846 m David Baldwin (dec 3 Feb 1898); lived near Roseburg, later near Fmt., but now in Fmt. since ca 1861; raised husband's nephew, Dr. Joseph W. Patterson; mbr Methodists; d 23 Aug 1901 (8/26/01)

BALDWIN, George F. - of W of Marion; age 55; d 2 Sep 1904, bur Marion IOOF Cem (9/6/04)

BALDWIN, Joseph - an early settler of Fmt. area (1/13/05); 1848, is first Fmt. merchant with his dry goods & grocery store on the NE corner of Washington St. & Main St. 1/20/05); his house, the 1st in Fmt., was built in 1849 for him by Joseph Peacock on the present site of the Borrey Blk. (6/20/05)

BALDWIN, Lank - of Marion; CW vet of 89th Ind. Inf. (10/10/05)

BALDWIN, Nettie - see Ed HOLLINGSWORTH

BALDWIN, Quincy - of Jonesboro; d last Sunday (7/1/02)

BALDWIN, Sarah (WILSON) - b Fmt. 12 Jun 1843; dt Nathan D. and Mary Wilson; 31 Oct 1863 m Cyrus Baldwin; mbr Friends; d 27 Oct 1903 at her home in Whittier, CA (11/3/03; 11/20/03)

BALDWIN, Thomas - 29 Oct 1833 bought NW 1/4 of Sec. 29, site of future Fmt. (1/13/05)

BALDWIN, Zoan - 10 Dec 1904 m Minnie B. Kelley; live in Fmt. (12/13/04)

BALLARD, __ - 1879 had dray in Fmt. (2/15/1879 as reprinted 1/29/04)

BALLARD, Frank - of Marion; age 40; s M/M Uriah Ballard, f of Fmt.; m; d 11 May 1905 (5/16/05)

BALLENGER, __ - infant of M/M John Ballenger of Fowlerton; d 15 Apr 1905 (4/18/05)

BALLENGER, Mrs. Alice - mbr Radley WCTU (7/29/02)

BALLENGER, Edna - dt Mrs. Alice Ballenger (7/29/02); 1903-04 tchr, Liberty Twp. Sch # 12 (9/11/03); of Anderson; becomes Bethel Sch tchr (3/3/05)

BALLINGER, John W. - of Upland; d 25 Feb 1901 (2/28/01)

BANNISTER, George - of Liberty Twp. 26 Aug 1903 m Lulu Wilson of Hackleman (9/22/03)

BARBER, Henry - serv Pvt., Co. D, 136th Ind. Inf. during CW (5/27/04; 5/26/05)

BARREN CREEK - mastodon is found near Lake Galatia (5/17/04), found in bed of the creek; is a mammoth instead of a mastodon (5/24/04), and was found on farm of Mrs. Dora Gift (6/17/04);

bones are sold to New York Museum of Natural History for $1,000 (8/5/04; 8/9/04); Gift farm tenants, Stephen R. and C.D. Smith, attempted to steal the bone sale proceeds; Mrs. Gift prevailed in court (1/17/05)

BARRY, Mrs. Eva - see William VINSON

BARTHOLOMEW, Mrs. Ann - b 3 Oct 1821 (8/12/04; 8/15/05)

BARTHOLOMEW, Ephraim - during CW was 1st Serg., Co. A, 19th Ind. Inf.; later was 1st Lieut., Co. I, 20th Ind. Inf. (5/26/05)

BARTHOLOMEW, William - age 78/79; came from Wales, UK ca 1854; m; d 13 Mar 1904, bur Park Cem (3/4/04; 3/15/04)

BARTLETT, Rev. M.V. - pastor, Fmt. U.B. Ch. (4/29/02; 1/15/04)

BASS, William - age ca 95; colored; serv army; d 31 Aug 1901, bur Weaver Cem (9/2/01)

BASTAIN, Emmet - of Gas City; 27 Apr 1902 m Elizabeth Turner of Fmt.; will live in Gas City (5/2/02)

BATES OIL/GAS WELL COMPANY - George Bates, founder; Directors are Lemuel Pearson, Pres.; Charles Childs, Treas.; George Mendenhall, Sect.; Bowman Pickard and Charles N. Graves; will drill a well ca 1 Sep 1901 (7/11/01); files for incorporation (8/5/01); will soon drill a gas well in N part of Fmt. (8/26/01); installs gas lines to customers, turns gas on (1/24/02)

BATES, George - helped get Bates Oil Co. started (7/11/01); serv Pvt., Co. D, 2nd Ind. Cav. during CW (5/27/04; 5/26/05)

BATES, John - of Fmt.; was fireman on Big Four passenger train that wrecked at Alexandria in Jan 1901; he is permanently injured (10/14/01)

BEALS, Enoch - dec; serv Pvt., 1st Ind. Cav. during CW (5/27/04; 5/26/05); 1 Jan 1887 is Pres., Fmt. Fair Assn. stockholders (12/15/05)

BEALS, Jacob - makes and repairs shoes in his Fmt. shop (5/9/01); 1881, is a shoe repairer (1/13/1881 as reprinted 3/29/04); sells his shoe shop (1/24/05)

BEALS, Lucy - see Lucy (Beals) LUNG

BEALS, Newton - serv Pvt., Co. K, 1st Ind. Cav. during CW (5/27/04; 5/26/05)

BEALS, R.J. - sells his grain elevators and coal bins (11/3/05)

BEALS, Mrs. R.J. - dt Mrs. __ Boynton (d 24 Feb 1902) (2/25/02)

BEALS, Ruth - 1 Aug 1905 is given party for her 6th birthday (8/4/05); dt M/M Robert Beals (12/15/05)

BEARD, __ - age 3 wks.; child of M/M Shelby Beard; d 3 Dec 1903; colored (12/4/03)

BEARD, Mrs. Shelby - age 22; d 25 Mar 1904, bur Park Cem; colored (3/29/04)

BEASLEY, William A. - Sect.-Treas., Roaring Gimlet Gold Mining Syndicate (9/26/02); stockholder, Fmt. Banking Co. (11/18/02); 11 Apr 1904, given party for his 40th birthday (4/15/04); Fmt. druggist since ca 1887 (5/27/04)

BEESON, Mrs. Ellen - of Butlerville; dt Rebecca Mote of Little Ridge area (8/23/04)

BEIDLER, James W. - mbr Fmt. Congregational Ch. (9/5/01); serv Pvt., Co. A, 156th Ind. Inf. during CW (5/27/04; 5/26/05)

BEIDLER, William - elected J.V.C., Beeson GAR Post 386 (1/24/02)

BELL, __ - age 4 mon.; s Amos Bell; d 19 Feb 1905 (2/21/05)

BELL, James - is new mbr of FFA Board of Trustees (12/23/01)

BELL, William - well on his farm 1 mi. W of Fmt. is producing 75 barrels of oil per day (11/11/02)

BELL CREEK - in NW Liberty Twp; Asa Wright contracted to re-ditch and clean out this creek (2/14/01)

BENBOW, Benjamin - from TN to Fmt. as early settler (1/13/05)

BENBOW, I.S. 'Ves' - b Monroe Twp., lives in Liberty Twp. (11/24/05)

BENNER, Charlie - 1905 Fowlerton Sch grad (5/12/05)

BENNETT, Elizabeth Emeline 'Emma' - of 7 mi. SE of Fmt.; b Grant Co. 29 Sep 1879; dt Charles W. and Minerva Bennett; d 18 Jul 1901 (7/22/01; 7/25/01)

BENNETT, Lawrence M. - and Maggie Viola are children of Charles W. and Minerva Bennett (7/25/01)

BETHEL CEMETERY - Asa Duling is bur (8/23/04)

BEVER, Mary - age 64; mother of William Bever; d 23 Apr 1904, bur Gas City IOOF Cem (4/26/04)

BEVINGTON, Fred - 13 Nov 1905 is his 11th birthday (11/17/05)

BEVINGTON, Grace - dt Mrs. O.M. Bevington; given party recently for her 13th birthday (12/1/03)

BEWLEY, Charles Arthur - mbr Cincinnati, OH Friends, in a letter read before Fmt. Friends on 14 May 1902, asked permission of the Meeting to m Isabel Hoskins (5/20/02); m Isabel Hoskins 25 Jun 1902 in Fmt. Friends MH in Quaker marriage ceremony (6/27/02)

BIDDLECUM, Homer - s Jason Biddlecum (12/5/05)

BIRELY, Jacob - of Marion; d 18 May 1901 (5/20/01)

BLAND, Fred - employee, Fmt. Glass Works (4/19/04)

BLAND, Mrs. William - age 46; m; d 31 Mar 1905, bur Park Cem (4/4/05)

BLUE, R.R. - of Fmt.; age ca 60; serv CW in Co. A, 82nd Ohio Inf.; d 21 Oct 1903, bur Hillsdale, MI (10/23/03)

BOGGESS, Randolph - serv Pvt., Co. C, 153rd Ohio Inf. during CW (5/27/04; 5/26/05)

BOGUE, Mrs. Amos - dt James Scott, aged man (7/8/02)

BOGUE, Burl - of 2 mi. SW of Fmt.; grad FFA 1900 (12/26/01)

BOGUE, Dora - tchr, Liberty Sch 1904-05 (12/27/04)

BOGUE, Elizabeth (Coggeshall) - of Fmt.; dt of Nathan Coggeshall (4/8/02)

BOGUE, Jesse - 1881, is a grocer (1/13/1881 as reprinted 3/29/04)

BOGUE, Leora - mbr Fmt. WCTU (8/8/02)

BOGUE, Mary - mbr Fmt. WCTU (6/3/02)

BOGUE, Nina - dt M/M Thomas Bogue (7/29/02); office worker, Fmt. Glass Works (4/29/04); att Earlham Coll 1904-05 (11/18/04)

BOGUE, Ora - mbr Back Creek [Friends] WCTU (5/16/02)

BOGUE, Ord - s Mrs. Elizabeth Bogue; 1903-05 att Purdue Univ (4/5/04; 9/6/04); att Ind. Univ 1904-05 (11/18/04)

BOGUE, Robert - 1 Jan 1887 is Supt., Fmt. Fair Assn. stockholders (12/15/05)

BOND, Asa - step-father of Elmer W. Jay (6/24/02)

BOND, Mrs. Asa - of Bethel area; 30 Jul 1905 celebrated her 73rd birthday (8/4/05)

BOOKOUT, Martha - of 2 mi. S of Fmt.; widow of Calvin Bookout; d 2 Feb 1901 (2/4/01)

BORREY, William - Mgr., American Window Glass Co. Factory # 28 at Albany; parents live on E. Washington St., Fmt. (7/25/01); Asst. Mgr., Bell Window Glass Factory (4/15/04)

BOSLEY, Miss Bernice - operator, Fmt. Telephone Co. (9/1/03)

BOWEN, Seth Hudson - old soldier who gave Jessie M. Jay a fine violin several yrs. ago; is dying in the Dayton, OH Soldier's Home (2/13/02)

BOWERS, Rev. George W. - performed m of M/M L.L. Fankboner in 1852 (8/5/02)

BOWERS, William - electrician for Fmt. Electric Light Plant; installs 7 arc lights at Wesleyan Camp Grounds (8/26/01); is now Water Works engineer (9/16/01); takes job in St. Marys, OH (7/15/02); is ill, returns to Fmt. with his wife (8/5/02); returns to his job in St. Marys, OH (9/2/02); will operate the Fmt. Waterworks (2/5/04)

BOWKER, Mrs. William - age 29; dt Mrs. Willard Adkinson of 3 mi. NW of Fmt.; m; 6 May 1905, bur Park Cem (5/9/05)

BOYD, James - colored; age ca 56; b Mississippi; Grant Co. coroner 1888-90; d 29 Aug 1902 (9/2/02)

BOYD, William - returns to his wife and son in Sweetser after 2 yrs. searching for gold in the Klondyke (12/5/01)

BOYER, A.J. - 1904-05 Fmt. HS tchr/Principal (9/2/04)

BOYNTON, Ray - s Mrs. __ Boynton (d 24 Feb 1902) (2/25/02)

BRADFORD, Gertrude - see Chauncey THORN

BRADFORD, Mrs. Malinda - see Paxton WILSON

BRANDEN, Phebe J. - see Alfred M. PRESNALL

BREWER, __ - b 19 Aug 1904; s M/M Mahlon Brewer of Little Ridge area (8/23/04)

BREWER, __ - b 2 Apr 1905; dt M/M Burl Brewer (4/4/05)

BREWER, Arthur - att Purdue Univ 1902-05 (9/12/02; 12/16/04)

BREWER, Mrs. Ellen - see John MARTIN

BREWER, Fred - of SW of Fmt.; his horse's tail was mutilated by a vandal last Friday (7/1/01); m Rebekah Clark last wk. (7/4/01)

BREWER, Pearl - see Percy DILLY

BREWER, William - age 31; s M/M Mahlon Brewer of SW of Fmt.; m Emily; d 6 Oct 1905 (10/10/05; 10/17/05)

BREWER, Willis - dec; serv Pvt., Co. C, 89th Ind. Inf. during CW (5/26/05)

BREWER, Mrs. Winnie - age 68; widow; d 9 Sep 1905 (9/12/05)

BRIGHT, Jesse - serv Pvt., Co. H, 142nd Ind. Inf. during CW (5/27/04; 5/26/05)

BRILES, __ - b 10 Jan 1905; s M/M Will Briles (1/13/05)

BRILES, __ - see Mrs. S.M. McCLEARY

BRILES, Adelbert - of Fmt.; m __, dt J.C. and Nancy (dec) McMasters (11/21/01)

BRILES, E.E. - is stenographer & typist at Fmt. Foundry & Machine Works (12/30/01)

BRILES, Mrs. Elizabeth - given party 11 Apr 1904 for her 80th birthday (4/12/04); f of NC (7/5/04)

BRILES, Jacob - Fmt. Town Clerk (6/20/02); came from NC ca 1872 (11/17/03); s Mrs. Elizabeth Briles (4/12/04)

BRILES, Mrs. Noah - of near Madison Co. line; d 7 Jul 1901 (7/11/01)

BRILES, Walter - 21 Mar 1905 is his 18th birthday (3/24/05)

BROOKS, Cora (Rush) - of Winchester; dt Susan Rush (2/16/04)

BROOKS, John - age 56; m; d 9 Mar 1904 (3/11/04), bur Back Creek Friends Cem (3/15/04)

BROOKSHIRE, __ - b 1 May 1904; dt M/M C.D. Brookshire (5/3/04)

BROOKSHIRE, __ - b 3 Mar 1905; s M/M Henry Brookshire of SW of Fmt. (3/14/05)

BROOKSHIRE, __ - see Mrs. Exum ELLIOTT; Mrs. John McCOMBS

BROOKSHIRE, Mrs. C.D. - accidentally shoots/wounds Pearl Eiber (7/8/04)

BROOKSHIRE, Clyde - age 20; s M/M Thomas Brookshire; f att FFA; d 5 Feb 1904, bur Park Cem (2/9/04)

BROOKSHIRE, Etta - see George CRONK

BROOKSHIRE, Eulalia - age 10; dt M/M Thomas Brookshire; d 8 Feb 1904, bur Park Cem (2/12/04)

BROOKSHIRE, Henry - s M/M Thomas Brookshire (2/9/04)

BROOKSHIRE, Leatha - see Nathan O. LOVE

BROOKSHIRE, Luther - of 2.5 mi. W of Fmt.; b Marion 26 Feb 1852; m in Henry Co. 25 Jul 1871 Louisiana Stinson; d 15 Feb 1904 (2/19/04; 2/23/04)

BROWN, __ - b 18 Oct 1904; dt M/M Lamont Brown (10/21/04)

BROWN, __ - b 10 Jun 1905; s M/M Lee Brown (6/13/05)

BROWN, __ - b 26 Oct 1905; s M/M Lamont Brown (10/31/05)

BROWN, Dr. C.N. - 7 Jun 1905 m Mrs. Pearl Hughes (6/9/05)

BROWN, Catherine - see Ottis WILBURN

BROWN, Mrs. Debbie A. - of Jonesboro; age 62; m 1st __ Wiley; m 2nd __ Brown; d 15 Apr 1902 (4/18/02)

BROWN, Edith - wife of Dr. C.N. Brown; d 21 May 1904, bur Park Cem (5/24/04)

BROWN, Frank C. - s William A. and Margaret A. Brown; dec (5/27/02)

BROWN, James - serv Pvt., Co. I, 2nd Ohio Cav. during CW (5/27/04; 5/26/05)

BROWN, Jephtha T. - s William A. and Margaret A. Brown; dec (5/27/02)

BROWN, Julia - see Julia (Brown) ICE

BROWN, Mrs. L. Amelia - f of Fmt.; age 78; 20 Jun 1905 d in TN (6/23/05)

BROWN, Lee - employee, Fmt. Tile Co.; 12 Dec 1903 m Miss Russel VanArsdall (12/15/03)

BROWN, Margaret A. - m William A. Brown; d 5 Jun 1899 (5/27/02)

BROWN, Mark - age 13; s Will F. and Lillie (Dean) Brown (3/18/025/27/02)

BROWN, P.T. - owns White House Saloon (7/7/05)

BROWN, Ralph - moves from Fmt. to Matthews to work for Winslow Glass Co. (2/17/02)

BROWN, Robert - of Alexandria; 30 Jan 1904 m Jesse Leach (2/2/04)

BROWN, Saloma - see Saloma (Brown) WILSON

BROWN, Susan - see Susan (Brown) LEACH

BROWN, Will F. - Fmt. real estate dealer; is injured when his horse runs away with his buggy (5/20/02); b near Fayetteville, TN 8 Jun 1864; s William A. (dec) and Margaret A. (dec) Brown; grew up 3 mi. E of Fmt.; 3 Apr 1886 m Lillie Dean in Fmt.; f cashier, Citizens Exchange Bank; d 21 May 1902 (5/23/02; 5/27/02); 6 Dec 1894 is Asst. Cashier, Citizen's Bank (12/15/05)

BROWN, Mrs. Will F. - dt Mrs. James Phillips (dec) (2/3/02)

BROWN, William A. - m Margaret A.; d 9 May 1894 (5/27/02)

BROYLES, Joe - during CW serv 14th Illinois Inf.; of Greeley, CO; is visiting here 1st time since he left his home 5 mi. SE of Fmt. on 15 Sep 1859 (3/25/04)

BRUMIT, Evelyn - see Lewis HOCKETT

BRUSHWILLER, Mrs. Robert - b 5 May 1883; dt M/M J. Burgess Hollingsworth; m 15 Apr 1903 Robert Brushwiller of Jonesboro; d 1 Mar 1904 (3/4/04)

BRYAN, Earl - s A.D. Bryan; 8 May 1905 m Zola Gray, dt Mrs. Emma Gray (5/12/05)

BRYAN, Mrs. Nannie - mbr Fmt. Congregational Ch. (9/5/01)

BRYAN, Thomas - Foreman, Wilson & McCullough Glass Factory; d 7 Oct 1901 (10/7/01)

BUCK, Charles F. - Commander, Beeson GAR Post 386 (1/24/02); serv Pvt., Co. C, 33rd Mass. Inf. during CW (5/27/04; 5/26/05)

BUCK, Mrs. Charles F. - dt Mrs. Mary/Ellen Carroll (of Marion; d at age 82 in Fmt. ca 20 Oct 1903, bur Marion IOOF Cem) (4/1/02; 10/23/03)

BUCK, Frank - flagman at Washington St. RR crossing (4/29/04)

BUCK, Lillian - dt Mrs. Charles Buck (7/4/02)

BUCK, Ray - s M/M C.F. Buck (7/28/05)

BULLER, __ - b last wk.; s M/M Clarence Buller of Summitville (2/14/05)

BULLER, Birchie M. (Rich) - b 22 Nov 1877; dt John and Martha Rich of Taylor Twp., Howard Co.; m W. Frank Buller 3 Mar 1900; f lived 2 mi. W of Fmt.; mbr Christian Ch.; d near Kokomo 14 Oct 1901, bur Kokomo cem (10/17/01; 10/21/01)

BULLER, Charles - is att 6-wk. embalming course in Cincinnati, OH (3/7/02); completes embalming course (4/1/02); s Harmon and Mary (Little) Buller (11/24/05)

BULLER, Elmer - s Harmon and Mary (Little) Buller (11/24/05)

BULLER, Harmon - serv Pvt., Co. C, 118th Ind. Inf. during CW (5/27/04; 5/26/05)

BULLER, John - arrested and charged with vandalizing the buggy and harness of C.M. Ratliff last Saturday night (6/17/01), charged with malicious trespass (9/5/01); is on trial (10/7/01); found guilty as charged, sentenced to 6 months in County jail and fined $100 (Attorney Charles M. Ratliff had represented Buller's wife in her successful suit for divorce) (10/10/01); is refused a pardon by Indiana Gov. Durbin (12/12/01); serv Pvt., Co. K, 47th Ind. Inf. during CW (5/26/05)

BULLER, Lydia A.C. - is awarded a divorce from husband, John Buller (3/7/01)

BULLER, Mary (Little) - b NC ca 1839; dt Nathan and Rachel Little; spring of 1865 m Harmon Buller; d 22 Nov 1905, bur Park Cem (11/24/05)

BULLER, Oliver - mbr, Fmt. Twp. Advisory Bd. (3/25/04); sells Fowlerton Canning Factory (10/24/05)

BULLER, Miss Stella - 1903-04 tchr, Liberty Twp. Sch # 5 (9/11/03); tchr, Liberty Twp. Sch 1904-06 (12/27/04; 7/28/05)

BULLER, W. Frank - a Director, Fmt. Fair Assoc. (1/12/04); Supt., Fmt. Fair Horse Dept. (8/15/05)

BUMPUS, Gabriel - dec; serv Pvt., Co. I, 33rd Ind. Inf. during CW (5/26/05)

BUMPUS, Mary - widow of Gabriel Bumpus; has CW pension of $12 per mon. (10/20/05)

BUNDY, Mrs. Elias - of Marion; dt Ivy and Sarah Luther (8/18/05)

BURDEN, __ - b 25 Aug 1904; s M/M Will Burden (8/26/04)

BURDEN, John W. - 1903-04 tchr, Liberty Twp. Sch # 3 (9/11/03); tchr, Liberty Twp. Sch 1904-06 (12/27/04; 7/28/05)

BURK, O.B. - purchases Frazier Hotel (9/16/01)

BURNS, Mrs. Nancy - of 1 mi. W of Fmt.; rents out her house; moves to Mills Corner, Jay Co. (12/4/03; 12/8/03)

BURNS, Virgil - of W of Fmt.; d 6 Nov 1902 (11/7/02)

BURNWORTH, __ - see Mrs. Martin WILTSIE/WILTSEE

BURWICK, John - dairyman; supplies milk to Fowlerton (8/26/01)

BUSING, J. Rhinehart - lives in Paris, IL (9/19/05)

BUSING, Mrs. J. Rhinehart - dt Robert Hasting (4/11/01)

BUSING, John - dec; Pvt., 153rd Ind. Inf. during CW (5/26/05)

BUTLER, Almeda - see Almeda (Butler) LITTLE

CAIN, Viony - grad Fowlerton Sch 1905 (5/12/05)

CALDERWOOD, C. - was a Van Buren Twp tchr for 5 yrs., is a specialist in music and in penmanship; 1905-06 Fowlerton Sch Principal/tchr (8/15/05)

CALHOUN, Will - 1881, Fmt. Twp. Sch grad (7/4/05)

CALIFORNIA, gone to - see Cyrus BALDWIN; Sarah (Wilson) BALDWIN; R.M. HIATT; R.K. JOHNSON; A.R. MOON; Mrs. Nancy NEWBY; Dr. Will N. RATLIFF; Levi SCOTT; Jackson STIVERS; Charles WEEKS

CAMMACK, Emma (Cox) - age 31; dt William and Elizabeth (Wilson) Cox; m Will Cammack; d Jun 1900 (1/28/01; 2/4/01; 6/17/01)

CAMMACK, Gertrude - of Jonesboro; recently divorced __Hill; 12 Feb 1902 m W.T. Cammack (3/21/02)

CAMMACK, James - 1848, built 1st sawmill in Fmt. (1/17/05)

CAMMACK, Verna - see Demetris HOWELL

CAMMACK, William T. - Grant County Clerk; 12 Feb 1902 m Gertrude Hill (3/21/02); Director, Roaring Gimlet Gold Mining Syndicate (9/26/02)

CAMMACK-GIBSON, Mattie - PHOTO; is Recording Sect., Indiana WCTU (4/8/01); mbr, Back Creek [Friends] WCTU (11/11/04)

CANUP, Thomas - [of Madison Co.]; 17 Mar 1904 att wedding anniv. dinner for M/M James Kirkpatrick (3/22/04)

CAREY, __ - b 18 Aug 1901; s M/M Newton Carey (8/19/01)

CAREY, Albert - 1848, ran a stage coach between Marion and Anderson through Fmt., later sold out to Philip Davis (1/20/05)

CAREY, Charles - Supt., Fmt. Tile Factory (11/17/05)

CAREY, Elias - of Marion; brother of Mrs. Susannah Elliott (4/28/05)

CAREY, Eliza - see Eliza [(Carey)] PIERCE

CAREY, Georgia - age 6; dt Newton Carey of W of Fmt.; is injured in farm accident (7/15/02)

CAREY, Gervas - is att Cleveland Bible Institute (1/1/04)

CAREY, Hattie Finney - mbr Fmt. WCTU (8/8/02)

CAREY, Dr. Isaac - of Marion; is age 93 (8/29/05)

CAREY, Stanley - grad, [Friends] Back Creek Sch 1904 (4/15/04)

CAREY, Susannah - see Mrs. Susannah (Carey) ELLIOTT; also see William SCOTT

CAREY, William - owner, Carey Manufacturing Co. (9/13/04)

CARPENTER, Mrs. Emory - of Memphis, TN; dt William Hasting (dec) (2/7/05)

CARPENTER, Pearl - dt Henry Carpenter of near Fowlerton; d 23 Sep 1903 (9/25/03)

CARROLL, __ - b 7 Oct 1904; dt M/M James Carroll of NE of Fmt. (10/11/04)

CARROLL, Mrs. Amy - 1904 Fmt. HS grad (5/17/04); 1904-06 Back Creek Sch tchr (10/11/04; 8/15/05)

CARROLL, Celia - and Ray Carroll are children of Mrs. Amy Carroll (8/18/05)

CARROLL, Edgar - recently joined US Navy (8/7/03)

CARROLL, Mabel - 5 Jul 1905 is given party for her 17th birthday (7/7/05); dt Mrs. Amy Carroll (8/18/05)

CARSON, M.G. - mbr, Fmt. M.E. Ch. (6/6/02)

CARTER, __ - b 9 Jun 1904; s Dr./M T.J. Carter (6/10/04)

CARTER, Chester - 1901 Liberty Twp. Dist. # 14 Sch grad (5/30/01); 1905-06 Liberty Twp. Sch tchr (7/28/05)

CARTER, Fern - dt M/M Robert Carter (7/28/05)

CARTER, Isaac - dec; serv Pvt., Co. G, 33rd Ind. Inf. during CW (5/26/05)

CARTER, J.E. - 29 Jul 1905 m Elizabeth, dt M/M Samuel Stewart (8/1/05)

CARTER, Mary - mbr, Fmt. WCTU (6/3/02)

CARTER, Myrtle - employee, Citizens Telephone Exchange (11/29/04)

CARTER, Ray - 1904 Fmt. HS grad (4/22/04)

CARTER, Robert - serv Pvt., Co. C, 51st Ind. Inf. during CW (5/27/04; 5/26/05)

CARTER, Mrs. Robert - sister of Calvin Rush (11/29/04)

CARTER, Thomas J. - m; is att medical sch in Chicago (7/25/01); recent grad Ind. Medical Coll, Indianapolis; will set up practice in Upland (5/2/02); takes over Fmt. practice of Dr. A. Holliday (12/5/02); had office in Borrey Blk., moves office to Rigdon (8/25/03); moves to Berrien Springs, MI (1/22/04)

CARTER, Mrs. Tom - sister of Palmer Edgerton (6/10/04)

CARTWRIGHT, __ - infant of Dr./M O.D. Cartwright; d recently, bur Park Cem (4/11/05)

CARTWRIGHT, Dr. Oz D. - and partner, Dr. Pearl Dickey, have dental offices in Borrey Blk. (6/20/01; 8/18/03)

CASEY, Rev. C.J. - pastor, Fmt. Baptist Ch. (8/7/03), resigns as pastor (5/2/05)

CASKEY, Bessie - see Bessie (Caskey) CORN

CASKEY, Lew - is a rural mail carrier; 23 Dec 1905 m Clara Stevens (12/26/05)

CASSELL, Marie - age 12; dt M/M Lew Cassell; in 6th grade, Fmt. Schs (6/17/04)

CASSELL, Susie J. (Winslow) - of Swayzee; dt Henry and Mary J. (Dillon) Winslow; wife of Lew Cassell (3/7/01; 3/25/01)

CECIL, Martha A. - see Henry LOVE

CENTER TOWNSHIP SCHOOLS - PUCKETT SCH (DISTRICT # 4) - 1901-02 tchr is Herman Wimmer (1/9/02)

CHAPMAN, Norine - dt M/M James Chapman of Gas City; freshman, FHS (6/13/05)

CHARLES, Dr. Etta - is Summitville physician (10/10/05); is sister of Dr. Olive Wilson of Paragould, AR (11/3/05)

CHARLES, Mrs. Mattie - mbr Fmt. Congregational Ch. (9/5/01); 1904-05 Fmt. Sch tchr (9/2/04)

CHASEY, __ - b recently; dt M/M L.O. Chasey (9/12/02)

CHICAGO PIPE LINE CO. - William D. Friend of Fmt. is an employee (2/17/02)

CHILD, Charles - Treas./Director, Bates Oil Co. (7/11/01); bought an interest in Cottage Steam Laundry (8/29/01)

CHILD, Etha - att Earlham Coll 1904-06 (12/16/04; 11/3/05)); dt M/M Charles Child (3/17/05)

CHILTON, Gladys - grad Fowlerton Sch 1905 (5/12/05)

CHRISTY, Hiram - age 4; s M/M William Christy of 4 mi. W of Fmt.; d 28 Mar 1904 (3/29/04)

CHURCHES
BACK CREEK FRIENDS - Benjamin F. Morris serv as pastor 1900-02 (10/14/02); now has an organ (1/1/04); J. Davis, pastor (1/10/05)
BACK CREEK WESLEYAN METHODIST (W.M.) - mbr, Maria Neal (11/4/02); new brick church to have slate roof (9/27/04); bricks are being laid by T.J. Pierce (10/25/04); date stone for new church is donated by Dye & Montgomery (10/28/04); roof on new bldg. is completed (12/2/04); is dedicated 22 Jan 1905; bldg. cost $2,500; pastor, Walter Thompson (1/24/05)
BETHEL METHODIST PROTESTANT (M.P.) - Rev. Iliff held funeral of Sylvester Smith here (3/7/01); will elect one Trustee 2 Dec 1901,

election committee chairman is J.C. McCashlin and secretary is J.B. Compton (11/11/01); Father G.P. Riley and a boy preacher will have 3 PM service next Sunday (6/27/02)
BETHEL FRIENDS - Benjamin F. Morris serv as pastor 1900-02 (10/14/02)
CENTER CHRISTIAN - in Liberty Twp.; pastor, __ Wilson (2/3/02)
EAST BRANCH FRIENDS - services discontinued here due to several mbrs moving (1/19/04); Meeting is being revived (3/8/04)
FAIRMOUNT AFRICAN METHODIST EPISCOPAL (A.M.E.) - has chapel/mission on E. Washington St. (12/12/01); mission to be remodeled (6/20/02); ch. bldg. being constructed on E. 7th St. (10/23/03), to be dedicated 24 Jan 1904 (1/15/04); is located at 7th St. & Buckeye (1/26/04); 1900, church is organized with 5 mbrs; 1st pastor, Rev. J.M. Nickles, is still pastor with 23 mbrs (1/24/05); pastor, Rev. T.J. White (11/24/05)
FAIRMOUNT BAPTIST - Rev. C.H. Fry to serv as pastor here and at Gas City Baptist at the same time (6/6/01); Mrs. Rachel Lewis, mbr (5/23/02); C.J. Casey, pastor (8/7/03); a f pastor is Rev. Lotus Aspy (2/9/04); 1886, organized by Rev. Moses Smith (10/4/04); organized 1888 as 5th church in Fmt.; 1st pastor, J.B. Summerville; now has ca 75 mbrs (1/24/05); C.J. Casey resigns as pastor (5/2/05)
FAIRMOUNT CHRISTIAN - mbr, Viola Dickey (11/4/02); located on corner of Walnut & Madison St. (11/10/05); pastor is J. Thomas W. Luckey (11/24/05)
FAIRMOUNT CONGREGATIONAL - Dec 1889, church bldg. is dedicated (12/15/05); J. Challen Smith, pastor resigns (3/18/01); 1 Sep 1901 Rev. Oscar Lowry to resume pastorate (6/13/01); is reorganized; new mbrs are Benjamin F. Stevens, Ida Ink, Frank W. Hathaway, Sarah F. Ink, Mrs. Jennie Hathaway, Mrs. Phoebe LaRue, M/M C.A. Cook, Mrs. Ella (Ink) Mart, Mrs. S. Stewart, Miss Leona Stewart, Miss M. Elizabeth Stewart, Mrs. Anna Engles, Mrs. Mattie Charles, Mrs. Nannie Bryan, Mrs. Ethel Shuey, Mrs. Ania Norton, Mrs. J. Wilson, M/M John Montgomery, James W. Beidler (9/5/01); church bldg. now has a large coal stove; mbrs are Mrs. D.P. Patterson (1/1/02), and Mrs. J. Stivers (9/12/02); Rev. Oscar Lowry resigns as pastor (9/23/02); Rev. Robert McNaughton is the new pastor (10/17/02); Walter B. Denny, acting pastor (5/27/04); 1888 is 4th church in Fmt., 1st pastor was William Wiedenhoeft; now has 140 mbrs (1/24/05); pastor, Harold Cooper (2/7/05); David Ice, att; Julia Ice, mbr (10/24/05)

FAIRMOUNT FRIENDS - Enos Harvey, pastor (1/17/01); Henry Love (dec) was mbr (7/8/01); Fmt. Mining Co. is drilling new gas well on the rear of MH lot (2/17/02), well is shot 24 Feb 1902 resulting in good flow of gas (2/25/02); Charles Arthur Bewley, mbr Cincinnati, OH Friends, in a letter read before Fmt. Friends on 14 May 1902, asked permission of the Meeting to m Isabel Hoskins (5/20/02); m Isabel Hoskins 25 Jun 1902 in Fmt. Friends MH in a Quaker marriage ceremony (6/27/02); mbr, Cynthia Winslow (11/4/02); Dempsey W. Presnall (dec) was a mbr prior to ca 1882 (4/5/04); 1853, 1st church in Fmt. (1/24/05)
FAIRMOUNT METHODIST EPISCOPAL (M.E.) - Millard Pell, pastor (1/17/01); Rev. Pell leaves for Lapel pastorate (4/18/01); Hansen C. Smith, pastor (5/9/01); new parsonage is under construction (5/20/01); work on parsonage progresses (6/3/01); new parsonage completed (7/22/01); church bldg. is now wired for/lighted by electricity (8/12/01); mbrs include John A. Hunt, M.G. Carson (6/6/02), Minnie Jay (11/4/02); J.M. Nickles, pastor (8/14/03); mbrs Hannah A. Winslow (3/22/04), and Elizabeth Weston are dec (3/25/04); Rev. O.V.L. Harbour, new pastor (4/15/04); built in 1885 at S. Walnut and E. Madison; now has 250 mbrs (1/24/05); Dec 1880, old M.E. Ch. bldg. on corner of Main & 2nd St., is now used as a pool hall (12/15/05)
FAIRMOUNT METHODIST PROTESTANT (M.P.) - organized 11 Jan 1902 with Rev. D.W. Eans(?) as pastor (1/13/02); mbr, Sina Latham (11/4/02)
FAIRMOUNT WESLEYAN METHODIST (W.M.) - C.S. Smith, pastor (1/17/01); oldest church bldg. in Fmt., will be remodeled this spring (4/4/01); renovated bldg. to be dedicated 28 Jul 1901 (7/22/01; 7/25/01); mbr, Caddie Kimes (11/4/02); recently baptized 2 new mbrs in Dare's gravel pit S of Fmt. (7/5/04); pastor, Rev. Walter L. Thompson (9/16/04); established 1867 as 2nd church in Fmt., with 50 mbrs and Isaac Meeks as pastor; Charles Smith is now pastor with 85 mbrs (1/24/05)
GAS CITY BAPTIST - pastor is Rev. Lotus Aspy (2/9/04)
GERMAN BAPTIST - mbr, Mary J. Dare (11/4/02)
HARRISBURG (later became GAS CITY) BAPTIST - 1883, organized by Rev. Moses Smith (10/4/04)
JONESBORO M.E. - cost $4,000, dedicated 4 Jul 1900; burned down 2 Dec 1901 (12/5/01); pastor is Rev. Arnold (2/12/04)
LITTLE RIDGE FRIENDS - pastor Stephen Scott leaves (2/25/02); Mahlon Harvey came to Little Ridge area 1855, he introduced singing

into Little Ridge Friends SS then into worship service, ca 1870 encouraged revival movement (8/22/05; 8/25/05)
MARION FRIENDS/MARION 1ST FRIENDS - Elwood Scott is new pastor (8/19/01)
MATTHEWS M.E. - new ch. is to be built soon (8/1/02)
OAK RIDGE FRIENDS - Benjamin F. Morris serv as pastor 1900-02 (10/14/02)
PLEASANT GROVE M.P. [GRANT CH.] - pastor is M.F. Iliff (8/12/01)
PT. ISABEL M.E. - Rev. J.W. Richey is pastor (9/25/03)
ST. CECILA'S CATHOLIC (RC) - in Fmt.; Mrs. James Keenan, mbr (2/28/01); Rev. Henry C. Kappel, pastor (7/15/01), and is still pastor (1/24/05); mbrs include Mrs. John Troy (6/20/02), Mrs. Anton Ulrich (10/20/03); church built in 1899 (1/24/05); H.C. Kappel leaves this pastorate (6/27/05)
SWAYZEE METHODIST - Rev. C.M. Hobbs, pastor (9/1/03)
UNION CHAPEL UNITED BRETHREN (U.B.) - pastor is __ Oxley (1/28/01); is near Pike School (7/1/01), S of Fmt.; is being repaired (9/16/01); mbr Mary A. Glover is dec (12/12/01); pastor, M.V. Bartlett (4/29/02; 1/15/04); 1.5 mi. S of Fmt.; bldg. is newly remodeled, to be dedicated 25 May 1902 (5/13/02); bldg. dedicated last Sunday (5/27/02); mbr, Lida Payne (11/4/02); has 75 mbrs (1/24/05); pastor, W.L. Crom (2/17/05; 8/22/05)
UPLAND FRIENDS - pastor 1898-1900 was Benjamin F. Morris (10/14/02)
VERMILLION FRIENDS - 5 mi. SE of Alexandria; MH cost $1,100; MH dedicated 3 Feb 1901, Enos Harvey spoke at dedication (2/7/01)

CLARK, Rebekah - see Fred BREWER

CLARK, Hugh - Fmt. Twp. Dist. #4 (East Branch Sch) 1901-02 tchr (2/10/02; 5/13/02)

CLARKE, __ - see Mrs. Perry WOOD

CLARKE, Simon - age 71; of 4 mi. NE of Fmt.; d 25 Aug 1903, bur Gas City IOOF Cem (8/28/03)

CLINE, Adam H.O.P. - suing Lydia A. Cline for divorce (12/16/01)

CLODFELTER, Noah J. - age 49; grew up in Montgomery Co.; d 1 May 1901 in Central State Hospital for the Insane, bur Crawfordsville Cem (5/2/01)

CLOTHIER, George - 21 Sep 1904 m Frances Scott, dt Rev./M Elwood Scott; will live in Marion (9/23/04)

CLOUD, Joseph - of Wayne Co.; brother of Mrs. Rachel Scott; 23 May 1904 will be age 86 (5/24/04); age 87, d this wk. (12/22/05)

CLOUD, Rachel - see Rachel (Cloud) SCOTT

COAHRAN, Ed - employee, Wilson & McCulloch Glass Factory (1/31/01)

COAHRAN, Jesse - att Purdue Univ 1904-05 (12/16/04)

COAHRAN, Katie - att Earlham Coll 1905-06 (12/5/05)

COAHRAN, Katie - see Katie (Coahran) DILLON

COAHRAN, Susan Frances 'Fanny' - b near Centersville, MD 23 Jan 1851; came to IN 1867; mbr Friends; d 21 Dec 1903 (12/25/03; 12/29/03)

COFFIN, __ - see Mrs. Walter S. LUSE

COGGESHALL, Elizabeth - see Elizabeth (Coggeshall) BOGUE

COGGESHALL, Nathan - of Marion; age 89; d 8 Apr 1902 (4/8/02)

COLEMAN, Anna - see Anna (Coleman) MASON

COLEMAN, Elizabeth - see Elizabeth (Coleman) BALDWIN

COLEMAN, Mary - see Mary (Coleman) HEAL

COLLINS, Mrs. John - dt M/M Fred Gass; f of Fmt.; f att FHS; d Gas City 11 Feb 1905 (2/14/05)

COLORADO, gone to - Joe BROYLES; Arthur Ernest SEALE; Trenton A. SHIELDS

COMER, __ - b 24 Jul 1904; s M/M Elmer Comer of S of Fmt. (7/26/04)

COMPTON, J.B. - Secretary, election committee, Bethel M.P. Ch. (11/11/01)

CONE, __ - b 13 Oct 1903; s M/M Vint Cone (10/16/03)

CONE, Vint - of Fmt.; had surgery at Marion Hospital 21 Apr 1902 (4/22/02)

CONLIFF, Julia - see James B. VALENTINE

CONNER, Nelson - of Starke Co.; f of Fmt.; during CW serv Co. G, 153rd Ind. Inf. (8/7/03)

CONNER, W.B. - Fmt. druggist for 12 yrs; sold out to Charles Daugherty and N.M. Mendenhall (9/30/01); is moving to Indianapolis (12/16/01)

COOK, Calvin B. - of Franklin Twp.; 5 Mar 1905 m Ida E. Moon; live W of Fmt. (3/10/05)

COOK, Charles A. - and wife are mbrs Fmt. Congregational Ch. (9/5/01); Director, Fmt. YMCA (6/6/02)

COOK, Isabella H. - see Isabella H. (Cook) PRETLOW

COOK, Lewis N. - representative/employee of Hoosier Mining Co. (10/3/01); Secretary, Hoosier Mining Co. (7/25/02)

COOK, Mrs. Lewis N. - d recently (4/21/05)

COOK, Lucile - 5 Dec 1903 is her 6th birthday (12/8/03)

COOK, Silas - CW vet (6/6/05)

COOMLER, __ - infant of M/M Sherman Coomler of Oak Ridge; d 28 May 1905 (5/30/05)

COOPER, __ - b 15 Mar 1902; dt M/M Roll Cooper (3/18/02)

COOPER, Elsie - see William H.H. TRASTERS

COOPER, Rev. Harold - pastor, Pond Creek, OK Congregational Ch.; is ordained recently (3/25/04)

COPELAND, Charles H. - 1897, is Supt., Fmt. Schs (12/19/05)

COPPOCK, Cyrus L. - of Jonesboro; 17 Apr 1905 m Miss Edith Ellis, dt Mrs. Jesse Haisley; will live in Jonesboro (4/21/05)

COPPOCK, Nora - see Mrs. Nora HAWORTH

CORN, Bessie (Caskey) - dt John Caskey; wife of Jacob Corn; d 11 Mar 1905 (3/17/05)

CORN, Lucinda - see Lucinda (Corn) LEACH

CORN, Rebecca (Ice) - dt Ransom and Sarah Ice (10/24/05)

CORY, Michael - Secretary, Farmer's Telephone Line of Matthews (3/14/01)

COTTRELL, Mrs. Jane - age ca 70; lived S near County line; d 17 Sep 1901 (9/19/01)

COULTER, Elizabeth - see Elizabeth (Coulter) WESTON

COWGILL, Anna - 1904 Earlham Coll grad (4/22/04)

COWGILL, Luzena T. - see Harry O. WHITNEY

COWGILL, Samuel C. - owns tile mill (10/21/01); Pres., National Drain Tile Co., Terre Haute (9/16/02); 13 Oct 1903 m Mrs. Alice Nixon (10/16/03); moves his family from Summitville to Montezuma (5/3/04)

COWGILL TILE CO. - 28 Dec 1890, factory burns (12/15/05); owned by Samuel C. Cowgill; largest tile mill in world; is in Madison Co. 2 mi. S of County line; started 20 yrs. ago with $2,500 in borrowed capital; bldgs. now cover 2,300 sq. ft., 100 workmen yr-round; 14 kilns; tile are 3.5" to 30" diameter; 100 RR car loads shipped each month; engine that brings dirt 1.5 mi. to factory has Matt Finnimore as engineer and Peter Schoonover as fireman (10/21/01); Harry O. Whitney, Co. bookkeeper/Co. partner, d 27

Oct 1901 (11/4/01); tile was sold to Queen Victoria during her lifetime and is now being sold to King Edward to drain royal parks and palace grounds (2/10/02)

COX, __ - b 5 Feb 1905; c M/M Eli Cox (2/10/05)

COX, __ - see Mrs. Clinton HAISLEY; also see Mrs. E.J. SEALE

COX, Abigail - see Abigail (Cox) WINSLOW

COX, Boyd - age 15; s M.H. Cox (8/4/05)

COX, Burl - of Fmt.; during CW serv in 160th Ind. Inf. (8/21/03)

COX, Charles - 1904 Liberty Twp. Sch grad (4/19/04)

COX, Clarence - of Summitville; 16 Sep 1905 m Eva, dt Willard Richardson of Fmt.; will live in Summitville (9/19/05)

COX, Eli J. - f of Fmt.; 12 Oct 1904 m Mrs. Ora Osborn, dt M/M W.S. Luse; will live in his orange grove in Gabriella, FL (10/14/04); brother of Nathan, John W. and Tilman Cox (9/26/05)

COX, Eliza Ann - see Eliza A. (Cox) SHIELDS

COX, Elizabeth (Wilson) - b Randolph Co., NC 22 Feb 1826; dt John and Mary Wilson; in IN 23 Oct 1846 m William Cox (dec 25 Jan 1901); d 12 Jun 1901 (6/13/01; 6/17/01)

COX, Emma - see Emma (Cox) CAMMACK

COX, Estella - files suit for divorce from Martin Cox; both f of Fmt. (10/21/02)

COX, Frank E. - of Fmt.; s Mrs. Martha Cox (dec) (2/28/01)

COX, Garfield - s Milton Cox (9/9/04)

COX, Josie - dt M/M Seth Cox (6/23/05)

COX, Mrs. Martha - of Sweetser; d recently, bur Park Cem (2/28/01)

COX, Mary - see Mary (Cox) HAISLEY

COX, Milton - brother of Nathan D., John W. and Tilman Cox (9/26/05)

COX, Mrs. Milton - sister of Henry Petty of Indianapolis (1/1/04)

COX, Muriel - f att FHS (5/20/04); see Ernest PEARSON

COX, Dr. N.S. - of NY; m; s M/M Alfred Cox of Indianapolis (10/7/01)

COX, Nathan D. - Park Cem sexton (10/10/02); Pvt., Co. A, 33rd Ind. Inf. during CW (5/27/04; 5/26/05); brother of Volley, John W. and Tilman Cox (9/26/05); gets $12 per mon. CW pension (10/13/05)

COX, Sallie - see Sallie (Cox) POWELL

COX, Seth - owns Cox Shoe Repair Shop (8/29/01)

COX, Tilman - brother of Nathan D., John W., Volley and Milton Cox (9/26/05)

COX, William - of 1.5 mi. SW of Fmt., Liberty Twp; b Randolph Co., NC 9 Nov 1824; s Joshua and Rachel; came to Morgan Co. ca 1829 and to Grant Co. ca 1844; m Elizabeth Wilson 23 Oct 1846; charter mbr Back Creek W.M. Ch.; d 25 Jan 1901, bur Park Cem (1/28/01; 2/4/01)

COYLE, __ - Mrs. James O'NEAL

COYLE, Arthur - s William Coyle (dec) (4/19/04)

COYLE, Gertrude - 1904-05 Fmt. Sch tchr (9/2/04)

COYLE, J.J. - of Fmt.; brother of William Coyle (dec) (4/19/04)

COYLE, John E. - f Fmt. glass worker; killed recently in Streator, IL (6/13/05)

COYLE, L.L. - of Fmt.; brother of William Coyle (dec) (4/19/04)

COYLE, M.L. - drilled gas well for Fmt. at Waterworks Pump Station, well came in 11 Dec 1901 (12/12/01); is contracted by Fmt. Sch Board to drill a gas well on the South Sch property (1/6/02)

COYLE, Rosa - widow of William Coyle, CW vet (6/9/05)

COYLE, W.S. - is shipping his well drilling outfits to OK and will work there (3/7/02)

COYLE, William - age 59; m; serv CW in 156th Pennsylvania Inf.; d 15 Apr 1904, bur Kokomo cem (4/19/04); wife is Rosa (6/9/05)

CRABB, __ - see Mrs. Roy SHERRON

CRABB, Thell - candidate for Fmt. Marshal (4/1/01)

CRAIG, Donald - age 2; s M/M C.G. Craig; d 9 May 1904, bur Park Cem (5/10/04)

CRAWFORD, Cyrus - dec; serv 1st Lieut., Co. D, 16th Ind. Inf. during CW (5/27/04; 5/26/05)

CRAWFORD, Mrs. Louisa - dt Nathan Little (7/22/02); is spending winter in State Soldier's Home, Lafayette (11/10/05)

CRAWFORD, Mamie - 1901 Fmt. Twp. Dist. #7 Sch grad (5/30/01)

CRAY, Fred - s Amos Cray, a Jonesboro banker; 27 Jan 1904 m Blanche Hasting, dt M/M Robert Hasting of 1 mi. S of Fmt.; will live near Jonesboro (1/29/04)

CREEK, Court/Cort - is a Fmt. drayman (2/28/01); Express Office agent (6/6/02); s Mrs. Martha Creek (dec) (10/27/05)

CREEK, Mrs. Cort - sister of Mrs. Samuel Tappan (dec 1 Sep 1904) (9/2/04)

CREEK, Della - dt Cort Creek (6/6/02)

CREEK, Mrs. Martha - of Summitville; age 77; d 25 Oct 1905 (10/27/05)

CREEK, Mary Ann - see Henry LOVE

CREEK, Xen - s Cort Creek (11/1/04)

CRILLEY, Grace Pierce - given party for her 21st birthday 6 Oct 1901 (10/7/01); b 6 Oct 1880; dt Thomas J. and Eliza Pierce; at death of her mother ca 1883, she was taken to raise by H.M. and C.M. Crilley; grad Fmt. HS 1900; mbr Fmt. W.M. Ch.; d 31 Dec 1901, bur Park Cem (12/30/01; 1/6/02; 1/16/02; 12/19/05)

CRILLEY, H.M. - mbr, Finance & Bldg. Committee raising money to build tabernacle for Billy Sunday revival to start 20 Mar 1902 (1/30/02); serv Corp., Co. C, 14th New Jersey Inf. during CW (5/27/04; 5/26/05)

CRISCO, Mark - m Mary Michaels 15 Apr 1901 (4/18/01)

CRISCO, Mrs. Winfield - dt Nathan Little (7/22/02)

CROM, Rev. W.L. - pastor, Fmt. U.B. Ch. (2/17/05)

CRONK, George - of Henry Co.; 28 Oct 1904 m Etta Brookshire, dt Mrs. Lou Brookshire (11/1/04)

CROWELL, Milton - dec; serv Pvt., Co. H, 12th Ind. Inf. and Co. K, 130th Ind. Inf. during CW (5/27/04; 5/26/05)

CROWELL, William P. - serv Co. H, 12th Ind. Inf. during CW (5/27/04; 5/26/05)

CULBERTSON, Mrs. Margaret - b 14 Dec 1818 (8/12/04); age 86 (8/15/05)

CUNNINGHAM, Mrs. Charles - of Pendleton, OR; dt Mrs. James Flanagan of Fmt. (4/15/01)

CURTIS, James W. - serv Pvt., Co. M and Co. A, 6th Ind. Cav. during CW (5/27/04; 5/26/05)

CURTIS, William - elected S.V.C., Beeson GAR Post 386 (1/24/02)

DAILY, Mrs. J.E. - of Fmt.; 11 Jun 1902 is given party for her 32nd birthday (6/13/02)

DALE, __ - b 21 Nov 1905; dt M/M Hal Dale (11/24/05)

DALE, Claude - of Dunkirk; s Dr. George R. Dale (12/1/05)

DALE, Dr. George R. - f Fmt. dentist; d recently (12/1/05)

DALE, Hal V. - enlisted in US Army 2 yrs. ago; serv in P.I. and in China; is now coming home (12/5/01); is home from China (12/26/01); serv Troop A, 6th US Cav.; serv at relief of Peking; is awarded US pension (6/14/04); s J.W. Dale; 11 Aug 1904 m Margaret Harkins (8/16/04)

DALE, J.W. - owner/operator of Dale Hardware (7/18/01)

DALE, Mabel - dt Mrs. J.W. Dale (12/30/01)

DALRYMPLE, Charles - is a barber in Acme Barber Shop (8/26/01)

DANE, Jacob - s Mrs. Sarah Venis of E of Fmt.; mail carrier for Rural Rte. # 1 (3/25/02); mail carrier, Fmt. Rural Rte. # 22 (8/8/02); resigned as mail carrier (8/19/02); is replaced as Fowlerton Postmaster (10/9/03)

DANIELS, Mrs. Will - of Muncie is dt M/M Robert Hasting of Fmt. (2/13/02)

DARE, Miss Addie M. - Fowlerton Sch tchr 1900-01 (3/28/01), and 1903-06 (8/28/03; 8/30/04; 8/15/05)

DARE, Mary J. - mbr German Baptist Ch. (11/4/02)

DARE, Robert - appointed Town Trustee from Ward 5 (1/10/01); serv Corp., Co. G, 69th Ind. Inf. during CW (5/27/04; 5/26/05); CW pension is increased $4 per mon. (6/6/05)

DARE, Mrs. Robert - sister of Caleb McQuoid (dec) (9/13/04)

DAUGHERTY, Bonnie - Tues. was her 11th birthday (8/14/03)

DAUGHERTY, Charles - and N.M. Mendenhall recently purchased Conner Drug Store (9/30/01); druggist (6/20/02)

DAUGHERTY, Nada - 23 Oct 1905, her 12th birthday (10/27/05)

DAUGHERTY, Nancy (Wilson) - dt John and Mary Wilson (6/17/01)

DAVIDSON, Charles E. - b 9 Oct 1887; s Nathan and Elizabeth; mbr Friends; d 13 Apr 1901 (4/15/01; 4/22/01)

DAVIDSON, Mary - young dt M/M Nathan Davidson (3/29/04)

DAVIDSON, Moses - of Hackleman area; d last wk., bur Park Cem (1/27/02)

DAVIDSON, Nathan - contracts to construct tabernacle for Billy Sunday revival (2/10/02); contracts to build new 10-room house on Ancil Winslow farm 2 mi. N of Fmt. (4/8/04)

DAVIS, __ - b 30 Jul 1901; dt M/M Joseph Davis of N of Fmt. (8/1/01)

DAVIS, __ - b 25 Dec 1903; dt M/M Luther Davis (12/29/03)

DAVIS, __ - b 17 Jan 1905; dt M/M Cy Davis of W of Fmt. (1/20/05)

DAVIS, __ - b 20 Feb 1905; s M/M Fred Davis (2/21/05)

DAVIS, __ - b 7 Jul 1905; s M/M Jasper Davis (7/11/05)

DAVIS, __ - b 19 Nov 1905; dt M/M Joe Davis of Bethel (11/28/05)

DAVIS, Arthur - is a Hackleman blacksmith (1/20/02)

DAVIS, Catherine - granddt Catherine Best (b NC 1742, d 1821) (2/19/04)

DAVIS, Charles - glass blower, Fmt. Glass Works; 15 Nov 1904 m Edith, dt M/M Thomas Flynn (11/18/04)

DAVIS, Clara - and Corda are dts Mrs. Frank Davis (9/9/02)

DAVIS, Earl F. - b 23 Oct 1902; s Luther and Mary E. Davis; d 20 Jul 1903 (8/4/03)

DAVIS, Effie - see Effie (Davis) LITTLE; also see Lin WILSON

DAVIS, Foster - a Director, Fmt. Hunting & Fishing Club (1/1/04); 1st Vice Pres., Fmt. Fair Assoc. (1/12/04); f of Fmt.; will soon m Mrs. Mary E. Higgins, widow of Rev. Higgins, f pastor Marion Presbyterian Ch. (4/26/04); Pvt., Co. H, 12th Ind. Inf. and 2nd Lieut., Co. G, 153rd Ind. Inf. during CW (5/27/04; 5/26/05)

DAVIS, Frank - owned W. Washington St. bldg. occupied by Morris & Childs Laundry (4/4/02)

DAVIS, Fred - is a baker in Shuey Bakery (1/19/04); leases Premium Bakery from Clyde Gossett (9/1/05)

DAVIS, Mrs. Fred - dt R.E. Overman (dec) (7/28/05)

DAVIS, George - of near Bethel; age ca 83; d 23 Jul 1901, bur Marion cem (7/25/01)

DAVIS, Georgia - grad Back Creek Friends Sch 1905 (5/12/05)

DAVIS, Harrison - b near Fmt. 18 Oct 1888; s David D. and Mary F. Davis; mbr Friends; d 4 Mar 1905 (3/7/05)

DAVIS, Harry - resigned from BeeHive after working there 14 yrs. (12/29/03)

DAVIS, Henry - Fmt. Mining Co. just completed a gas well on his farm (9/12/02)

DAVIS, Joe S. - is a sailor/'Jackie' aboard the cruiser, USS Yankee (8/25/03), is a USN quartermaster (9/9/04)

DAVIS, Joseph - pastor, Back Creek Friends (1/10/05)

DAVIS, Leroy - and Melvin and Lucile and Russell are children of David D. and Mary F. Davis (3/10/05)

DAVIS, Luther - s M/M Frank Davis (8/19/04)

DAVIS, Mrs. Luther - dt Nathan W. and Tamer Hunt (8/16/04)

DAVIS, Merlie - dt David D. and Mary F. Davis; FHS senior (3/7/05)

DAVIS, Myrtle - FFA grad; f missionary to Matamoras, Mexico (9/15/03); see Vaughn GOODYKOONTZ

DAVIS, Myrtle - 1904 Liberty Twp. Sch grad (4/19/04)

DAVIS, Philip - ran stage coach between Marion and Anderson through Fmt. until he sold it in 1861 (1/20/05)

DAVIS, Phillip - age 66; m; 28 Dec 1904 accidentally killed by interurban car (12/30/04); bur Park Cem (1/3/05)

DAVIS, Stella - dt Mrs. Frank Davis (9/9/02); 1904-05 Fmt. Schs tchr (9/2/04)

DAVIS, Verling W. - grad Stetson Univ Law Sch 1902 (5/30/02); s Foster Davis; to be his father's law partner in Marion (6/10/02); recently m Alta Loretta, dt M/M A.W. Nickle; will live in Marion (7/5/04)

DAVIS, W.F. - of Fmt.; s George Davis (7/25/01)

DAVIS, Webster - 1901-02 FFA science tchr (10/3/01)

DAVIS, Will - s Kelly Davis; 25 Sep 1904 d at Treaty; bur Back Creek Friends Cem (9/27/04)

DAY, ___ - b 31 Oct 1905; s M/M Isaac Day (11/3/05)

DAY, Aquilla - of Green Twp.; serv 34th Ind. Inf. during CW (10/10/05)

DAY, Isaac - s Mrs. Willard Day (d 23 Jan 1905) (1/24/05)

DAY, Mrs. Isaac - dt J.B. Eaton (11/21/05)

DAY, John M. - mail carrier, Fmt. Rural Rte. #22 (8/14/03)

DEALY, G.W. - dec; serv Pvt., Co. F, 32nd Ind. Inf. during CW (5/27/04; 5/26/05)

DEAN, A.K. - brother of Cal and Joab Dean; d at Summitville 6 Sep 1901 (9/9/01)

DEAN, Alfred - of near Summitville; age 52; brother of Cal Dean; d 21 May 1905, bur Vinson Cem (5/26/05)

DEAN, Amanda - see Amanda (Dean) WILSON

DEAN, Cal - auctioneer (9/2/02)

DEAN, Glenn - resigns as barber in Acme Barber Shop (8/26/01); is working in TX; s Mrs. James Phillips (dec) (2/3/02)

DEAN, Harrison - dec; Pvt., 22nd Ind. Inf. during CW (5/26/05)

DEAN, Job - of 3 mi. SE of Fmt.; age 59; m Mollie; brother of Cal Dean; d 16 Oct 1905, bur Park Cem (10/17/05; 10/20/05)

DEAN, Lillie - see Will F. BROWN

DEAN, Purl - s Cal Dean; both are auctioneers (3/7/02)

DEAN, R.E. - 1901-02 FFA commercial/shorthand tchr (10/3/01)

DEBRUCQUE, B. - and Henry are Directors, Industrial Window Glass Co. of Fowlerton (10/14/01)

DEEREN, Alex - dec; serv Pvt., Co. C, 172nd Ohio Inf. during CW (5/27/04; 5/26/05)

DeHOFF, Ida [(Mason)] - 17 Mar 1904 att wedding anniv. dinner for M/M James Kirkpatrick (3/22/04)

DELPH, James - b 4 Feb 1818 (8/12/04); age 87 (8/15/05)

DENNING, ___ - b 8 Oct 1905; dt Chris and Mabel (Winslow) Denning of Jonesboro; Mabel f of Fmt. (10/13/05)

DENNY, Walter B. - Acting Pastor, Fmt. Congregational Ch. (5/27/04)

DeSHON, __ - young dt of M/M Will DeShon; d 7 Apr 1902 (4/8/02)

DeSHON, __ - see Mrs. George KESSEL

DeSHON, Amos - dec; serv Pvt., Co. D, 79th Ind. Inf. during CW (5/27/04; 5/26/05)

DeSHON, Anna (Rush) - of Fmt.; dt Susan Rush (2/16/04); is granted a divorce from Frank DeShon (6/24/04)

DeSHON, Bert - s Mrs. Frank DeShon of Fmt. (3/18/02)

DeSHON, Frank - and wife and family move to Rising Sun 4/29/01); s Mrs. Phoebe DeShon; is Farm Mgr., Jeffersonville Reformatory (12/2/04)

DeSHON, Glen - age 12 (10/17/05)

DeSHON, Kate - see Kate (DeShon) SHIELDS

DeSHON, Phoebe - age 57; widow of Amos DeShon (dec 4 Aug 1876); d 17 May 1905, bur Park Cem (5/19/05)

DeSHON, Will - of Piqua, PA; s Amos and Phoebe DeShon (5/19/05)

DeSHON, Zen - age 12 (10/17/05)

DEVINE, John - of N of Fmt.; 14 Nov 1902 lost right hand in farm accident (11/14/02)

DICKENS, Gabriel - colored; age 81; d 13 Apr 1905, bur Park Cem (4/18/05)

DICKERSON, __ - infant of M/M Arthur Dickerson of 4 mi. SE of Fmt. d recently, bur Park Cem (4/21/05)

DICKERSON, R.H. - serv Pvt., Co. F, 32nd Ind. Inf. during CW (5/27/04; 5/26/05)

DICKEY, A.V. - opens blacksmith shop at 312 W. Washington St. (7/25/05); moves his blacksmith shop to N. Main St. (12/12/05)

DICKEY, Mabel - age 14; dt M/M Abner Dickey; d 4 Dec 1904, bur Park Cem (12/6/04)

DICKEY, Oren - tchr, Liberty Twp. Sch 1904-05 (12/27/04)

DICKEY, Dr. Pearl - and partner, Dr. Oz Cartwright, have dental offices in Borrey Blk. (6/20/01)

DICKEY, Viola - mbr Fmt. Christian Ch. (11/4/02)

DICKEY, Mrs. Walter - of 4 mi. SE of Fmt.; m; d 27 Jan 1905, bur Park Cem (1/31/05)

DICKS, Mary - dt Rev. John Pennington (recently dec); mbr, Fmt. WCTU (9/16/02)

DICKS, Nathan - s Allen Dicks (12/25/03)

DIEFENBACH, Fred - of Fmt.; d 15 May 1902 (5/16/02)

DILLON, Agnes - dt Mrs. Margaret Dillon (6/16/05)

DILLON, Claude - and A.J. Morris own Cottage Laundry (5/30/01); sold his interest in laundry to Charles Childs (8/29/01); and wife intend moving to Colorado (9/5/01); s Julia Ann Dillon (9/1/03)

DILLON, Mrs. Claude - dt Mrs. M.H. Nelson of Fmt. (11/4/04)

DILLON, Katie - see Verlie JONES

DILLON, Katie (Coahran) - 1881, Fmt. Twp. Sch grad; m Arthur Dillon; later dec (7/4/05)

DILLON, Mary - dt M/M Richard Dillon; 7 Jul 1905 is given party for her 12th birthday (7/18/05)

DILLON, Mary J. - see Henry WINSLOW

DILLON, Mrs. Richard - sister of Miss Susan F. Coahran (12/25/03)

DILLY, Percy - 2 Jan 1905 m Pearl Brewer; live in Fmt. (1/6/05)

DITCH - John Flanagan et al. petitioned for construction of New Prairie Ditch across sections 33, 28, and 27, Fmt. Twp. (7/8/02)

DOHERTY, Mrs. Henry - of Little Ridge area; dt Mrs. Millicent Haisley (12/4/03)

DOHERTY, Katherine - age 4; dt M/M Cyrus Doherty (3/21/05)

DOLMAN, W.A. - sold his Lunch Room to Samuel Mart (12/30/01); serv Pvt., Co. C, 89th Ind. Inf. during CW (5/26/05)

DOUGLASS, __ - see Mrs. Frank ELDRIDGE

DOUGLAS, Emma - see Emma (Douglass) NOSE

DOUGLASS, John L. - serv Pvt., Co. F, 40th Ind. Inf. during CW (5/27/04; 5/26/05); age 61; m; d 7 Sep 1905, bur Jonesboro IOOF Cem (9/12/05)

DOUGLASS, Mattie - widow of John L. Douglass (9/15/05)

DOVE, Levi - serv Pvt., Co. A, 19th Ind. Inf. during CW (5/26/05)

DOWNS, Miss Belle - cashier, Bee Hive Cash Store (3/7/02)

DOWNS, Ethel Charlotte - see Ethel Charlotte (Downs) SHUEY

DOWNS, Frank Elmer - b Pt. Isabel 11 Nov 1867; d Fmt. 13 Jun 1902, bur Knox Chapel Cem (6/13/02; 6/17/02)

DOWNS, Phebe A. (Pence) - b Champaign Co., OH 29 Jan 1829; dt Martin and Elizabeth Pence; m OH 1 Feb 1849 Allen B. Downs; mbr Fmt. Congregational Ch.; d 8 Jan 1901 (1/10/01; 1/14/01)

DRIGGS, Fred - and Harry are sons Mrs. Asa Driggs (7/21/05)

DuBOIS, Nestor - of Alexandria is a Director, Industrial Window Glass Co. of Fowlerton (10/14/01)

DuBOIS, Pearl - see Albert KAMMER

DUCKWALL, Nelson E. - of Van Buren; 17 Oct 1903 m Alta L. Ward of Fmt.; will live in Upland (10/20/03)

DULING, ___ - see Mrs. Charles M. HOBBS

DULING, Asa - of Jonesboro; s Edmund and Eliza Ann (Hubert) Duling (2/18/01); d recently, bur Bethel Cem (8/23/04)

DULING, Blanch - see Jacob LEACH

DULING, Della - dt Thomas Duling; d at her home 2 mi. E of Fmt. 27 Feb 1901, bur Park Cem (2/28/01)

DULING, Edmund - of E of Fmt.; age 83 (2/4/01); b Coshocton Co., OH; age 83 yr., 10 mon, 2 da; s Edmund and Mary; lived 4 mi. E of Fmt.; 1 Nov 1842 m Eliza Ann Hubert; came to Grant Co. Sep 1845; mbr M.P. Ch.; early Fmt. Twp. sch tchr; d 11 Feb 1901 (2/18/01)

DULING, Emily - of Fmt.; dt Edmund and Mary Duling (2/18/01)

DULING, Georgia - dt Mrs. Caroline Duling of E of Fmt. (4/12/04)

DULING, J.O. - Fmt. Twp. Assessor (6/27/01); is Fmt. Twp. Trustee (7/25/02; 8/7/03); replaced as Trustee 1 Jan 1905 (11/29/04)

DULING, Maria - see Maria (Duling) HOLLINGSWORTH

DULING, Sina M. - see Sina M. (Duling) LATHAM

DULING, Solomon - of 4 mi. E of Fmt.; s Edmund and Eliza Ann (Hubert) Duling (2/18/01)

DUNBAR, Lillian May - given party for 19th birthday 26 Jun 1902 (7/4/02); - see Clyde SCOTT

DUNCAN, Elmer - of Summitville; brother of John Duncan of Fmt.; d 27 Sep 1902 (9/30/02)

DUNCAN, Emanuel - serv Pvt., 5th Ind. Cav. during CW (5/26/05)

DUNLAP, Mrs. John - of E of Fmt.; age ca 61 (11/21/05)

DURNION, John - age 40; m; 27 Oct 1905 committed suicide with morphine, bur Park Cem (10/31/05)

DYSON, Daisy (Starr) - dt M/M C.A. Starr (4/22/04)

DYSON, James - age 31; s Thomas Dyson of near Little Ridge; d 21 Sep 1905, bur Park Cem (9/26/05)

EARNEST, Dr. A.O. - f of Knightstown; veterinary surgeon, new office is over Citizens Exchange Bank (2/7/05); his home burned last wk. (9/8/05)

EASTES, Lucinda - see Lucinda (Eastes) WARD

EASTES, M.P. - of Markle; brother of Lucinda (Eastes) Ward (1/26/04)

EASTES, Sallie - see Sallie (Eastes) KELSAY

EASTES, Dr. William - of Gaston; brother of Lucinda (Eastes) Ward (1/26/04)

EATON, __ - see Mrs. Isaac DAY

EATON, J.B. - of Hackleman; age 69; d recently, bur Park Cem (11/21/05)

EATON, Porter - s M/M Otto Eaton of Hackleman (9/16/01)

EDGERTON, __ - see Mrs. Tom CARTER

EDGERTON, Palmer - att Purdue Univ 1904-05 (12/16/04); s Mrs. Sallie Edgerton (12/23/04)

EDGERTON, Sallie - mbr, Fmt. WCTU (9/16/02)

EDWARDS, Gladys - 1903-04 att Miami Coll, Oxford, OH (1/8/04)

EDWARDS, Lydia - see Harvey F. PRESNALL

EDWARDS, Nathan W. - 1881, Fmt. druggist (1/13/1881 as reprinted 3/29/04); a Trustee, Fmt. Schs (6/10/04)

EDWARDS, Mrs. Nathan W. - 7 Mar 1901 is given party for her 41st birthday (3/11/01)

EDWARDS, Orville - f clerk in Edwards Drug Store; brother of N.W. Edwards; d recently in Muncie (12/13/04)

EDWARDS, Walter - age 32; s William and Anna Edwards; not m; d 4 Mar 1904 (3/8/04)

EDWARDS, Xen H. - grad DePauw Univ 1902 (8/26/01; 6/13/02); s M/M N.W. Edwards; is engaged to Ora Ethel, dt Rev./M Enos Harvey (12/30/04); 25 Jan 1905 m Ethel (1/27/05)

EDWARDS, Mrs. Xen H. - mbr Shakespeare Club (4/14/05)

EIBER, Pearl - age 17; s Henry Eiber of Hackleman; is accidentally shot/ wounded by Mrs. C.D. Brookshire (7/8/04)

ELDRIDGE, Mrs. Frank - sister of John Douglass (9/15/05)

ELKINS, Mrs. Willard - of PA; dt John and Mary (Hiatt) Baker (5/9/05)

ELLIOTT, Anson - of Marion; s Elijah and Deborah (Wilson) Elliott (8/30/04)

ELLIOTT, Deborah (Wilson) - b 26 Jun 1845; dt Nathan D. and Mary Wilson; 22 Nov 1865 m Elijah Elliott; mbr Friends; d 28 Aug 1904 (8/30/04)

ELLIOTT, Mrs. Exum - of Fmt.; dt Luther Brookshire (2/19/04)

ELLIOTT, Nathan D. - of Salem, OR; s Elijah and Deborah (Wilson) Elliott (8/30/04)

ELLIOTT, Rachel - see Ora FOWLER

ELLIOTT, Samuel - s William S. Elliott of Radley (2/24/05)

ELLIOTT, Mrs. Samuel - dt William Hartley of Radley; m; d 22 Feb 1905, bur Knox Chapel Cem (2/24/05)

ELLIOTT, Susannah (Carey) - sister of Elias Carey of Marion (4/28/05)

ELLIOTT, William S. - of Radley recently purchased a Star Windmill from Fmt. Buggy Co. who erected it (5/2/02); s Mrs. Rebecca Elliott of Harveyville, KS (9/18/03); serv Corp., Co. C, 89th Ind. Inf. during CW (5/27/04; 5/26/05)

ELLIS, __ - see Mrs. Clint WINSLOW

ELLIS, Arthur - and Cressie, both of Richmond; children of Rev./M Elwood O. Ellis (11/15/04)

ELLIS, Dora - of Richmond; dt Rev./M Elwood O. Ellis (12/27/04); grad Earlham Coll 1905 (4/28/05)

ELLIS, Edith - 1904-05 Fmt. Sch tchr (9/2/04); - see Cyrus L. COPPOCK

ELLIS, Rev. Elwood O. - of Richmond; s M/M James Ellis (1/21/01); replaced as Richmond Friends pastor due to relationship with Miss Bessie Slick; 3 M.D.'s declare him insane, he is committed into a hospital in Oxford, OH (7/22/04); he does not enjoy being confined but makes no complaint (7/29/04); has disappeared from Oxford, OH sanitarium (9/9/04); is dropped from rolls of Richmond Friends (9/20/04); was found in Cincinnati, OH; is brought to home of Clinton Winslow E of Fmt., mentally ill (11/15/04); temporary clerk, Gold Mine # 9 Grocery Store (1/31/05); and wife live on E. Washington St. (3/10/05); and wife move to S. Vine (6/16/05); resigns from A.D. Stech Grocery to sell aluminum ware (8/29/05); advertises for traveling salespersons, male or female, to work for $21 per wk. plus expenses (9/1/05)

ELLIS, Mrs. Elwood O. - of Richmond; is ill (8/30/04); is now in Fmt. with husband (11/15/04)

ELLIS, Frank - of OH; 2 Nov 1904 m Alice, dt M/M Thamer Winslow; will live in Camden, OH (11/4/04; 2/19/05)

ELLIS, Lydia - see Lydia (Ellis) JONES

ELLIS, Mayme - tchr, Liberty Twp. Sch 1904-05 (12/27/04); Pike Sch tchr 1905-06 (8/15/05)

ELLIS, Rachel A. - see Rachel A. (Ellis) NOLDER

ELLIS, Robert T. - of Jonesboro; s M/M James Ellis (1/21/01); d 24 Jan 1902 (1/24/02)

ELLIS, Walter - of Jonesboro; s M/M James Ellis (1/21/01)

ELSON, O.C. - a Director, Fmt. Hunting & Fishing Club (1/1/04)

ENGLAND, came from - see William BARTHOLOMEW; James FENTON; John SEALE, Sr.; William SEALE

ENGLE, Mrs. Charles - of Matthews; dt M/M Samuel Stewart of Fmt. (5/16/02)

ENGLE, Roy - employee of Fmt. Machine & Tool Works (1/15/04)

ENGLE, William - sold his W. Washington St. shoe shop; is moving to Dunkirk (1/20/02)

ENGLES, Mrs. Anna - mbr Fmt. Congregational Ch. (9/5/01)

ENGLISH, John H. - employee, Bell Window Glass factory; 7 May 1904 m Lucy Pickard, will live in Fmt. (5/13/04)

EVINGER, Hortense - see Hortense (Evinger) FORAKER

FAIRMOUNT, TOWN of - 1879, Will Winslow had the nicest house in town, the streets were muddy, 1 RR ran N-S and had 1 depot, 2 flour mills, 1 flax factory, 1 planing mill, 2 warehouses, 1 woolen factory, 1 sawmill, 1 sch, 2 millinery shops, 1 hotel, 3 churches, a plank walk from Levi Scott's Dry Goods Store to a warehouse, Walker Winslow had a livery stable, Levi Winslow had a boarding house, many streets were graveled, 1 printing shop (Fmt. News) run by

[William] Seaford (tchr, Fmt. Sch) and Stout, Bogue's Dry Goods Store, __ Ballard had a dray, and one drug store (2/15/1879 as reprinted 1/29/04); Robert Dare appointed Town Trustee from Ward 5 (1/10/01); Pat T. O'Brien of Elwood contracts to brick Main St. from Washington St. S to Henley Ave., then Henley Ave. S. to Taylor St. (2/11/01); sewers under Main St. to Harrison St. will empty directly into Back Creek (5/27/01); brick for Main St. was made in Veedersburg (6/17/01); 24 Jul 1901 brick laying began on Main St. (7/25/01); J.A. Spencer resigns as Water Works engineer, is replaced by William Bowers (9/16/01); brick laying starts on W. Washington St. (9/30/01); brick laying starts on Henley Ave. (10/31/01); bricking of Henley Ave. is completed (11/21/01); bricks are laid on S. Main St. (11/28/01); gas well drilled by M.L. Coyle for the town at Waterworks Pump Station came in 11 Dec 1901 with 66 lbs. pressure; 100 electric Christmas lights are strung 4' apart on Main St. downtown (12/12/01); Water Works well was shot with poor results (1/9/02); C.D. Overman re-appointed postmaster (2/10/02); Town Marshal is Esom O. Leach (3/28/02); Jacob Briles, Town Clerk (6/20/02); Charles T. Parker is Town Attorney (6/24/02); Police have a pair of bloodhounds that "couldn't trail a hot sausage from the stove to the table" (7/29/02); George A. Fletcher is Town Civil Engineer (9/26/02); 26 Nov 1903 Marshal James Payne is murdered by Harry Hooper (11/27/03); Clifford V. Hadley appointed new Marshal (12/4/03); William Bowers will operate waterworks (2/5/04); horse watering troughs, out of service during winter, are now installed at Big Four RR, at 8th & Main St., and in front of Fritz Meat Market; a drinking fountain is on Post Office corner (5/13/04); Dr. W.M. Warner is appointed Health Officer replacing Dr. S.G. Hastings (9/23/04); site of Fmt. 1st settled in 1833; Thomas Baldwin bought NW 1/4 of Sec. 29 on 1 Oct 1833, then came Daniel Baldwin from NC, Benjamin Benbow from TN, then Joseph Winslow, Seth Winslow, Joseph Baldwin, David Stanfield, William Hall, Thomas Powell, Nathan Vinson, John Wilson and his s Micajah; William Hall had 1st tanyard in S part of Fmt.; Nathan Little had tanyard near Fmt. center (1/13/05); James Cammack built 1st sawmill 1848, later William Lindsey has sawmill that burned in 1900; Winslow & Rau Glass Factory was established 1888; Main St. was 1st graveled in 1862 (1/17/05); beginning 1848, Albert Carey drove stage coach between Marion and Anderson through Fmt., he sold stage to Philip Davis who sold it to Walker H. Winslow in 1861, who then operated it for 14 yrs.; I.B. Rush had 1st velocipede in Fmt.; Ira Neely owned 1st auto; 1848, 1st merchant, Joseph Baldwin, had dry goods/grocery store on NE corner of Washington & Main; 1st Postmaster was William Hall; 1863, Milton Henley had 1st harness shop; 1882, Levi Scott had 1st bank (1/17/05); 28 Dec 1850, Fmt. is platted by David Stanfield (1/17/05); f home of David and Elizabeth Stanfield stood on corner of Main & Madison St., burned 20 May 1905 (5/23/05); Joseph Peacock, now of Kokomo, in 1849, built 1st house in Fmt. for Joseph Baldwin at site of present Borrey Blk. (6/20/05); R.K. Johnson helped William Neal lay out 1st Fmt. plat (6/27/05); R.E. Overman (dec) had a music store here for several yrs. (7/28/05); 15 Feb 1879 there were 9 steam mills and factories in Fmt.; 11 Jan 1883, one telephone in Fmt., J.H. Wilson was 1st person to telephone from Fmt. to Indianapolis (12/15/05)

ACME BARBER SHOP - Bert Sherwin is a barber (2/7/01); Glenn Dean resigns as barber, Charles Dalrymple takes his place (8/26/01); Will Rudicil resigns as barber (10/31/01)

ADAMS EXPRESS CO. - has office in C.I.&E. station (1/17/05)

AMERICAN EXPRESS CO. - office is on N. Main St. (3/2/02); O.M. Harris, agent (3/28/02); Cort Creek is now the agent (6/6/02); Chester VanArsdall resigns as agent, is replaced by George A. Fletcher (3/25/04); 1888, had office in C.W.&M. depot (1/17/05)

AMERICAN WINDOW GLASS FACTORY # 27 - A.L. Reed, Mgr. (7/25/01); Fred D. Oakley works in office (8/29/01); drilled a new gas well that is an excellent producer (1/30/02)

BEAL SHOE SHOP - located on N side of Washington St. a half block W of Main St.; owner/operator is Jacob Beals (5/9/01); 1881, Jacob Beals does shoe repair (1/13/1881 as reprinted 3/29/04)

BEASLEY DRUG STORE - H.I. Wheeler is a f clerk (1/13/05)

BEEHIVE CASH STORE - Miss Belle Downs, cashier (3/7/02); Harry Davis resigns after working here 14 yrs. (12/29/03); Olive Rittenhouse, employee (4/11/05); Miss Zola Wilson, cashier (10/13/05)

BELL WINDOW GLASS FACTORY - Fred Miller, employee (5/2/01); has a new gas well (2/3/02); Sim Pearson, employee (3/29/04); William Borrey, Asst. Mgr. (4/15/04); John H. English (5/13/04), and Charles Oakley, employees (7/26/04)

BIG FOUR BARBER SHOP - is purchased by Marion Love (8/26/01); is closed by M. Love (10/3/01)

BIG FOUR RESTAURANT - re-purchased by Ike Lemon (11/21/02)

BIG FOUR WINDOW GLASS FACTORY - John Shaughnessy, employee since ca 1894, resigns (8/29/01); factory is closed for indefinite period, employees seek work elsewhere (2/3/02); A.L. Reed, Supt.

(7/18/02); was 1st window glass factory in Fmt.; 1st owners were Al Reed, Harry Gable, B.F. Zieglar; now owned by American Window Glass Co.; idle ca 3 yrs., burned 16 Apr 1905 (4/18/05)

BILLY SUNDAY TABERNACLE - Rev. Oscar Lowry leads drive to build a tabernacle seating 1,200 people for the 4-wk. W.A. Sunday revival starting 20 Mar 1902; 100 shares being sold at $5 each; Finance & Bldg. Committee mbrs are Oscar Lowry, C.R. Small, Carl P. Rau, H.M. Crilley (1/30/02); revival to begin 25 Mar 1902; funds are raised, construction of bldg. to begin soon on the Odd Fellows lot just N of Sutton Blk. (2/3/02), on S. Main St. (2/3/02), lot is 44' X 132' (4/4/02); contract to construct bldg. is given to Nathan Davidson (2/10/02); tabernacle framework is up ready for roof (2/28/02); revival starts Sunday 30 Mar 1902 (3/21/02); 4 large electric arc lights & several gas jets are installed (3/25/02); a rented piano will be used during revival (3/28/02); a chorus of 75 to 100 voices are performing during the revival; tabernacle will be sold at close of meetings 28 Apr 1902 (4/1/02); standing room only at revival (4/4/02); Newt Allen bought tabernacle for $151, to tear it down at end of revival (4/8/02); at least 1,300 people in tabernacle with 500 people turned away on some nights (4/15/02); PHOTOS of Billy Sunday & his song leader, F.G. Fischer (4/22/02); 609 conversions during 4-wk. revival that ended 27 Apr 1902 (4/29/02); next wk. Newt Allen begins tearing down tabernacle, lumber will be used in 2 new houses in S part of Fmt. (5/2/02); new converts church prefer-ences are: Friends-195; Methodist-150; Congregational-71; Baptist-24; Wesleyan Methodist-53; United Brethren-11; rest of 609 indicated no preference (5/2/02)

BOGUE GROCERY - 1881, Jesse Bogue, prop. (1/13/1881 as reprinted 3/29/04)

BORREY BLOCK - has dental offices of partners Dr. Pearl Dickey and Dr. Oz Cartwright (6/20/01); houses telephone exchange (3/18/02); Dr. T.J. Carter moves his office out (8/25/03); Dr. J.P. Seale has office here (6/2/05)

BORREY HALL - is rented by newly formed Fmt. YMCA (5/13/02)

CAREY MANUFACTURING CO. - established on W. 3rd St. in spring of 1904; William Carey, owner; makes automobiles using 10 horse-power Leo gasoline engines (9/13/04)

CIGAR & SUNDRY STORE - sold to Buck Mann by M. West (9/26/01)

CITIZEN'S EXCHANGE BANK - John Selby, Cashier (3/7/01); stockholders are Nixon Winslow, A.A. Ulrey, John Selby (3/18/02); Will F. Brown (dec), f cashier (5/27/02); above bank is office of Dr. S.G. Hastings (6/6/02), and office of new veterinary surgeon, Dr.

A.O. Earnest (2/7/05); Dec 1894, Gilbert LaRue is Cashier, John Winslow and Will Brown are Asst. Cashiers (12/15/05)

CITIZEN'S TELEPHONE COMPANY - S.B. Hill, Mgr., says phone lines soon to extend to Hackleman and Rigdon (1/10/01); new employee is Ralph Fletcher (2/4/01); has station in Jonesboro (4/8/01); Miss Alta Ward, telephone exchange operator (5/30/01); has device that rings calls without operators doing the ringing (9/26/01); phone lines to be extended into country as far as Rigdon (9/26/01); phone lines now extend to 2.5 mi. S of Fmt. and W to Rigdon; 200 phones are in use (10/21/01); Co. purchased by H.O. Miller of United Telephone Co., S.B. Hill to be retained as Mgr. (1/9/02); Supt./Mgr. is H.O. Miller (3/7/02; 4/1/04); exchange is moved to Borrey Blk. (3/18/02); telephone is installed in YWCA rooms (6/6/02); operators are Miss Bernice Bosley and Miss Margaret Harkins (9/1/03); S.B. Hill resigns (9/16/04); Elizabeth (Pretlow) Baldwin, f employee (11/4/04); Myrtle Carter and Blanche Yerkey are employees (11/29/04); Aaron Newby, Supt. (1/3/05); began in 1897 with 14 telephones (1/24/05)

COLUMBIA HOTEL - is sold by H.A. Scott to H.D. Thomas of Jonesboro (4/25/01); was owned/operated several yrs. ago by Robert Malott and his son Nate (7/18/01); is again owned by Mrs. George Thomas (6/24/04); J. Maddy is a f Mgr. (12/2/04)

COTTAGE PHOTOGRAPHY GALLERY - is at Jefferson St. & Washington St.; photographer is S.Y. Pearson (10/21/01)

COTTAGE STEAM LAUNDRY - owned by A.J. Morris and Claud Dillon (5/30/01); C. Dillon sells interest to Charles Childs (8/29/01)

COX SHOE REPAIR SHOP - owned by Seth Cox; also sells ready-made shoes (8/29/01)

CRESCENT BAKERY - purchased by Andy Gangwisch; Al Shuey remains as baker (4/18/05)

CRYSTAL ICE & BOTTLING WORKS - H.E. Johnson, Mgr. (1/31/01); makes and sells ice cream (4/29/01); John Tomlinson, employee (7/22/01); Joe Patterson, employee (8/26/01); to be dismantled and taken from Fmt. to Chicago Heights (3/14/02)

DALE HARDWARE - owned by J.W. Dale; Hort Ribble is an employee (7/18/01)

DICKEY BLACKSMITH SHOP - at 312 W. Washington St.; owned by A.V. Dickey (7/25/05); is moved to N. Main St. (12/12/05)

DOLMAN LUNCH ROOM - sold by W.A. Dolman to Samuel Mart (12/30/01)

DRUG STORE - run for 12 yrs. by druggist W.B. Conner, now sold to Charles Daugherty and N.M Mendenhall (9/30/01)

DYE & MONTGOMERY CEMETERY MONUMENTS - donated date stone for new Back Creek W.M. Church building (10/28/04)

EDWARDS DRUG STORE - 1881, N.W. Edwards, druggist (1/13/1881 as reprinted 3/29/04)

ENGLE SHOE SHOP - on W. Washington St.; sold by William Engle (1/20/02)

FAIRMOUNT BANKING CO. - 2nd Fmt. bank; started by Will F. Morris of Pendleton (11/11/02); Aaron Morris, Pres.; John Flanagan, Vice Pres.; R.A. Morris, Cashier; C.R. Small, Asst. Cashier; stockholders are Aaron Morris, R.A. Morris, W.F. Morris, John Flanagan, F. Mason, W.A Beasley, John A. Hunt, C.R. Small (11/18/02)

FAIRMOUNT BLOCK - is new; contains offices of Walter L. Jay, Attorney and of Dr. C.M. Wilson, Dentist (11/7/01); John A. Hunt's business is on 1st floor; YWCA rented the front rooms above Hunt, will be a reading room and a parlor (5/30/02); telephone is installed in YWCA rooms (6/10/02)

FAIRMOUNT BUGGY CO. - erects 2 Star Windmills on the Henry Wise farm E of Gas City (8/22/01); recently erected a Star Windmill for Al Shields (3/25/02); recently erected a Star Windmill for William S. Elliott of Radley (5/2/02); includes a harness shop (1/20/05); opens a blacksmith & repair shop on S. Walnut St. (4/11/05)

FAIRMOUNT DAILY JOURNAL - established 1900 by E.A. Morgan (1/24/05)

FAIRMOUNT ELECTRIC LIGHT PLANT - Will Bowers, plant electrician, has installed 7 arc lights at the Wesleyan Camp Grounds (8/26/01); is sold by LaRue & Patterson to Francis M. Ingler of Indianapolis (10/14/04); a deisel engine is installed (1/20/05)

FAIRMOUNT FLOURING MILL - 4 Dec 1904 is slightly damaged by a fire (12/6/04)

FAIRMOUNT FOUNDRY & MACHINE WORKS - E.E. Briles is employed as a stenographer & typist (12/30/01); is merged into Machine & Tool Works (10/21/02)

FAIRMOUNT GAS CO. - Mgr., H.H. Hughes (8/26/04)

FAIRMOUNT GLASS WORKS - Factories No 1-4 employ 625 men (9/15/03); Fred Bland, employee (4/19/04); Nina Bogue, office employee (4/29/04); Frank Stewart, glassblower (6/10/04); had 500-625 employees during winter of 1903-04, is now shut down for summer (6/17/04); William Harvey replaces Charles Rau as Supt. (6/21/04); William E. Armfield, employee (7/8/04); Factories 1,3 & 4 started work 15 Sep 1904 with ca 500 employees; Factory 2 is dismantled, moved to Indianapolis (9/16/04); Ray Apple (dec) was employee (10/4/04); Charles

Davis, glass blower (11/18/04); Clayton Johnson, bookkeeper (12/23/04); Harmon T. Newby, employee (11/7/05)
FAIRMOUNT GRAIN CO. - purchases R.J. Beal's Grain Elevator & Coal Bins (11/3/05)
FAIRMOUNT MINING CO. - brought in a good gas well at S end of Fmt. (8/26/01); J.C. Overman, plant Supt. (8/26/01); Ed S. Leach, Asst. Supt. (9/5/01); gas well at crossing of C.I.&E. RR and Pike S of Fmt. is full of salt water, is abandoned (11/28/01); drilling more gas wells (12/19/01); struck gas 1 Jan 1902 in their new well in NE part of Fmt. (1/1/02), well has now been shot (1/6/02); 1902 officers are Alex Myers, Pres.; John Flanagan, Sect.; Nixon Winslow, Treas.; J.C. Overman, Supt.; Eddie Leach, Asst. Supt. (1/16/02); now drilling new gas well in S part of Fmt. (1/30/02), on S. Henley Ave., is completed (2/10/02); drilling gas well on rear of Friends MH lot (2/17/02), is shot 24 Feb 1902 with a resulting good flow of gas (2/25/02); new gas well on S. Henley Ave. 18 Feb 1902 filled with water (2/20/02); 1st gas well brought in was 'Jumbo'; its property is sold to John R. Pearson of Indianapolis Gas Co. for $20,000 (7/8/02); just completed a gas well on Henry Davis farm (9/12/02); J.C. Overman resigns as Supt. (9/19/02); natural gas discovered in Fmt. in Apr 1887 by drilling the gas well 'Jumbo' by Fmt. Mining Co. whose investors were Dr. A. Henley, Levi Scott, Jonathan P. Winslow, C.R. Small, John Flanagan, Thomas J. Nixon, Dr. Hubbard, M. Mark, and the Kimbrough Bros. (1/17/05)
FAIRMOUNT NEWS - 1881, Charles and Emma Stout, editors (1/13/1881 as reprinted 3/29/04); 1st established by editor, Joel Reece (1/24/05); 1st issue was 22 Dec 1877 (12/22/05)
FAIRMOUNT TILE CO. - Lee Brown, employee (12/15/03); Supt., Dr. M.E. Ratliff (9/23/04); S.E. Haisley, employee (8/4/05); is purchased by C.R. Small and John A. Hunt (9/1/05); Charles Carey, Supt. (11/17/05); John A. Hunt, business Mgr. (11/21/05)
FLANAGAN DOUBLE STORE - cashier, Gertrude Winslow (2/20/02); John Flanagan, prop.; sells clothing, carpets, blankets (9/22/05)
FLAXMILL - 15 Feb 1879, T.J. Nixon sells his interest in mill to J.P. Winslow (12/15/05)
FRAZIER BARBERSHOP - on W. Washington St.; Steve Frazier, prop. (4/1/04)
FRAZIER HOTEL - on E. Washington St.; owned/run by Mrs. Sallie Frazier since ca 1883; now sold to O.B. Burk (9/16/01); is again owned by Sallie Frazier, is managed by her son, Benjamin Frazier (9/2/02)

FRITZ MEAT MARKET - has a horse watering trough in front (5/13/04)
GOLDMINE # 9 GROCERY STORE - Elwood O. Ellis is a temporary clerk (1/31/05)
GOSSETT BLACKSMITH SHOP - on E. 1st St.; is sold by prop., Will Gossett to H.L. Perry (7/29/04)
GROVES GAS FITTINGS & TIN SHOP - recently opened on Walnut St. by Will Groves (8/22/01)
HANE MEAT MARKET - located east of RR; is closed by owner, Adam Hane (7/18/02)
HASTING LIVERY STABLE - on W. Washington St.; C.A. Hasting, prop. (8/8/05)
HEADLEY GLASS FACTORY - start production 1 Apr 1901 (2/7/01); is incorporated; Directors are Joseph E. Headley, Carl W. Headley, Richard Knight (4/18/01); Jake Hardwick, employee (6/6/01); John Shaughnessy, new employee (8/29/01); moved to Danville, IL; is now dissolved (1/22/04)
HIATT HARNESS SHOP - owned by M.A. Hiatt (1/20/05)
HOCKETT PHOTOGRAPHY STUDIO - being set-up in Wilson Blk. (3/25/04)
HOTEL BLOCK - C.C. Lyons is selling out his merchandise here (6/24/02)
IOOF LODGE 381 - Lawrence Osborn (dec) was a mbr (7/8/01); 11 Sep 1901 Cy Nicholson became a mbr (9/12/01); - see ODD FELLOWS BLOCK (4/4/02)
KLONDYKE SALOON - on E. Washington St.; prop. John Venitz, dec (9/8/03)
KNIGHTS OF PYTHIAS (K of P) LODGE - in past met in a room in the Sutton Blk., now have lodge room in J.H. Parker's hall (12/5/01), above Parker's Hardware (1/16/02)
LANGSDON & HUNT FURNITURE & UNDERTAKING - co-owner John Langsdon d last wk. (8/30/04)
LaRUE & PATTERSON ELECTRIC LIGHT PLANT - is about complete; has a Corless engine (5/27/02); 1 Jun 1902, started by Gilbert LaRue (1/24/05); - see FAIRMOUNT ELECTRIC LIGHT PLANT
LATHAM BLOCK - 2-story brick bldg.; sold by Mrs. S.M. Latham to F.O. Gephart (3/18/02)
LEACH RESTAURANT - is recently sold by E.O. Leach to W.E. Mackay of Danville (2/28/02)
LEASE CIGAR STORE - on Main St., Bert Lease, prop. (6/14/04)
LEWIS & PARRILL - their new store opened Saturday (6/24/02); have an elevator in their new bldg. (7/25/02)

LINDSEY MILLING & LUMBER - operated by William Lindsey for ca 20 yrs.; sold to A.C. Kies (8/15/01), for $17,000 (8/22/01); is having a gas well drilled nearby, depth is now at 800' (1/6/02)
McCULLOUGH GLASS FACTORY - is gone; site in N. Fmt. is almost all cleaned up (11/17/05)
MACHINE & TOOL WORKS - absorbs Fairmount Foundry & Machine Works; Thomas R. Stoner is in charge (10/21/02); T.R. Stoner sells his interest to James Otto Fink (11/27/03); William Lindsey purchased an interest in Works from J.O. Fink (12/4/03); Roy Engle is an employee (1/15/04)
MARION CONSERVATORY OF MUSIC - opens branch in Borrey Blk., will teach piano, violin, elocution, physical culture (10/13/05)
MASONIC LODGE - contractor John S. Baker builds a brick Masonic Temple on N. Main St. (6/10/04); hollow cornerstone, containing newspapers, etc., is laid for new Temple (7/1/04); Masonic Blk. adjoins the Borrey Blk. (7/22/04); 2 Nov 1904 new Masonic Hall is dedicated (11/4/04)
MECCA SALOON - operated by Victor Roehm of Marion (5/16/05)
MENDENHALL & DAUGHERTY DRUG STORE - Charles Daugherty is druggist (6/20/02)
MILLER & HAAS DRY GOODS STORE- employees include Miss Flossie Anderson (1/6/02), Jesse Leach (2/2/04)
MORRIS POOL HALL - Dec 1880, Andy Morris rented old M.E. Ch. bldg. on corner of Main & 2nd St. to use as a pool hall (12/15/05)
MORRIS & CHILDS LAUNDRY - is on W. Washington St. in bldg. owned by Frank Davis (4/4/02)
NEW CENTRAL HOTEL - Dec 1886, J.H. Mull is prop. (12/15/05)
NIXON WAREHOUSE - 1881, owned by T.J. Nixon (1/13/1881 as reprinted 3/29/04)
NORTON GROCERY - cashier is Miss Bernice Oakley (2/3/02)
ODD FELLOWS BLOCK - 2-story brick bldg. to be built by IOOF on their lot when the Billy Sunday Tabernacle is removed; Blk. will be 44'X70' (lot is 44'X 132'); Blk. S wall will be present N wall of Sutton Blk. (4/4/02); John S. Baker drew up plans for new Hall (7/25/02); bricks laid for new Hall by Isaac Wooten (10/24/02)
PALACE MEAT MARKET - is purchased by Elmer Gates (9/16/01); Morton Jones, prop. (5/20/04); on Main St.; M.P. Jones sells out to S.B. Hill (9/16/04); James T. Hill, partner of S.B. Hill (2/28/05)
PARKER HARDWARE - owned by J.H. Parker (10/21/01); 1881, owner J.H. Parker sells groceries & hardware (1/13/1881 as reprinted 3/29/04)

PARKER'S HALL - owned by C.T. Parker; is at corner of 1st & Main (1/9/02); Prohibition Alliance to meet here Mon. night (2/28/02)
PARKER'S OPERA HOUSE - "Society Minstrels in Black Faces called Honolulu Belles" will be given 21 Jun 1901 by the Rebekah Lodge (6/13/01); now called 'Parker's Hall,' 21 Oct 1905 is site of a political meeting (10/20/05)
PARKER OPERA HOUSE BLOCK - Dec 1892 is being built by J.H. Parker (12/15/05)
PICKARD WALLPAPER STORE - on N. Main St.; prop., Otto Pickard, hangs wall paper (3/29/04)
PREMIUM BAKERY - on E. Adams St.; prop., Clyde Gossett; burned 17 Jul 1904, will be rebuilt (7/19/04); new bldg. is of concrete blks. (8/19/04); is leased from Clyde Gossett by Fred Davis (9/1/05)
RAU BROTHERS/FAIRMOUNT GLASS FACTORY - employees include Jess Stibbs and his s, Will (dec) (5/2/01); having gas well drilled on their property within 300 ft. of 'Jumbo' well (4/11/02); their new gas well near Big Four tracks is full of salt water (4/25/02); Levi Frazier and John McGrath are employees (6/13/02); - see FAIRMOUNT GLASS WORKS
RIBBLE TAILOR SHOP - owned by Lafe and Hort Ribble, is in Masonic Temple (8/22/05)
RIGDON GROCERY - 1881, prop. is B.T. Rigdon (1/13/1881 as reprinted 3/29/04)
SAGE TAILOR SHOP - in Borrey Blk.; operated by Ira S. Sage (5/16/01)
SCOTT DRY GOODS - 1881, Levi Scott, prop. (1/13/1881 as reprinted 3/29/04)
SCOTT DRY GOODS - 1881, Lindley Scott and O.R. Scott, propriators (1/13/1881 as reprinted 3/29/04)
SHUEY BAKERY - owned by Clyde Gossett; Fred Davis is baker (1/19/04); - see PREMIUM BAKERY
SKINNER SALOON - on E. Washington St.; owned by J.P. Skinner (7/21/05)
SPENCE BLACKSMITH SHOP - is on E. Washington St.; owned by W.H. Spence; Will Gossett is employed as a blacksmith (3/28/01)
STAR HOTEL - existed in 1878 (9/28/1878 as reprinted 2/26/04); 1881, Nathan Johnson, prop. (1/13/1881 as reprinted 3/29/04)
STECH GROCERY - owned by A.D. Stech; employee Elwood O. Ellis resigns (8/29/05)
SUTTON'S HALL - is on S. Main St. near Adams St. (10/24/02)

SWAIM LUMBER & PLANING MILL CO. - is enlarging its bldg. (1/6/02); gas was struck at nearby well (1/9/02); sells lumber wholesale and retail; filed incorporation papers; A.C. Kies of Jonesboro is a Director (1/24/02); 25 May 1904 partially burned; to be reconstructed (5/27/04); rebuilt and running (8/5/04)
THOMAS ICE CO. - Lon Thomas, owner, has stored 400 tons of clear ice to sell to Fmt. customers (3/4/02); from pits S of Fmt., harvested and stored 350 tons of ice in 3 bldgs. (2/10/05)
ULREY FLOUR MILL - Fred Pearson is an employee (12/22/03)
VENITZ SALOON - is on E. Washington St. (10/17/05)
VINSON ORGAN & SEWING MACHINE SHOP - owned by Ezra Vinson; located in Winslow's Livery Stable (9/23/01)
WESLEYAN METHODIST CAMP GROUNDS - has electric lights, 58 unfurnished rooms, 24 furnished rooms (8/25/03); Dec 1894, land for camp grounds is purchased from Nixon Rush (12/15/05)
WHEELER & STEVENSON SALOON - opened in Gephart Bldg. 19 Apr 1902 (4/22/02)
WHEELER MILL - operated by W.S. Luce (7/25/01); built ca 1845; its chimney is being torn down, mill is being repaired (3/22/04)
WHITE HOUSE SALOON - owned by P.T. Brown; closes because license expires (7/7/05)
WI-DA-ME SALVE CO. - office is moved from Wilson Blk. to corner of Walnut & Washington St.; Walter L. Jay, Secretary (8/18/05)
WILSON BLOCK - site of new Hockett Photography Studio (3/25/04)
WILSON & McCULLOCH GLASS FACTORY - Ed Coahran is an employee (1/31/01); Thomas Bryan, Foreman, d 7 Oct 1901 (10/7/01)
WINSLOW & RAU GLASS FACTORY - established in 1888 (1/17/05)
WINSLOW LIVERY STABLE - horse thief is captured here with 2 horses he had stolen in White Co. (1/31/01)

FAIRMOUNT CORNET BAND - mentioned (11/3/05)

FAIRMOUNT FAIR ASSOCIATION - fair opens next Mon. with 8 electric arc lights on grounds (8/5/02); 1st fair held 1884 (8/19/02); T.J. Lucas, Pres. (8/14/03); Dr. A. Henley, Pres.; Foster Davis, 1st Vice Pres.; Dr. Glenn Henley, 2nd Vice Pres.; C.V. Hadley, Treas.; Jep Wilson, Secretary; Lin Wilson, Supt.; Directors are Frank Buller, John Kelsay, John A. Jones, Luther Morris, Dr. John Pearl Seale, Solomon Johnson, Jackson Stivers, John S, Baker, Carl P. Rau, Richard Henley, Thomas W. Moore, Adam Hane (1/12/04); 1 Jan 1887, Fair Assn. stockholders are Enoch Beals-Pres., J.H. Parker and John Simons-Vice Presidents, Levi Scott-Treas., Robert Bogue-Supt. (12/15/05)

FAIRMOUNT FRIENDS ACADEMY (FFA) - W.E. Schoonover, Principal (4/15/01); L.L. Tyler, new Principal (8/1/01); 1901-02 faculty include Leon L. Tyler, Principal; Minnie Tyler, History & English; Sidney J. Lockner, Science; Gertrude C. Mills, Literature & Language; E. Leona Wright, Music (8/19/01), Webster Davis, Science; R.E. Dean, Commercial & Shorthand (10/3/01); new mbrs, Board of Trustees are James Bell and Will W. Ware (12/23/01); Murton Woolen organized a basket supper for the FFA Athletic Association held last night at Back Creek Sch (2/17/02); Lewis Richards to teach science 1902-03 (6/24/02); Leon L. Tyler, 1903-04 Principal (9/4/03); Minnie Haisley (dec) was 1902 grad (4/1/04); Ernest Pearson, 1903 grad (5/20/04); 100 students att FFA; Miss Julia Kelsay, music tchr (9/20/04); enrollment is 116 (1/10/05); enrollment is 101 (9/15/05); enrollment is 112 (10/20/05)

FAIRMOUNT GUN CLUB - 28 Mar 1901 Shoot winners were Charles Parker, E.E. Hiatt, Mark Parker, George Vaughn, John Montgomery (4/1/01)

FAIRMOUNT HUNTING & FISHING CLUB - is now incorporated; Directors are F. Davis, F. Shimel, O.C. Elson (1/1/04)

FAIRMOUNT LADIES SHAKESPEARE CLUB - mbrs include Mrs. Carl P. Rau (dec) (9/12/02), and Osha Starr (9/30/02); celebrates 7 yrs. in existence 2 Mar 1905; Miss Opha Swaim, mbr (2/28/05); mbrs dec in past 7 yrs. are Mrs. Rachel Nolder, Mrs. Al Reed, Mrs. Gilbert LaRue, Mrs. Harry Whitney (3/7/05); Mrs. Xen Edwards, mbr (4/14/05)

FAIRMOUNT SCHOOLS - Isaac Hiatt, janitor (2/4/01); John S. Baker contracts to construct new HS bldg. (7/25/01); Sch Board contracted M.L. Coyle to drill a gas well on sch property at South Sch (1/6/02), gas well is shot 24 Feb 1902 resulting in a good flow of gas (2/25/02); slate roof is installed on new HS bldg. (2/25/02); Adam M. Highley of Converse is tchr in Fmt. HS (9/12/02); Grace Hobbs is 1903-04 tchr (9/8/03); Harriett Winslow is mbr HS senior class (12/15/03); John Starr (dec) was 1900 FHS grad (4/15/04); 1904 FHS grads: Opha Swaim, Lutie Presnall, Zoe

Wiley, Hazel Fletcher, Mabel Mathis, Glen Pearson, Ray Carter, Harry Smith, Tony Payne, John Rau, Homer Thompson, Mrs. Amy Carroll (4/22/04; 5/17/04); Trustees are: John Flanagan, Dr. J.W. Patterson, N.W. Edwards (6/10/04); Miss Ellen Hastings is a kindergarten tchr (7/15/04); 1904-05 Sch tchrs: Dea Nolder, Glenn Moon, Edith Ellis, Stella Davis, Nettie Maloney, Anna Freeman, Elizabeth Stewart, Grace Hobbs, Gertrude Coyle, Lucia Parrill, Osha Starr, Mrs. Mattie Charles; 1904-05 HS tchrs: A.J. Boyer-Principal, Avis E. Hughes, Josephine Abel, L.C. Robey (8/30/04); HS has 98 students (9/16/04); 1853, 1st sch was in Friends MH, tchr was Thomas Knight; High Sch established 1896 (1/24/05); 1881, Erasmus Nelson, Principal, Fmt. Schs (7/4/05); Forest Foraker, HS tchr; Nell Fear, tchr (10/17/05); John D. Ferree was HS Principal for 2 yrs. sometime in past (12/8/05); HS began in fall 1896, R.W. Himelick was a tchr, Edward Monahan was Principal fall 1896 until Jan 1899 when he dec, 1897 Charles H. Copeland became Supt., in 1st graduating class of 1900 were Emma Parrill, Grace Hobbs, Grace Crilley, Verna Hardwick, Eliza Frazier, Irvin Winslow, Moses Morrison, Albert Knight, John Starr (12/19/05)

FAIRMOUNT TOWNSHIP - Benjamin F. Stevens, Justice of Peace (11/28/02); J.O. Duling, Trustee (8/7/03); Twp. Advisory Bd. mbrs are Henry Morrish and Oliver Buller (3/25/04); 1881, Trustee was Lemuel Pearson (4/4/05)

FAIRMOUNT TOWNSHIP SCHOOLS - W.W. Ware was a tchr in twp. for 14 yrs. (9/15/03); 1881, 1st graduates were Katie Coahran, Ora Winslow, Dorothy Luther, Myra Rush, Frank Presnall, Will Calhoun (4/4/05)
DISTRICT #1 (BACK CREEK) - 1901 grad, Amanda Stone (5/30/01); last night was basket supper organized by Murton Woolen for FFA Athletic Assoc., Edna Overman is voted prettiest girl in attendance (2/17/02); Herman Wimmer, 1903-05 tchr (9/4/03; 8/30/04); has 35 students (9/11/03); Stanley Carey is 1904 grad (4/15/04); Mrs. Amy Carroll replaces Herman Wimmer as 1904-05 tchr (10/11/04); John Hasting att log sch; T.B. McDonald was log sch tchr prior to 1870 (2/14/05); 1905 grads: Georgia Davis, Walter West (5/12/05); Mrs. Amy Carroll, 1905-06 tchr (8/15/05); 29 pupils att (10/6/05)
DIST. #2 (PIKE) - Ben Jones, 1903-05 tchr (9/4/03; 8/30/04); 1905 grads: Frank Underwood, Clarence Kitterman, Hershel Neal,

Ernest C. Hiatt (5/12/05); Mayme Ellis, 1905-06 tchr (8/15/05)
DIST. #3 (GRANT) - Oscar B. Hockett, 1900-02 tchr (1/3/01; 2/10/02); John R. Little, 1903-06 tchr (9/4/03; 8/30/04; 8/15/05); students include Arthur Wyckoff (1/5/04); Miss Addie Wright, substitute tchr (4/18/05); 1905 grad, Eli Jones (5/12/05)
DIST. #4 (EAST BRANCH) - 1901 grad is John Morrish (5/30/01); Murton Woolen, 1901-02 tchr (8/19/01); Hugh Clark, 1901-02 tchr (2/10/02; 5/13/02); Nellie Simons, 1903-05 tchr (9/4/03; 8/30/04); Lavina French, 1905-06 tchr (8/15/05)
DIST. #5 (LEACHBURG) - 1901 grad is Lula Leach (5/30/01); Leonard Little, 1903-04 tchr (9/4/03); Willard Hastings, 1904-05 tchr (8/30/04); substitute Ina Ratliff is tchr while W. Hastings is ill (1/17/05); modern brick sch with indoor water is to be built (3/31/05); William Henley is awarded contract to build new sch (4/28/05); new sch is ready for plasterers; total cost of bldg. to be ca $3,500 (7/25/05); Leonard Little, 1905-06 tchr (8/15/05); new sch bldg. is completed (8/29/05)
DIST. #6 (LAKE) - 1901 grad is Iva Arnett (5/30/01); Elgie Leach,1902-03 tchr (8/29/02); 1903-04 tchr, Ben Frazier (9/4/03); has 59 students (11/10/03); Leonard Little, 1904-05 tchr (7/26/04); L. Little becomes Principal, Fowlerton Sch, is replaced by Miss Vina French (1/24/05); Preston Lucas, 1905-06 tchr (8/15/05)
DIST. #7 (FOWLERTON) - William Ware and Miss Dare, 1900-01 tchrs (3/28/01); 1901 grads, Glenn Smith and Mamie Crawford (5/30/01); Trustee J.O. Duling lets contract for new sch house (7/25/02); 1903-04 tchrs: Oscar B. Hockett (Principal), Elgie Leach, Addie Dare, Carrie Simons, Mary Pearson (9/4/03); two-room addition is being added to sch bldg. (4/5/04), addition will not be built (5/27/04); 1904-05 tchrs: Oscar B. Hockett (8/9/04), Myrtle Reeve, Addie M. Dare, Mary E. Pearson (8/30/04); O.B. Hockett resigns, replaced as Principal by Leonard Little (1/24/05); 1905 grads: Violet Wall, Isa Templeton, Emma Swartz, Viony Cain, Charlie Benner, Gladys Chilton, Maude Reeve (5/12/05); 1905-06 tchrs: Miss Myrtle Reeve, Miss Addie Dare, Miss Mary Pearson, and C. Calderwood, a specialist in music and penmanship, is Principal (8/15/05); Miss Treva Seale, substitute tchr (10/24/05)

FAIRMOUNT YOUNG MENS CHRISTIAN ASSOCIATION (YMCA) - is formed with rented space in Borrey Hall (5/13/02); incorporated;

Directors are: J. Edward Headley, Pres.; Walter Jay (5/23/02), Fred D. Oakley, Secretary (6/3/02), Ira Neely, Carl P. Rau, Harry D. Wood, Jackson Stivers, Charles A. Cook, John A. Hunt, Cornelius Small (6/6/02); W.A. Sunday will dedicate the Hall when completed (7/8/02); C.V. Hadley, Sectretary, places gym equipment in YMCA rooms (10/21/02); J.E. Headley and Jack Stivers are replaced on the Board by John Kelsay and R.A. Morris (8/28/03); Directors include C.V. Hadley, Elwood Miller, H.F. Hardin (12/18/03); is closed (3/18/04); furniture/furnishings being sold (4/29/04)

FAIRMOUNT YOUNG WOMENS CHRISTIAN ASSOCIATION (YWCA) - rented the front rooms over John A. Hunt's business in the Fmt. Blk.; to be reading room and parlor (5/30/02); telephone is installed in rooms (6/6/02)

FANKBONER, __ - see Mrs. E. Lawrence McDONALD/McDONNELL

FANKBONER, L.L. - b 1827 in Tuscarawas Co., OH; 1849 walked all the way to Jonesboro in 10 days; 1852 m by Rev. George W. Bowers; settled 2 mi. E of Fmt. with "wife and a chopping ax"; lives in Fmt.; 2 Aug 1902 celebrated 50th wedding anniv with wife (8/5/02)

FARLOW, Mary P. (Peacock) - b Grant Co. 20 Jan 1854; dt Joseph and Caroline (dec) Peacock; 31 Oct 1878 m Lindley M. Farlow; mbr/ Elder, New London Friends, Howard Co.; d 19 Sep 1902 (9/23/02)

FARR, Edna - see Morton JONES

FEAR, Eva - see Eva (Fear) HAMILTON

FEAR, Mrs. N. Jane - age 61; widow of James Fear (dec ca 1899); mbr Wesleyan Ch.; d 13 Nov 1905, bur Park Cem (11/17/05)

FEAR, Nellie - dt James and N. Jane Fear; Fmt. Schs tchr (11/17/05)

FEAR, William - s James and N. Jane Fear (11/17/05)

FELTON, __ - age 15 months; child of M/M George Felton; d 11 Jul 1905 (7/14/05)

FELTON, Almeda - see William E. ARMFIELD

FELTON, Arlin - b 26 Mar 1901; s George and Ada M. Felton; d 4 Jul 1902 (7/8/02)

FELTON, George - his horse was stolen 28 Dec 1901 from the hitch rack near the old mill (12/30/01)

FELTON, Jacob E. - of S of Fmt. on Co. Line; d last wk., funeral in Back Creek Wesleyan Church (11/11/02)

FELTON, Joseph - had surgery for a fistula (8/22/01)

FELTON, Samuel - age 68; d 3 May 1905, bur Back Creek Friends Cem (5/5/05)

FENTON, James - b England; m; glass blower; came to Fmt. ca 1894; d 20 Sep 1904, bur Park Cem (9/23/04)

FERREE, __ - b recently; s M/M John Ferree (8/30/04)

FERREE, __ - b 19 Jan 1905; s M/M Evan H. Ferree of Marion (1/24/05)

FERREE, Alvin - and Charles A., of Fmt.; are sons John and Rebecca (Harvey) Ferree (12/15/03)

FERREE, Evan H. - of Marion; s John and Rebecca (Harvey) Ferree (12/15/03)

FERREE, Jessie - see Mart TRADER

FERREE, John D. - of Marion; s John and Rebecca (Harvey) Ferree (12/15/03); grad FFA 1891; grad Earlham Coll 1895 (11/17/05); b Liberty Twp.; age 34; for 2 yrs. was Principal, Fmt. HS (12/8/05)

FERREE, Lydia - see Lydia (Ferree) HIATT

FERREE, Rebecca (Harvey) - b Clinton Co., OH 16 Apr 1828; dt William and Ruth Harvey; 18 Oct 1850 m John Ferree of Morgan Co. in Oak Ridge Friends MH; d 11 Dec 1903, bur Park Cem (12/15/03)

FERREE, Sarah - dt John and Rebecca (Harvey) Ferree; d 1859 (12/15/03)

FERREE, William E. - of Pittsburgh, PA; s John and Rebecca (Harvey) Ferree (12/15/03)

FIELD, Mrs. Ella - age ca 28; d in Fmt. 9 Nov 1902 (11/11/02)

FINK, James Otto - buys Fairmount Machine & Tool Works from T.R. Stoner (11/27/03)

FINNIMORE, Mike - engineer on engine that brings dirt 1.5 mi. to Cowgill Tile Mill (10/21/01)

FISCHER, F.G. - PHOTO; song leader for Billy Sunday during his Fmt. revival (4/22/02)

FLANAGAN, Dora - see Dora (Flanagan) KIMES

FLANAGAN, John - s James and Mary (Morley) Flanagan (4/15/01; 4/18/01); Secretary, Fmt. Mining Co. (1/16/02); et al. petitioned for construction of New Prairie Ditch (7/8/02); V. Pres./Director, Fmt. Banking Co. (11/18/02); brother of Dora (Flanagan) Kimes (4/26/04); a Trustee, Fmt. Schs (6/10/04); Apr 1887 was mbr, Fmt. Mining Co. (1/17/05); April 1879 started a Fmt. business (9/22/05)

FLANAGAN, Mary (Morley) - b Mayo Co., Ireland 6 Jan 1825; m 1844 James Flanagan (dec 31 Aug 1875); came to USA in 1848; came to Grant Co. in fall of 1865 from Preble Co., OH; mbr RC Ch.; d 11 Apr 1901, bur Jonesboro Cem (4/15/01; 4/18/01)

FLETCHER, George A. - Civil Engineer for Town of Fmt. (9/26/02); local agent for American Express Co. (3/25/04)

FLETCHER, Hazel - 1904 FHS grad (4/22/04)

FLETCHER, Ralph - new employee, Citizen's Telephone Co. (2/4/01)

FLOREA, Lake - 1905-06 Liberty Twp. Sch tchr (8/28/05)

FLORIDA, gone to - see Eli J. COX; Asa J. GASKILL

FLYNN, __ - infant of M/M Thomas Flynn d 9 Aug 1902 (8/12/02)

FLYNN, Edith - see Charles DAVIS

FORAKER, Prof. Forest - Fmt. HS tchr (10/17/05)

FORAKER, Hortense (Evinger) - b Perrysville 7 Oct 1879; m Prof. Forest Foraker 5 Jul 1904; att Northern Univ, Ada, OH; d 14 Oct 1905, bur Savona, OH (10/17/05)

FORD, Mollie E. - 1 Jan 1896 m John K. Ford; now sues John for divorce (3/7/01); is granted a divorce(4/1/01)

FOSTER, Henry - serv 3 yr. during CW in 84th Ind. Inf., is granted $12 per mon. pension (11/8/04)

FOUST, Mrs. Laura - age 74; d 24 Apr 1905, funeral in Back Creek Friends MH, bur Back Creek Friends Cem (4/25/05; 4/28/05)

FOUST, Thomas - s Mrs. Laura Foust (4/28/05)

FOWLER, Mrs. Daniel - of Fmt.; dt Mrs. Caroline Tinn (dec) (6/13/02)

FOWLER, Ora - of North Grove; 2 Jan 1905 m Rachel Elliott of Salem, OR; will live near Jonesboro (1/6/05)

FOWLER, Rachel (Elliott) - grad FFA 1903; wife of Ora Fowler (1/6/05)

FOWLER, Steve - s Mrs. Daniel Fowler (7/4/02)

FOWLERTON, Town of - John Burwick, dairyman, is supplying citizens with milk (8/26/01); a frame bldg. hotel burned 20 Dec 1901, at a loss of $3,000 (12/23/01); new C.I.&E. RR depot is completed (1/30/02); old C.I.&E. passenger depot is hauled to Fmt. on a flat car, to be a freight house (8/19/02); Allen Virgin replaces Jacob Dane/Dame as Postmaster (10/9/03)
CITIZEN'S TELEPHONE CO. - of Fmt. has a Fowlerton switchboard; 40 telephones are being hooked up (8/21/03)
FOWLERTON BANK - opens next wk.; counters and other woodwork is installed by J.L. Swaim & Co. (1/10/05); banker, George E. Hopkins

of Chicago; 30 May 1905 bank closed for Decoration Day and Hopkins disappeared with $4,000 of deposits; all that is left are $15.52 in pennies, a few furnishings, and notes drawn for $1,080 (5/23/05; 6/6/05)
FOWLERTON CANNING FACTORY - is sold by Oliver Buller (10/24/05); Levi Simons, employee (11/21/05)
FOWLERTON LAND & GAS CO. - is now incorporated; Directors are William J. Leach, Charles E. Leach, Chalmer Kerr (4/1/01)
FOWLERTON WINDOW GLASS CO. - employs ca 75 men (1/10/05)
INDEX - editor is Cal Sinninger (5/23/02)
INDUSTRIAL WINDOW GLASS CO. - Directors: B. Debrucque, Eugene Romain, Lucien Mayer, Henry Debrucque, Alfred Mirior, Nestor Dubois of Alexandria, and Leon Quinet of Matthews (10/14/01)
MODERN WOODMEN CAMP # 10035 LODGE - took in 7 new mbrs 18 Jan 1902 (1/24/02)
ROYAL GLASS CO. - drills a dry gas well on L.P. Simons farm (1/5/04); factory is being dismantled and shipped to Caney, KS (8/30/04)
SEALE FURNITURE STORE - owner M. Luther Seale is stocking it with furniture and caskets (2/6/02); has a new funeral car (9/27/04); M.L. Seale moves undertaking business to Summitville (9/15/05)
ST. CLAIR & MORRISON - Frank Smith is employed as a blacksmith (5/23/02)

FRAZIER, __ - b recently; weight is 11 lb.; ch M/M Ananias Frazier; colored (7/15/01)

FRAZIER, __ - b 30 Sep 1904; s M/M Ben Frazier (10/4/04)

FRAZIER, __ - b 5 Nov 1904; s M/M Levi Frazier (11/8/04)

FRAZIER, Benjamin F. - s Mrs. Sallie Frazier; att Ind. Univ Law Sch 1901-02 (9/16/01); manages Frazier Hotel for his mother (9/2/02); 1903-04 tchr, Fmt. Twp. Sch # 6 (9/4/03); recently m Harriett Winslow (12/15/03); and wife disappear (5/13/04); arrested in CA, charged with embezzlement from Fmt. American Express office (5/20/04); states that he somehow lost the purse of American Express money and panicked (5/31/04); is held in Marion jail (6/3/04); out on bail (6/7/04); disappears just before his trial (11/29/04); still missing, may forfeit bond of $1,000 put up by his mother and by his father-in-law (12/2/04); is captured in Oklahoma City, Indian Territory; to be brought back by Grant Co.

Sheriff (12/30/04); is in Marion jail (1/13/05); his trial is underway (1/20/05); is sentenced to 2-14 yrs. in Jeffersonville Reformatory (1/24/05); prisoner, is bookkeeper for Reformatory (5/23/05)

FRAZIER, Eliza _ grad Fmt. HS 1900 (12/19/05)

FRAZIER, Levi - employee of Rau Glass Factory (6/13/02)

FRAZIER, Mrs. Sallie - owned/ran Frazier Hotel ca 18 yr., now sells it to O.B. Burk (9/16/01); again owns Frazier Hotel (9/2/02)

FRAZIER, Steve - prop., Frazier Barbershop (4/1/04)

FRAZIER, William A. - b Culpepper Co., WV 25 Dec 1828; m Mary Burden, dt Austin and Emily Burden 2 Oct 1857; came to Fmt. ca 1868; d 7 Jan 1901; colored (1/7/01; 1/10/01; 1/14/01)

FREDERICK, Mrs. Alexander - age 35; m; d 31 Dec 1903, bur Park Cem (1/5/04)

FREEMAN, Anna - 1904-05 Fmt. Sch tchr (9/2/04)

FREEMAN, Prof. Daniel - FFA tchr (11/28/05)

FREEMAN, India - dt Prof. Daniel Freeman (11/10/05)

FRENCH, Miss La*vina* - tchr, Lake Sch 1905 (1/24/05); East Branch Sch tchr 1905-06 (8/15/05)

FRIEND, Jasper A. 'Jap' - mail carrier, Rural Rte. #1 (3/21/02); mail carrier, Fmt. Rural Rte. # 18 (8/8/02; 8/14/03); 1 Feb 1905 will m Millie, dt M/M Eugene Goodykoontz (1/31/05)

FRIEND, Martha Belle - see Benjamin THOMPSON

FRIEND, Mathias S. - b Warren Co., OH 9 Jun 1836; wounded in CW, Pvt., Co. K, 79th Ohio Inf.; moved to Liberty Twp. in 1865, to Fmt. in 1888 (12/1/03; 5/26/05); his CW pension is increased to $30 per mo. (3/25/04); elected Adjutant, Beeson GAR Post (5/20/04)
FRIEND, William D. - employee of Chicago Pipe Line Co.; 15 Feb 1902 m Myrtle A. Winans, will live in Fmt. (2/17/02)

FRY, Rev. C.H. - will be pastor for both Fmt. and Gas City Baptist Churches jointly (6/6/01)

FRY, Mrs. Charles - of Kentland; dt M/M Roland Smith (11/14/01)

FRY, S.T. - is a Swayzee blacksmith (5/30/02)

FRY, Vanessa - dt M/M Charles Fry, f of Fmt., now of Kentland; d 7 Nov 1901 (11/14/01)

FURNISH, Cleave - of E of Fmt., 3 Jun 1904 m Sarah Sparks (6/7/04)

FURR, L.A. - of Matthews; intends to raffle off his new Furr Hotel, Matthews (9/5/01)

GABLE, Harry - one of 1st owners of Big Four Window Glass Factory (4/18/05)

GADDIS, Georgia - dt M/M Marcus Gaddis (12/5/05)

GADDIS, Marcus - Lafayette Gas Co. drilled and shot a well on his farm W of Fmt.; well produces gas and oil (10/21/02)

GADDIS, Wauneda - dt M/M Marcus Gaddis (12/5/05)

GALLOWAY, Irvin - and wife were in buggy struck 19 May 1902 by Union Traction car in Fmt.; wife was bruised (5/20/02)

GAMBRIEL, John R. - serv Co. D, 34th Ind. Inf. during CW (5/27/04; 5/26/05); lives in Liberty Twp. (10/10/05)

GANGWISCH, Andy - purchases Crescent Bakery (4/18/05)

GARDENER, Henry - serv Pvt., Co. K, 130th Ind. Inf. during CW (5/27/04; 5/26/05)

GARDINER, __ - b 6 Aug 1904; s M/M Will Gardiner (8/9/04)

GARNER, Prof. __ - Liberty Twp. Dist. # 11 Sch tchr (2/25/02)

GARNER, Elwood H. - 1903-04 tchr, Liberty Twp. Sch # 6 (9/11/03); tchr, Liberty Twp. Sch 1904-05 (12/27/04); resigns from Bethel Sch to be tchr in Mill Twp. (3/3/05)

GARNER, Mervin - of Oak Ridge; 27 Sep 1905 m Caroline Gemmer of Marion; will live on farm near Oak Ridge (10/10/05)

GARRISON, Henry - Pvt., Co. A, 8th Ind. Inf. during CW (5/26/05)

GARRISON, Orpha - infant dt M/M John Garrison; d 1 Apr 1904, bur Park Cem (4/5/04)

GAS CITY, Town of -
AMERICAN TIN PLATE CO. - Asst. Mgr., Richard Henley (10/6/03)
MISSISSINEWA HOTEL - hotel Mgr., Henry W. Hess, has skipped town with $3,000 (12/12/01)

GAS WELLS - Fmt. Mining Co. just completed one on the Henry Davis farm (9/12/02); Royal Glass Co. of Fowlerton drills a dry well on the L.P. Simons farm (1/5/04); Apr 1887, gas was discovered in Fmt. area when 'Jumbo' was drilled by Fmt. Mining Co. (1/17/05)

GASKILL, Asa J. - of Marion; 20 Dec 1903 m Grace Mart; to live in Fmt. with Grace's grandmother Rachel Scott (12/22/03); and wife move to Tampa, FL (5/6/04)

GATES, Elmer - purchases the Palace Meat Market (9/16/01); m 12 Jun 1904 Mrs. Nora Haworth; will live in Fmt. (6/14/04)

GATES, Miss Ida - of Fmt.; d this wk., bur Mt. Carmel Cem, Franklin Co. (5/27/02)

GAUNT, Mrs. Will - f of Fmt.; d Matthews 24 Jul 1904 (7/26/04)

GEEDING, Leander - serv Pvt., Co. G, 136th Ind. Inf. during CW (5/26/05)

GEMMER, Caroline - see Mervin GARNER

GEORGE, Elizabeth Jane - see Elizabeth Jane (George) NELSON

GEORGIA, gone to - see Emma C. STOUT

GEPHART, F.O. - of Marion; bought Latham Blk. in Fmt. (3/18/02)

GIBSON, Georgia - dt M/M Charles Gibson (1/1/02)

GIBSON, John - dec; serv Pvt., Co. K, 130th Ind. Inf. during CW (5/26/05)

GIBSON, Mattie C. - see Mattie CAMMACK-GIBSON

GIBSON, Minnie - see Minnie (Gibson) MILLER

GIBSON, Nece - of Hackleman; s Mrs. Ruth Gibson of Jonesboro (12/23/01)

GIFT, Charles W. - of Jonesboro; age 66; d 22 Sep 1902 in Marion Soldier's Home (9/26/02); serv Pvt., Co. I, 159th Ohio Inf. during CW (5/27/04; 5/26/05)

GIFT, Mrs. Dora - owner of Barren Creek farm where mammoth bones were discovered (6/17/04); won case against her tenants, the Smith brothers, who tried to steal proceeds from sale of mammoth bones (1/17/05)

GIFT, Mrs. P.E. - sells her 80-acre farm located E of Fmt. to H.U. Abbot (9/26/05)

GIMMEL, Andrew 'Andy' - mail carrier, Fmt. Rural Rte. #20 (8/8/02)

GLASS, James F. - farmer near Fmt.; last Sun. m Mellia Hill of Gas City (8/19/02)

GLOVER, Mary A. (Laberman) - b Dayton, OH 21 Jul 1867; dt J.B. and Amie Laberman; m William R. Glover 14 Apr 1886; mbr Fmt. U.B. Ch.; d 7 Dec 1901 (12/12/01)

GLOVER, William R. - candidate for Fmt. Marshal (4/1/01)

GOLDTHWAIT, E.L. - quoted in the Marion Chronicle as reprinted in The Fairmount News: Many yrs. ago a Grant County citizen rode out of the forests and swamps to Marion to pay his taxes. After paying his tax of $8.13 he started drinking and thinking about the obvious widespread corruption in a government that would require him to pay out $8.13. Riding into the hallway of the old Grant County courthouse and stopping in front of the Treasurer's Office, he yelled "I want to know where all this @#%&# money goes that we pay in for taxes!" He ended this with an Indian war whoop! The old Citizen would have been ignored except that Judge Biddle was holding court in the second floor courtroom. Angry at the interruption, the Judge sent the Bailiff downstairs to bring upstairs the violator of public peace. The Bailiff dragged the old Citizen off the mare and took him up to the Judge. The Culprit was about 4' 3" tall dressed in homespun with a coonskin cap on his head. The Culprit, awestruck, was silent before the Judge. Attorney Brownlee suggested that the Judge go downstairs to see the horse. Downstairs the Judge and Court observed a placid, flybitten beast waiting for her Master. Judge Biddle sent the Bailiff to fetch the old Citizen who was then ordered to mount his beast. The old man was fat and so was his mare. The Judge saw the humor in the spectacle and the old man's breach of the peace was forgiven by the Court. The Citizen rode off filled with awe and Court resumed filled with merriment. (2/6/02)

GOODYKOONTZ, Mrs. Eugene - 19 Aug 1905 is given party for her 50th birthday (8/25/05)

GOODYKOONTZ, Millie - see Jasper FRIEND

GOODYKOONTZ, Vaughn - of W of Jonesboro; 13 Sep 1903 m Myrtle Davis (9/15/03)

GOSSETT, Clyde - owns Shuey Bakery (1/19/04), now called Premium Bakery (7/19/04); leases Premium Bakery to Fred Davis (9/1/05)

GOSSETT, Mrs. Elmer - dt M/M Leander Smith (2/16/04)

GOSSETT, Jesse - dt Mrs. Zep Gossett (6/20/05)

GOSSETT, L.C. - mail carrier, Fmt. Rural Rte. #22 (8/19/02)

GOSSETT, Will - is a blacksmith in W.H. Spence's Blacksmith Shop (3/28/01); helped Ira Neely build his automobile (9/12/01); sells his blacksmith shop located on E. 1st St. to H.L. Perry (7/29/04)

GOSSETT, Z.M. - investor, Roaring Gimlet Gold Mining Syndicate (9/26/02)

GRAND ARMY OF THE REPUBLIC (GAR), Beeson Post 386, Fmt. - officers are Charles Buck, Commander; William Curtis, S.V.C.; William Beidler, J.V.C.; Lewis Moon, Chaplain; George Allred, Quartermaster; Frank Jones, Adj.; William Smith, O.D.; Roland Smith, O.G.; Jude Smithson, Surgeon (1/24/02); John F. Jones, Commander; Mathias S. Friend, Adj. (5/20/04)

GRANT COUNTY ROADS - last toll road in county ended when toll road from Fmt. S to Madison Co. Line recently became a free pike (1/7/01)

GRAVES, Charles N. - Director, Bates Oil Co. (7/11/01)

GRAY, Zola - see Earl BRYAN

GREEN, Charles - of near Back Creek Friends MH; 16 Mar 1904 is given party for his 43rd birthday, that date is also his wedding anniv. (3/22/04)

GREEN, Hazel - age 12; dt M/M Charles Green of 4 mi. NW of Fmt.; d 7 Jan 1905, funeral in Back Creek Friends MH, bur Park Cem (1/10/05)

GREY, John - s Mrs. Oskie Grey (8/1/02)

GRINDLE, William - dec 23 Sep 1903 (9/25/03)

GROSE, Mrs. T.D. - age 26; of Summitville; d recently, bur Park Cem (12/13/04)

GROVES, Will - has new gas fittings & tin shop on Walnut St. (8/22/01)

HADLEY, Clifford V. - Secretary, Fmt. YMCA (10/21/02); is appointed new Fmt. Marshal (12/4/03); is reelected as a Director, Fmt. YMCA (12/18/03); Treas., Fmt. Fair Assoc. (1/12/04)

HADLEY, Zilpha - see Mahlon HARVEY

HAHNE, Helen - dt Mrs. Henry Hahne of Fmt. (10/6/03); 10 Oct 1903 is given party for her 7th birthday (10/13/03)

HAINES, Mrs. Azariah - m; d 21 Jan 1901, bur Marion IOOF Cem (1/21/01; 1/24/01)

HAISLEY, __ - b 6 Jun 1904; dt M/M Sylvester Haisley (6/10/04)

HAISLEY, Mrs. Clinton - of near Jonesboro; dt Nathan Cox (12/27/04)

HAISLEY, Dennis - Trustee, Liberty Twp. (8/22/02); retires as Trustee 1 Jan 1905 (12/27/04)

HAISLEY, Emory V. - of Burr Oak, KS; s David Haisley; grandson Cyrus Haisley (11/8/04)

HAISLEY, Glenn - of Matthews; m; s Mrs. Otto Haisley (9/30/02)

HAISLEY, Jesse - Pvt., Co. F, 139th Ind. Inf. during CW (5/26/05)

HAISLEY, Linus - and wife move from their farm near Back Creek Friends MH to Muncie where he will sell patent churns (1/20/02)

HAISLEY, Mary (Cox) - sister of Nathan, John W. and Tilman Cox (9/26/05)

HAISLEY, Millicent (Rush) - sister of Calvin Rush (11/29/04)

HAISLEY, Minnie - age 20; dt M/M Dennis Haisley of NW of Fmt.; grad, FFA 1902; att Marion Business Coll; d 30 Mar 1904, bur Park Cem (4/1/04)

HAISLEY, Murven - 1904 Liberty Twp. Sch grad (4/15/04)

HAISLEY, Otto - att Earlham Coll 1904-05 (12/16/04)

HAISLEY, S.E. - employee, Fmt. Tile Co. (8/4/05)

HAISLEY, Mrs. S.E. - dt R.E. Overman (dec) (7/28/05)

HAISLEY, Vernie - dt Jesse Haisley of near Oak Ridge (12/20/04)

HAISLEY, Waldo - is attorney living in Marion; s Mrs. Millicent Haisley of Fmt. (3/7/02)

HAISLEY, Dr. Walter D. - s Jesse Haisley of Liberty Twp.; has dental office in Dunkirk; to m Maude Peryl Hawkins of Lynn (12/18/03); 31 Dec 1903 m Maude P. Hawkins (1/8/04)

HAISLEY, Wilson - 1904 Liberty Twp. Sch grad (4/15/04)

HALL, Daisy - see Burr JONES

HALL, William - an early Fmt. area settler; in S part of Fmt. had its first tanyard (1/13/05); 1st Fmt. Postmaster (1/20/05)

HAMAKER, Martha - widow of Jefferson Hamaker; 13 Sep 1902 d at her Washington Twp. home (9/16/02)

HAMILTON, Eva (Fear) - dt James and N. Jane Fear (11/17/05)

HAMILTON, Miss Myrtle - Trask postmistress (5/9/01)

HAMMOND, Emeline - see Emeline (Hammond) LECKENBY

HANE, Adam - closes his Fmt. meat market east of RR (7/18/02); a Director, Fmt. Fair Assoc. (1/12/04)

HANE, Homer - age 12; s Adam Hane (8/18/03)

HANE, Joseph - age ca 22 yr.; s Adam Hane; d 9 Jul 1902 while at work in his father's meat market (7/11/02)

HANES, Alma - 6 Jul 1905 her 17th birthday (7/11/05)

HARBOUR, Rev. O.V.L. - new pastor, Fmt. M.E. Ch. (4/15/04)

HARBOUR, Vena - dt Rev./M O.V.L. Harbour (6/16/05)

HARDIN, H.F. - is an attorney; a Director, Fmt. YMCA (12/18/03)

HARDWICK, Jake - Headley Glass Factory employee (6/6/01)

HARDWICK, Verna - grad Fmt. HS 1900 (12/19/05)

HARKINS, Miss Margaret - operator, Fmt. Telephone Co. (9/1/03), for 2 yrs.; dt M/M John Harkins (8/16/04); - see Hal V. DALE

HARRIS, __ - see Mrs. David WINSLOW

HARRIS, __ - b recently; dt M/M Otto Harris of 1 mi. S of Fmt. (9/19/01)

HARRIS, Benjamin - s John Harris (recently dec); ex-Grant Co. Commissioner (4/22/04)

HARRIS, G.W. - of near Matthews; came to Grant Co. ca 1864 (2/12/04)

HARRIS, John - d at Summitville 19 Oct 1901 (10/21/01)

HARRIS, John - of near Jonesboro; d recently (4/22/04)

HARRIS, O.M. - is Fmt. agent for American Express Co. (3/28/02)

HARRISON, __ - b 1 Nov 1904; dt M/M R.C. Harrison of Matthews (11/4/04)

HARSHBARGER, Arletta - Secretary, Fmt. WCTU (3/1/04)

HART, Robert - Pvt., Co. G, 101st Ind. Inf. during CW (5/26/05)

HARTLEY, __ - see Mrs. Samuel ELLIOTT

HARTLEY, Owen - of Radley; d 17 Aug 1903 (8/21/03)

HARVEY, __ - see Mrs. Ancil RATLIFF; Mrs. Clayton WRIGHT

HARVEY, __ - infant of M/M Austice M. Harvey of W of Fmt.; d 12 Nov 1902, bur Park Cem (11/14/02)

HARVEY, Albert - s Mahlon and Zilpha (Hadley) Harvey; d long ago at age 3 (8/25/05)

HARVEY, Amy (Wright) - b Highland Co., OH 4 May 1824; dt Joab and Ruth Wright; m 24 Nov 1842 Eli Harvey in Friends wedding in Sulphur Springs Sch house, Morgan Co.; f mbr Bethel Friends,

Morgan Co.; came to Grant Co. 1882; d near Fmt. 18 Apr 1901 (4/25/01)

HARVEY, Arthur - s M/M W.H. Harvey (5/27/02)

HARVEY, Dr. Austic M. - is an osteopathic physician in Versailles, KY (4/18/02)

HARVEY, Mrs. Ed - of Little Ridge area; dt M/M Irvin Taylor of Elwood (11/24/05)

HARVEY, Eli - s Mahlon and Zilpha (Hadley) Harvey; d 1891 (8/25/05)

HARVEY, Ella - see Fred PEARSON

HARVEY, Emlen - dt Mahlon and Zilpha (Hadley) Harvey; d 1865 (8/25/05)

HARVEY, Enos - Fmt. Friends pastor (1/17/01); 30 Mar 1904 is given party for his 50th birthday (4/1/04), and 3 Apr 1905 for his 51st birthday (4/7/05); s Mahlon and Zilpha (Hadley) Harvey (8/22/05)

HARVEY, Mrs. Enos - mbr Fmt. WCTU (6/3/02)

HARVEY, Helen J. - 1905 Fmt. Twp. Sch grad (5/12/05)

HARVEY, Mrs. Hiram - mbr, Radley WCTU (8/23/04)

HARVEY, J.W. - of Little Ridge; s Mahlon and Zilpha (Hadley) Harvey (8/22/05)

HARVEY, Jonathan - 29 Dec 1904 m Mrs. Nancy Mart (1/3/05)

HARVEY, Lucetta - see Lucetta (Harvey) RONEY

HARVEY, Mahlon - of Fmt.; s William and Ruth (Hadley) Harvey (12/15/03); b Clinton Co., OH 26 Feb 1826; at Mooresville m Zilpha Hadley 24 Dec 1846; came to Little Ridge area 1855; mbr Little Ridge Friends, introduced singing into Little Ridge Friends SS then into worship service, ca 1870 encouraged revival movement; d 18 Aug 1905, bur Park Cem (8/22/05; 8/25/05)

HARVEY, Mary - mbr Fmt. WCTU (6/3/02); - see Mary RUSH; also see Mary (Harvey) WRIGHT

HARVEY, Milton - of Marion; s Mahlon and Zilpha (Hadley) Harvey (8/22/05)

HARVEY, Nettie - see Charles TREON

HARVEY, Ora Ethel - see Xen H. EDWARDS

HARVEY, Rebecca - see Rebecca (Harvey) FERREE

HARVEY, Robert - age 3; s M/M Will Harvey of Little Ridge (12/19/05)

HARVEY, Ruth - see Ruth (Harvey) RATLIFF

HARVEY, Mrs. Sadie B. - mbr Radley WCTU (5/13/02), and/or Hadley WCTU (10/24/02)

HARVEY, Sidney - of near Marion; s William and Ruth (Hadley) Harvey (12/15/03); lives near Roseburg (8/25/05)

HARVEY, William - of Fmt.; s William and Ruth (Hadley) Harvey (12/15/03); Supt., Fmt. Glass Works (6/21/04); of Cumberland (8/22/05)

HARVEY, Zilpha (Hadley) - wife of Mahlon Harvey; d 1889 (8/22/05)

HASTING/HASTINGS, __ - b 12 Apr 1904; s M/M Ralph Hastings (4/15/04)

HASTING, __ - see Mrs. J. Rhinehart BUSING; also see Mrs. Emory CARPENTER; also see Mrs. Will DANIELS

HASTING, Blanche - see Fred CRAY

HASTING, C.A. - prop., livery stable on W. Washington St. (8/8/05)

HASTING, Dewit - s Mrs. Robert Hasting (7/18/02)

HASTINGS, Ellen - kindergarten tchr, Fmt. Schs (7/15/04); dt Dr. S.G. Hastings; tchr, Gas City Schs (11/8/04)

HASTINGS, Mrs. Jane - b 1 Jan 1815 (8/12/04; 8/15/05)

HASTING, John - b 28 Dec 1859; s William Hasting (dec), step-s Mrs. Cyrus Winslow; m; att Back Creek Friends Sch (a log sch); d 2 Feb 1905, bur Park Cem (2/3/05; 2/7/05; 2/14/05)

HASTING, Lola - see Clarence SHOEMAKER

HASTING, Mada - dt Robert Hasting; 21 Oct 1903 m Orly Moles; will live in Middletown, OH (10/23/03)

HASTING, Robert W. - his sheep got on the C.I. & E. RR tracks today, 7 killed, 4 maimed (4/27/01); b Grant Co. 28 Nov 1840; s Carter and Elizabeth Hasting; serv Pvt., Co. H, 8th Ind. Inf. 16 Aug 1861-6 Sep 1864 (11/13/03; 5/27/04; 5/26/05)

HASTINGS, Dr. S.G. - has office over Citizen's Exchange Bank; is in general practice; fits glasses (6/6/02); is Secretary, Prohibition Alliance (6/20/02); has moved his office to next to his home on E. Washington St. one block E of Bank corner (7/8/02); is replaced as Fmt. Health Officer (9/23/04)

HASTINGS, Willard - 1904-05 tchr, Fmt. Twp. Sch # 5 (8/30/04)

HASTY, Ethel - see Charles YOUNG

HASTY, Eva - sues Nancy J. Osborn for tearing down Fmt. house that Osborn bought at tax sale (9/23/01); case dismissed (10/17/01)

HASTY, George - 1904 Liberty Twp. Sch grad (4/19/04)

HASTY, Harry Joseph - b 8 Nov 1901; s Thomas M. and Carrie A. Hasty; d 31 Jan 1902, bur Park Cem (3/18/02)

HASTY, Hazel Dena - b 8 Nov 1901; dt Thomas M. and Carrie A. Hasty; d 8 Mar 1902 (3/18/02)

HASTY, Mrs. Lou - of Fmt.; dt Mrs. Winnie Brewer (9/12/05)

HATHAWAY, Frank W. - mbr Fmt. Congregational Ch. (9/5/01)

HATHAWAY, Mrs. Jennie - mbr Fmt. Congregational Ch. (9/5/01)

HAVENS, Mrs. Gabrilla - b 25 Feb 1820 (8/12/04; 8/15/05)

HAWKINS, Maude Peryl - see Dr. Walter D. HAISLEY

HAWORTH, Mrs. Nora - sister of Ebon Coppock of Jonesboro (6/14/04); - see Elmer GATES

HAYNES, F.M. - serv Pvt., 2nd Ind. Light Artillery during CW (5/27/04; 5/26/05)

HAYWORTH, Charles - recently enlisted in a Cavalry Co., US Army (7/18/01)

HAYWORTH, Herbert - 1901 Jefferson Twp. Dist. # 9 Sch grad (5/30/01)

HEADLEY, Carl W. - Director, Headley Glass Co. (4/18/01)

HEADLEY, Joseph Edward - Director, Headley Glass Co. (4/18/01); Pres., Board of Directors, Fmt. YMCA (5/23/02; 6/3/02); s George Headley (11/28/02); leaves Fmt. YMCA Board (8/28/03)

HEAL, Mont - 17 Apr 1905 killed in a boiler explosion near Jonesboro, bur New Cumberland Cem (4/21/05)

HEAL, Mary (Coleman) - dt Thomas Coleman (8/26/01)

HEAVENRIDGE, Elizabeth - see Bernard McDONALD/McDONELL

HENLEY, Dr. Alpheus - Vice Pres. of Board of Directors, Roaring Gimlet Gold Mining Syndicate (9/26/02); Pres., Fmt. Fair Assoc. (1/12/04); Pvt., unassigned, 79th Ind. Inf. during CW (5/27/04; 5/26/05); Apr 1887 was Pres., Fmt. Mining Co. (1/17/05)

HENLEY, Dr. Glenn - is returning home from att medical sch in Buffalo, NY (12/5/01); is a squirrel hunter (6/24/02); 2nd Vice

Pres., Fmt. Fair Assoc. (1/12/04); 25 Feb 1904 m Margaret May James, dt M/M Robert James of Louisville, KY (3/1/04)

HENLEY, Jane - see Jane (Henley) WINSLOW

HENLEY, John R. - CW vet (6/6/05)

HENLEY, Milton - 1863, had 1st Fmt. harness shop (1/20/05)

HENLEY, Richard - of Fmt. is Asst. Manager, American Tin Plate Co., Gas City (10/6/03); a Director, Fmt. Fair Assoc. (1/12/04)

HENLEY, Vivian - dt M/M Will Henley (12/11/03)

HENLEY, William L. - has contract to build new Leachburg Sch (4/28/05); came to Fmt. in 1882; is contractor and builder (11/7/05)

HENLEY, William P. - f of Fmt.; m; is working in Nicaragua (12/18/03), as US Commercial Agent (1/29/04)

HERREN, J.J. - of Summitville; purchases tailor business from Ira S. Sage (2/3/05)

HESS, Henry W. - Mgr. of Gas City's Mississinewa Hotel, has skipped with $3,000 (12/12/01)

HESS, Mabel - dt Mrs. Sadie Hess (6/20/02)

HIATT, Cuthbert - b Guilford Co., NC 17 Jan 1822; s Cuthbert and Hannah; m 1st 4 Mar 1851 Clementina Mendenhall (dec 1880); came to Hendricks Co. 1861; came to Little Ridge area 4 mi. SW of Fmt. 1866; 28 May 1881 m 2nd Asenath Reeder; d 4 Mar 1902 (3/7/02; 3/7/02)

HIATT, E.E. - a winner in recent Fmt. Gun Club Shoot (4/1/01); Fmt. night policeman (3/7/02)

HIATT, Ernest C. - grad Pike Sch 1905 (5/12/05)

HIATT, George W. - of Roseburg; brother of Elmer E. Hiatt of Fmt.; d 13 Jul 1902 (7/15/02)

HIATT, Georgia - att Earlham Coll 1901-04 (8/26/01; 11/27/03); dt Lydia (Ferree) Hiatt (12/15/03); 1904 Earlham Coll grad (4/22/04)

HIATT, Isaac - janitor for Fmt. Schools (2/4/01)

HIATT, Jesse - of Dublin; age 90; 1880's lived in Fmt.; d 29 Sep 1903 (10/2/03)

HIATT, Lucille - 5 Oct 1905 is her 11th birthday (10/10/05)

HIATT, Lydia (Ferree) - of Fmt.; dt John and Rebecca (Harvey) Ferree (12/15/03)

HIATT, M.A. - s Cuthbert and Clementina (Mendenhall) Hiatt (3/4/02; 3/7/02); has a Fmt. harness shop (1/20/05)

HIATT, Mary - see Mary (Hiatt) BAKER

HIATT, R.M. - of Fresno, CA; s Cuthbert and Clementina (Mendenhall) (3/7/02)

HIGGINS, Mrs. Mary E. - see Foster DAVIS

HIGHLEY, Adam M. - of Converse is tchr in Fmt. HS (9/12/02)

HIGHLEY, Mrs. Annie - of Swayzee; dt Mrs. Jennie Moon of Hackleman (10/3/01)

HIGHLEY, David F. -appeals judgement against him for $1,000 to be paid to Martin Rutherford and William Miller for saving his wife from drowning in Pipe Creek; case is in Wabash Circuit Court (4/15/01); court rules that he must pay the $1,000 to Rutherford and Miller (10/24/01); his Richland Twp. 80-acre farm was sold to pay $450 demanded by court to Marion Retherford and William Miller; rest of income from sale of farm went to Sarah V. Highley (12/12/01)

HIGHLEY, Sarah V. - wife of [David] F. Highley (10/24/01)

HILDRETH, George W. - age 81; d 29 Jul 1905, bur Park Cem (8/1/05)

HILL, Chris - of Jonesboro; d 17 Mar 1902 (3/18/02)

HILL, Dan - CW vet (6/6/05)

HILL, Mrs. George - of 2 mi. N of Fmt.; age 38; dt Thomas Little; m; d 20 May 1905, funeral in Back Creek Friends MH, bur Park Cem (5/23/05)

HILL, Mrs. Gertrude - of Jonesboro was recently granted a divorce (3/21/02); - see William T. CAMMACK

HILL, James T. - of Troy, OH; is partner of S.B. Hill in Palace Meat Market (2/28/05); s Mrs. S.J. Hill of Warfordsburg, PA (10/17/05)

HILL, Mellia - see James F. GLASS

HILL, S.B. - Mgr., Fmt. Telephone Co. (1/9/02); resigns from Telephone Co., purchases Palace Meat Market (9/13/04); s Mrs. S.J. Hill of Warfordsburg, PA (10/17/05); bagged 12 rabbits while hunting on Thanksgiving Day (12/5/05)

HIMELICK, R.W. - Fmt. HS tchr 1896-97 (12/19/05)

HOBBS, Rev. Charles M. - f Fmt. area tchr; pastor, Swayzee Methodist Ch. (9/1/03; 2/3/05)

HOBBS, Mrs. Charles M. - dt John Duling of SE of Jonesboro (4/4/05)

HOBBS, Grace - 1903-05 tchr, Fmt. Sch (9/8/03; 9/2/04); grad Fmt. HS 1900 (12/19/05)

HOBBS, O.M. - of Upland is s Mrs. Jane Hobbs of Fmt. (3/4/02)

HOBBS, Thomas - dec; serv Pvt., 32nd Ind. Inf. during CW (5/27/04; 5/26/05)

HOCKETT, Caroline - of near Hackleman; aged; d 11 Aug 1901, bur Park Cem (8/15/01)

HOCKETT, Isaac - and Jacob are sons of Josiah Hockett (3/31/05)

HOCKETT, Mrs. Jacob - of 0.25 mi. SW of Fmt.; has Barred Plymouth Rock chickens for sale (4/8/01)

HOCKETT, John - of Wabash; s Joseph Hockett (3/31/05)

HOCKETT, Joseph - b Clinton Co., OH 19 Sep 1841; s Josiah Hockett; lived in Liberty Twp. 51 yrs.; m; d 28 Mar 1905, bur Park Cem (3/31/05); serv Pvt., Co. F, 139th Ind. Inf. during CW (5/26/05); wife was Phoebe Ann (7/21/05)

HOCKETT, Leona - see Leonard LITTLE

HOCKETT, Lewis - s Josiah Hockett (3/31/05); wife is Susannah (5/2/05)

HOCKETT, Lewis - s M/M Jacob Hockett; 12 Apr 1905 m Evelyn Brumit of near Hemlock (4/18/05)

HOCKETT, Oliver J. - 1903-04 tchr, Liberty Twp. Sch #7 and Principal, Liberty Twp. Schs (9/11/03; 12/8/03); tchr, Liberty Twp. Schs 1904-06 (12/27/04; 7/28/05); s Joseph Hockett (3/31/05)

HOCKETT, Oscar B. - Fmt. Twp Dist. #3 Sch tchr 1900-02 (1/3/01; 2/10/02); is att State Normal at Terre Haute (4/4/01); 1903-04 Fowlerton Sch Principal (9/4/03); 1904-05 Fowlerton Sch tchr (8/9/04); brother of Louis Hockett (10/21/04); resigns as Fowlerton Sch Principal to be tchr in Greenfield (1/24/05)

HOCKETT, Phoebe Ann - widow of Joseph Hockett; gets US CW pension of $8 per month (7/21/05)

HODSON, __ - b 20 Dec 1905; s M/M Daniel W. Hodson (12/22/05)

HODSON, Effie - 4 Mar 1900 m Daniel W. Hodson; now files for divorce (9/26/05)

HODSON, Irvin - age 13; s Aaron Hodson (10/13/05)

HOLDING, __ - see Mrs. Palmer WINSLOW

HOLLIDAY, __ - b 31 Jan 1905; s M/M Dale Holliday (1/31/05)

HOLLIDAY, Dr. D.A. - has purchased an auto (5/30/02); his Fmt. medical practice is taken over by Dr. T.J. Carter (12/5/02)

HOLLIDAY, L. Doyte - s Dr./M D.A. Holiday; is att Ind. Medical Coll (9/30/01; 2/3/02; 11/27/03; 11/25/04)

HOLLINGER, Mrs. Ida - of Fmt.; dt Mrs. Winnie Brewer (9/12/05)

HOLLINGSWORTH, __ - see Mrs. Robert BRUSHWILLER

HOLLINGSWORTH, Cyrus - architect; draws up plans for several Fmt. houses (9/12/01); completed plans for new $2,000 house in Matthews (2/20/02); serv Pvt., Co. I, 101st Ind. Inf. and Pvt., 32nd Ind. Inf. during CW (5/27/04; 5/26/05)

HOLLINGSWORTH, Ed - 6 Dec 1888 m Nettie Baldwin in Marion (12/15/05)

HOLLINGSWORTH, Gilmore - dec; serv Musician, Co. H, 12th Ind. Inf. during CW (5/27/04; 5/26/05)

HOLLINGSWORTH, J. - sells Rhode Island Reds, S.C.B. Leghorns, Golden Wyandottes, and Brown Leghorns [all are breeds of chickens] (4/4/02)

HOLLINGSWORTH, John Burgess - b Hudson Co., OH 6 Aug 1836; came to IN 1854; serv Pvt., Co. K, 8th Ind. Inf. 23 Apr 1861-6 Aug 1861; Pvt., Co. H, 12th Ind. Inf. 1 Oct 1861-18 May 1862; Pvt., Co. H, 8th Ind. Inf. 10 Aug 1862-14 Jun 1865; Fmt. marble cutter/monument maker until retired 1897; has US pension (10/23/03; 5/27/04; 5/26/05)

HOLLINGSWORTH, Kenneth - 7 Dec 1903 is given party for his 10th birthday (12/11/03)

HOLLINGSWORTH, Maria (Duling) - of Fmt.; dt Edmund and Eliza Ann (Hubert) Duling (2/18/01)

HOLLINGSWORTH, Wesley - dec; serv Musician, Pvt., Co. K, 130th Ind. Inf. during CW (5/27/04; 5/26/05)

HOLLOWAY, __ - b 19 Jun 1905; dt M/M Uriah Holloway (6/23/05)

HOLLOWAY, Abner - dec; serv Pvt., Co. E, 83rd Ind. Inf. during CW (5/26/05)

HOOSIER MINING COMPANY - Directors include C.C. Lyons and F.B. Zeigler (7/1/01); owns a mine at Dewey, ID (10/10/01); employee/representative is Lewis N. Cook (10/3/01); Alva Renbarger is an employee (3/7/02)

HOPKINS, Fay - see Preston LUCAS

HORN, Dr. Brose - [of Jonesboro] Michigan City State Prison physician; is accused of gouging State on cost of medicene (4/15/02)

HOSIER, Polk - serv Pvt., 36th Ind. Inf. during CW (5/27/04; 5/26/05)

HOSIER, Wiley - 1903-04 tchr, Liberty Twp. Sch # 14 (9/11/03); Liberty Twp. Sch tchr 1904-05 (12/27/04)

HOSKINS, Charles - of N of Fmt.; 22 Oct 1903 given party for his 21st birthday (10/27/03); 23 Nov 1904 m Florence, dt M/M Rom Poole (11/25/04)

HOSKINS, Isabel - see Charles Arthur BEWLEY

HOWE, Armada J. - see Armada J. (Howe) REED

HOWELL, Demetris - 26 Jun 1904 m Verna, dt M/M Willis Cammack of 8 mi. NW of Fmt. (6/28/04)

HOWELL, Donnie - 1904 Liberty Twp. Sch grad (4/19/04)

HOWELL, Glenn E. - is att Medical Sch, Indianapolis (9/23/01); f of Fmt.; has medical practice in Carson City, NV (6/20/02)

HOWELL, J.T. - s Riley Howell of W of Fmt. 7/15/04)

HOWELL, Thurza (Arnett) - sister of Lindley Arnett (9/15/03)

HOYT, Caroline - see John PICKARD

HUBBARD, Dr. __ - Apr 1887 was investor in Fmt. Mining Co. (1/17/05)

HUBBARD, Mrs. Charles - of Matthews; dt Mrs. William Lindsay (1/12/04)

HUBERT, Eliza Ann - see Edmund DULING

HUBERT, Rev. John - of 6 mi. NE of Fmt.; came to Fmt. Twp. ca 1845-46 from Guernsey Co., OH; serv Mexican War and CW; M.E. Ch. minister; d 21 Jan 1904, bur Jonesboro cem (1/26/04); serv Corp., Co. B, 3rd Ohio Inf. during Mexican War; Corp., Co. C, 54th Ind. Inf. during CW (5/27/04; 5/26/05)

HUGHES, Avis E. - 1904-05 Fmt. HS tchr (9/2/04)

HUGHES, H.H. - Mgr., Fmt. Gas Co. (8/26/04)

HULLEY, Samuel - of Marion; age ca 82; d 26 Aug 1901 (8/29/01)

HUNT, __ - b 5 Oct 1905; weighs 9 lb.; s M/M John A. Hunt (10/7/01)

HUNT, __ - see Mrs. Luther DAVIS

HUNT, John A. - mbr Fmt. M.E. Ch.; mbr, Board of Directors, Fmt. YMCA (6/6/02); stockholder, Fmt. Banking Co. (11/18/02); and C.R. Small purchase Fmt. Tile Factory (9/1/05); PHOTO; b near Rigdon; att Danville Normal Coll 2 yrs.; non-practising mbr Grant County Bar; business Mgr., Fmt. Tile Co. (11/21/05)

HUNT, Nathan W. - serv Pvt., Co. C, 12th Ind. Inf. during CW (5/27/04; 5/26/05)

HUNT, Tamer - b Wabash Co.; age 48; wife of Nathan W. Hunt; ca 1893 came to Fmt.; d 11 Aug 1904, bur Lafontaine Cem (8/16/04)

HUNT, Mrs. Wilson - b near Alexandria 21 Nov 1880; dt Leroy and Clara Jones; m Wilson Hunt 15 Aug 1900; mbr Mt. Pisgah Baptist Ch.; d 24 Mar 1904, bur Mt. Pisgah Cem (3/29/04)

HUNTER, Will - 10 Jan 1904 m Alice Maxey (1/12/04)

ICE, David - b Delaware Co. 30 Apr 1855; s Ransom and Sarah Ice; 1874 m Julia Brown; was Fmt. Marshal for 8 yrs.; att Fmt. Congregational Ch.; d 19 Oct 1905, bur Park Cem (10/20/05; 10/24/05)

ICE, Florence - dt David and Julia (Brown) Ice (10/20/05)

ICE, George - s Ransom and Sarah Ice (10/24/05)

ICE, John W. - of Lawrence, SD; s Ransom and Sarah Ice (10/24/05)

ICE, Julia (Brown) - dt William A. and Margaret A. Brown; of Fmt.; 1874 m David Ice; mbr Fmt. Congregational Ch. (5/27/02; 10/24/05)

ICE, Palmer - investor, Roaring Gimlet Gold Mining Syndicate (9/26/02); s David and Julia (Brown) Ice (10/20/05)

ICE, Rebecca - see Rebecca (Ice) CORN

ICE, Sanford - s David and Julia (Brown) Ice (10/20/05)

ILIFF, Rev. M.F. - of Jonesboro (3/7/01); pastor, Pleasant Grove M.P. Ch. (8/12/01); of Johnson Co.; f pastor of Jonesboro Circuit of M.P. Ch. (4/25/05)

ILLINOIS, gone to - see J. Rhinehart BUSING

INK, Ella - see Ella (Ink) MART

INK, Ida - mbr Fmt. Congregational Ch. (9/5/01)

INK, Sarah F. (Nelson) - dt John M. and Elizabeth J. (George) Nelson (8/5/01); mbr Fmt. Congregational Ch. (9/5/01)

IOWA, gone to - see T.B. McDONALD; Dempsey W. PRESNALL; Mrs. Elsworth WHINNERY

IRELAND, came from - see Mary (Morley) FLANAGAN; Bernard McDONALD/McDONELL

JACKSON, Mrs. Elizabeth - b 9 May 1823 (8/12/04; 8/15/05)

JAMES, Lucille - see Lucille (James) RAU

JAMES, Margaret May - see Dr. Glenn HENLEY

JAY, __ - dt b recently to M/M Walter L. Jay (7/15/02)

JAY, __ - b 8 Feb 1904; s M/M Walter L. Jay (2/9/04)

JAY, Cynthia - see Cynthia (Jay) WINSLOW

JAY, Elisha - of Jonesboro; d recently (4/11/05)

JAY, Elmer W. - of Fmt.; is bald; m; step-son of Asa Bond; 22 Jun 1902 is given dinner for his 40th birthday (6/24/02)

JAY, Ernest - is in US Navy (9/22/03), aboard cruiser 'Buffalo'; s M/M Elmer Jay (7/12/04); aboard battleship 'Olympia' (5/5/05)

JAY, Harlie - age 14; s M/M Riley Jay of Marion; d recently, bur Park Cem (1/3/05)

JAY, Jesse - of Jonesboro; brother of Susan (Jay) Ratliff (dec) (3/25/04)

JAY, Jessie M. - b Fmt.; gives violin recital in Friends MH (2/10/02); was given a fine violin several yrs. ago by Seth Hudson Bowen, an old soldier (2/13/02); dt Rev./M Isaiah Jay (5/13/02)

JAY, Joseph - walked from Fmt. to Franklin Coll in 1845 with John Morris, John Ratliff and Nelson Turner; all att Franklin Coll 1845-46 (2/12/04)

JAY, May - age 20; dt Roy and Cerena (Wright) Jay of Hamilton Co.; d 29 Oct 1905, funeral in Back Creek Friends MH (10/31/05)

JAY, Minnie - mbr, Fmt. M.E. Ch. (11/4/02)

JAY, Roy - of Hamilton Co.; m Cerena Wright, dt Joel B. Wright (10/31/05)

JAY, Susan - see Susan (Jay) RATLIFF

JAY, Walter L. - 1901 Ind. Law Sch grad (5/9/01); m; to set up law office in Fmt. (6/3/01); moves office to new Fmt. Blk. (11/7/01); mbr Fmt. YMCA committee (5/23/02); Secretary, Wi-da-me Salve Co. (8/18/05)

JAY, Mrs. Walter L. - dt M/M John Sanders of near Matthews (4/8/04)

JEFFERSON TOWNSHIP SCHOOLS - 1903-04 Principal, Township Schs is Morton Kline (12/8/03)
DIST. # 5 - 1901 grad is Oscar Jones (5/30/01)
DIST. # 7 - 1901 grad is Effie M. Jenkins (5/30/01)
DIST. # 9 - 1901 grads are Dory Smiley and Herbert Hayworth (5/30/01)

JEFFREY, Henry - serv Corp., Co. H, 118th Ind. Inf. during CW (5/27/04; 5/26/05)

JEFFREY, Mrs. William - of SE of Rigdon; d 2 Sep 1904, bur Forrestville Cem (9/6/04)

JENKINS, Effie M. - 1901 Jefferson Twp. Dist. # 7 Sch grad (5/30/01)

JENKINS, Tom - 1903-04 tchr, Liberty Twp. Sch # 9 (9/11/03); tchr, Liberty Twp. Sch 1904-05 (12/27/04)

JENKINS, Valerie - 1904 Liberty Twp. Sch grad (4/19/04)

JESSUP, __ - b 6 Aug 1902; s M/M Austin Jessup (8/8/02)

JOHNSON, __ - b 27 Nov 1905; dt M/M Clayton Johnson (11/28/05)

JOHNSON, Annette - att Earlham Coll 1904-05 (12/16/04)

JOHNSON, Clayton - 1903-04 tchr, Liberty Twp. Sch # 8 (9/11/03); s M/M Barclay Johnson of Liberty Twp.; bookkeeper, Fmt. Glass Works; 28 Dec 1904 will m Emma, dt Mrs. Rebecca Rau (12/23/04)

JOHNSON, Elizabeth - age 6; dt M/M Elwood Johnson; d 9 Oct 1904, bur Park Cem (10/14/04)

JOHNSON, Elizabeth - wife of James Johnson; d at her home SE of Upland 26 Jan 1902 (1/30/02)

JOHNSON, Elizabeth S. - see Henry LOVE

JOHNSON, Elva - b near Fmt. 4 Jun 1886; dt Gabriel (dec ca 1900) and Ursula Johnson; Fmt. HS student; d 13 Mar 1901, bur Park Cem (3/18/01; 3/21/01)

JOHNSON, Gabriel - dec; serv Pvt., Co. A, 8th Ind. Inf. during CW (5/27/04; 5/26/05)

JOHNSON, Mrs. Gabriel - granted CW widow pension of $8 per mon. (9/16/01)

JOHNSON, H.E. - Mgr. of Crystal Ice Plant (1/31/01)

JOHNSON, H. Sophia - 1903-04 tchr, Liberty Twp. Sch # 1 (9/11/03); tchr, Liberty Twp. Sch (Oak Ridge) 1904-05 (12/27/04; 3/3/05)

JOHNSON, Mary Alice - att Univ of IL 1904-05 (12/16/04) - see Charles WEEKS

JOHNSON, Nathan - 1881, prop., Star Hotel (1/13/1881 as reprinted 3/29/04)

JOHNSON, Otis - 1904 Liberty Twp. Sch grad (4/19/04)

JOHNSON, R.K. - of near Escondido, CA; age 76; helped William Neal lay out 1st plat of Fmt. (6/27/05)

JOHNSON, Solomon - a Director, Fmt. Fair Assoc. (1/12/04)

JOHNSON, Will - att Univ of IL 1904-05 (12/16/04)

JONES, __ - b 6 May 1904; dt M/M Ottis Jones (5/10/04)

JONES, __ - see Mrs. Wilson HUNT

JONES, Ben - 1903-04 tchr, Fmt. Twp. Sch # 4 (9/4/03); 1904-05 tchr, Fmt. Twp. Sch # 2 (8/30/04); s M/M David Jones (10/14/04); is given party 2 Jul 1905 for his 21st birthday (7/4/05); is att Ind. Medical Coll, Indianapolis (11/10/05)

JONES, Burr - 1 Jan 1905 m Daisy, dt M/M George Hall of Marion; live in Fmt. (1/3/05)

JONES, Eli - 1905 grad Grant Sch (5/12/05)

JONES, Hiram - serv Pvt., Co. C, 89th Ind. Inf. during CW (5/27/04; 5/26/05)

JONES, John - serv Pvt., Co. C, 89th Ind. Inf. during CW (5/26/05)

JONES, John A. - mail carrier, Fmt. Rural Rte. #22 (8/14/03); a Director, Fmt. Fair Assoc. (1/12/04)

JONES, Mrs. John - dt Mrs. Laura Foust (4/28/05)

JONES, John **Frank** - Adjutant, Beeson GAR Post 386 (1/24/02); b Henry Co. 16 Mar 1840; came to Mill Twp. 1852; Pvt., Co. H, 12th Ind. Inf. 2 Sep 1861-May 1862; Capt., Co. C, 89th Ind. Inf. Aug 1862-19 Aug 1865; came to Fmt. 1868 (10/20/03; 5/27/04; 5/26/05); Commander, Beeson GAR Post 386 (5/20/04); pension is increased to $24 per mon. (2/7/05)

JONES, Mrs. Lemuel - of S of Fmt.; age 72; d 13 Mar 1905 (3/17/05)

JONES, Mrs. Lew - dt Joseph and Malinda Kirk (3/17/05)

JONES, Lydia (Ellis) - of West Milton, OH; dt M/M James Ellis (1/21/01)

JONES, Mrs. Maria - of W of Fmt.; is age 76 (2/24/05)

JONES, Morton P. - prop., Palace Meat Market; 19 May 1904 m Edna Farr of near Bath (5/20/04); sells Palace Meat Market (9/16/04)

JONES, Oscar - 1901 Jefferson Twp. Dist. # 5 Sch grad (5/30/01)

JONES, Thomas - dec; serv Pvt., Co. G, 129th Ohio Inf. during CW (5/27/04; 5/26/05)

JONES, Tom - recently enlisted in US Army (7/18/01)

JONES, Verlie - s Squire/M J.F. Jones; 14 Jun 1905 m Katie, dt Mrs. Margaret Dillon (6/16/05)

JONES, Will - s M/M David Jones; FFA grad; Madison Co. sch tchr; 12 Oct 1904 m Lucy, dt M/M Webster Winslow; will live E of Summitville (10/14/04)

JONESBORO, Town of - 10th Street bridge for wagon and foot across Mississinewa River is completed by County Commissioners (2/3/02); Elam H. Neal is re-appointed postmaster (2/10/02); Jonesboro HS burned 3 Oct 1902 (10/7/02)
JONESBORO HERALD - Elon Tucker, Editor (12/18/03)

KAMMER, Albert - 9 Mar 1904 m Pearl, dt M/M E.J. DuBois (3/11/04)

KANSAS, gone to - see Lizzie (Winslow) WRIGHT

KAPPEL, Rev. Henry C. - of Walkerton; 21 Jul 1901 becomes pastor of St. Cecelia RC Ch. (7/15/01); leaves this pastorate (6/27/05)

KEEFER, Miss Alma - of Matthews; dt M/M Charles Keefer of Fmt. (6/20/02)

KEELEY, George - of Fmt.; age 56; d 2 Sep 1903, bur Gas City Cem (9/4/03)

KEENAN, Mrs. James - mbr of St. Cecila's RC Ch. (2/28/01)

KEEVER, Jay - att Univ Michigan Law Sch 1902-05 (9/16/02; 12/16/04), 1905 grad (5/23/05)

KELLAR, David H. - of Liberty Twp.; age ca 25; Spanish-American War vet; 1901 is kicked by a horse causing(?) present insanity, is in Marion jail (2/3/02)

KELLEY, James 'Spider' - famous featherweight pugilist; handyman for Columbia Hotel and for Mendenhall & Daugherty Drug Store; stole a watch in drugstore, pawned it for $6.50 in Alexandria, is in Marion jail; is an alcoholic (5/9/02; 5/23/02); 28 May 1902 is taken to State Prison to begin 2 to 14 yr. term (5/30/02)

KELLEY, Josephine (Shields) - 8 Jul 1902 m George Kelley, Matthews glass worker (7/11/02)

KELLEY, Minnie B. - see Zoan BALDWIN

KELSEY, A.W. - investor, Roaring Gimlet Gold Mining Syndicate (9/26/02); serv Pvt., Co. H, 12th Ind. Inf. and Corp., Co. K, 153rd Ind. Inf. during CW (5/27/04; 5/26/05)

KELSAY, Adin - is att Purdue Univ (9/16/01); b Fmt. 16 Dec 1880; s John and Luvenia Kelsay; FFA grad; att Purdue Univ 1900-03; d 7 Jan 1904, bur Park Cem (1/8/04; 1/12/04)

KELSAY, Guy H. - s County Commissioner John Kelsay; electrician for Marion Transit Railway Co.; 12 Jun 1901 m Cassie E. Wiltsee (6/13/01); grad Purdue Univ in mechanical engineering; moves to Richmond to work (6/6/02); s John and Luvenia (12/8/03)

KELSAY, John - Fmt. YMCA Board mbr (8/28/03); a Director, Fmt. Fair Assoc. (1/12/04)

KELSAY, Josephine - b 8 Jul 1899; dt John and Luvenia Kelsay; d 2 Dec 1903, bur Park Cem (12/4/03; 12/8/03)

KELSAY, Miss Julia - PHOTO, 1904-05 FFA music tchr (9/20/04)

KELSAY, Robert - age ca 42; s Mrs. Rezepha Kelsay; d 2 May 1904, bur Park Cem (5/3/04)

KELSAY, Sallie (Eastes) - of Fowlerton; sister of Lucinda (Eastes) Ward (1/29/04)

KELSAY, Smith - of Marion; d 1 May 1902, bur Park Cem (5/2/02); serv Pvt., Co. K, 130th Ind. Inf. and Co. H, 8th Ind. Inf. during CW (5/26/05)

KENTUCKY, came from - see Margaret J. KIMES; Lucinda (Corn) LEACH; Lucille (James) RAU

KEPLER, Henry D. - b 10 Oct 1823 Knox Co., OH; serv CW, Pvt., Co. E, 57th Ind. Inf.; 1888 moved to Fmt. (10/13/03; 5/27/04; 5/26/05); age 81 (8/15/05)

KERR, Chalmer - a Director in Fowlerton Land & Gas Co. (4/1/01)

KESSEL, Mrs. George - dt Amos and Phoebe DeShon (5/19/05)

KETCHCART, Miss Cora - d Fmt. 16 Jan 1904, bur Huntington Cem (1/19/04)

KIBBEY, John - of 7 mi. E of Fmt.; m; d 24 Aug 1904 (8/26/04)

KIBBEY, Mrs. Sarah - age 85 (8/15/05)

KIERSTEAD, __ - b 28 Aug 1903; dt M/M Aaron Kierstead (9/1/03)

KIES, A.C. - of Jonesboro, paid William Lindsey $17,000 for his sawmill (8/22/01)

KIMBROUGH, __ - see Mrs. James STEWART; Mrs. Samuel STEWART

KIMBROUGH, Eli - of Liberty Twp. was 81 11 Nov 1902; grandson of Elizabeth Mendenhall (dec) of Guilford Co., NC (11/28/02); age 82; d 21 May 1904 (5/24/04)

KIMBROUGH, Owen C. - of near Radley is Indian agent for Klamath Reservation in southern Oregon (8/22/05)

KIMES, __ - b 25 Jul 1904; s M/M Ed Kimes (7/26/04)

KIMES, C.R. - lives 4 mi. E of Fmt.; men and boys killed 221 rats on his farm last Sunday with clubs, revolvers, dogs (4/4/01)

KIMES, Caddie - mbr, Fmt. W.M. Ch. (11/4/02)

KIMES, Charles - 21 Sep 1901 m Carrie Royal (9/30/01)

KIMES, Clarence - clerk in Big Four depot (6/13/02)

KIMES, Dora (Flanagan) - age 41; m Albert Kimes; sister of John Flanagan; lived 6 mi. SW of Fmt.; mbr Hadley WCTU; d 23 Apr 1904, bur Park Cem (4/26/04; 4/29/04)

KIMES, Ed - 18 Jul 1905, and wife celebrate 19th wedding anniv (7/21/05)

KIMES, Fred - is Big Four RR brakeman (10/10/05)

KIMES, Howard - att Ind. Univ 1904-05 (12/16/04)

KIMES, Inez - 31 Jan 1905 is her 13th birthday (2/3/05)

KIMES, Margaret J. - b Montgomery Co., KY 1827; m KY 18 Oct 1855 Ephraim M. Kimes (dec 16 Oct 1891); d 4 Sep 1901 (9/9/01)

KIMES, Millard - and wife had their 20th wedding anniv last Sat (4/4/01)

KINCH, George F. - of Fmt.; d 22 Jun 1902 (6/24/02); b PA 26 Mar 1872; s Martin and Caroline (both dec); 1889 came to IN; 29 Apr 1893 m Elizabeth McCoy; mbr Fmt. Friends; d Fmt. (7/1/02)

KIRK, __ - see Mrs. Lew JONES

KIRK, Carlos - 1903-04 tchr, Liberty Twp. Sch # 11 (9/11/03); tchr, Liberty Twp. Sch 1904-06 (12/27/04; 7/28/05)

KIRK, Malinda - b Center Co., PA 10 Feb 1817; m Joseph Kirk (dec several yrs. ago); came to Grant Co. ca 1852; d at her Liberty Twp. home 14 Mar 1905, bur Back Creek Friends Cem (3/17/05)

KIRK, Samuel - s Joseph and Malinda Kirk (3/17/05)

KIRKMAN, Robert F. - of Liberty Twp.; is sentenced to 1 yr. in prison for assault on Chlystia 'Lesta' Addison (6/13/01); is serving 1 to 21 yrs. (7/4/01), in Michigan City Prison (7/8/01)

KIRKPATRICK, Bessie - and William, Emory, Etta, Harvey, Lindley, and Nora are children M/M James Kirkpatrick (3/22/04)

KIRKPATRICK, Della - mbr, Back Creek WCTU (11/11/04)

KIRKPATRICK, James - and wife 17 Mar 1904 were given a surprise dinner for their 24th wedding anniv.; att were: their children, William (and wife), Etta, Nora, Emory, Bessie, Lindley and Harvey; M/M William Mason and their children, Florence and Charles; M/M John Mason; Mrs. Anna Mason; Mrs. Ida (Mason) DeHoff and her children, Hazel Parks and Pearly Parks; Thomas Canup; M/M Newton Lucas and M/M Leslie Lemons (3/22/04)

KIRKPATRICK, William - last Sat. m Della Morris at home of Robert Wilson (8/14/03); and wife 17 Mar 1904 att wedding anniv. dinner for his parents, M/M James Kirkpatrick (3/22/04); 24 Sep 1904, and wife are chivareed (9/27/04)

KIRKWOOD, Elmer - last Sun. m Cora Zeek (both of Radley area) (8/14/03)

KIRKWOOD, John - of 3 mi. S of Matthews; age 78; d 6 May 1905 (5/9/05)

KITTERMAN, Clarence - grad Pike Sch 1905 (5/12/05); age 16; s M/M Ennis Kitterman; d 5 Oct 1905, bur Park Cem (10/6/05)

KLINE, Morton - 1903-04 Principal, Jefferson Twp. Schs (12/8/03)

KNIGHT, Albert - grad Fmt. HS 1900 (12/19/05)

KNIGHT, Bennett - s Abel and Anna Knight (9/22/05)

KNIGHT, Charles - of Marion; adopted s of Calvin and Elizabeth (Winslow) Rush (11/29/04)

KNIGHT, Clara - mbr, Back Creek [Friends] WCTU (11/11/04); dt Abel and Anna Knight (9/22/05)

KNIGHT, Cly - 17 Jun 1904 is her 9th birthday (6/21/04)

KNIGHT, Emmet C. - b 5 Oct 1875; s Abel and Anna Knight; FFA grad; d 20 Sep 1905, bur Park Cem (9/22/05; 10/3/05)

KNIGHT, Richard - Director, Headley Glass Co. (4/18/01)

KNIGHT, Mrs. Shelby - dt J.R. Smith of Knox (7/29/04)

KNIGHT, Shell W. - of Fmt.; brother of John Knight (of Summitville; 5 May 1901 killed by Big Four freight train) (5/6/01)

KNIGHT, Thomas - 1853, tchr in 1st sch in Fmt. (1/24/05)

KURTH, Charles - of Toledo, OH; 14 Oct 1905 m Mabel, dt M/M Fremont Roush (10/17/05)

LABERMAN, Mary A. - see Mary A. (Laberman) GLOVER

LAKE GALATIA - is frozen to depth of 18 inches (2/28/05)

LAMM, William G. - serv Pvt., 24th Ind. Battery during CW (5/27/04; 5/26/05)

LANGSDON, John - b Anthony, IN 8 May 1861; m Mattie Norris 15 Apr 1889; and wife were parents of Rae, Fred, Mary, and Hal; co-owner of Langsdon & Hunt Furniture & Undertaking; d 26 Aug 1904 (8/30/04; 9/20/04)

LARKINS, Mrs. James - dt W.C. Thompson (11/3/05)

LaRUE, __ - b 15 Aug 1903; s M/M Will LaRue (8/18/03)

LaRUE, __ - infant of M/M Gilbert LaRue d recently (2/9/04)

LaRUE, Mrs. Eugene - dt Elias M. (dec) and Lucetta (Harvey) Roney (2/28/02)

LaRUE, Gilbert - 21 Sep 1905 m Mrs. Bessie Smith, f of Vincennes (6/27/05); Dec 1894 is Cashier, Citizen's Bank (12/15/05)

LaRUE, Paul - age 16; s Gilbert and Phebe (2/14/01); 27 Jun 1905 m Nettie Maloney; will live in Fmt. (7/4/05)

LaRUE, Phoebe - sues husband, Gilbert LaRue, for divorce (2/14/01); divorce suit is dismissed, couple are reconciled (3/28/01); mbr Fmt. Congregational Ch. (9/5/01); b Lincoln Co., MO 18 May 1860; m Gilbert LaRue 18 Oct 1879; came to Fmt. ca 1883; d 22 Feb 1904, bur Park Cem (2/26/04; 3/1/04); dec mbr, Shakespeare Club (3/7/05)

LaRUE, Victor - age 9; s Gilbert and Phebe (2/14/01)

LATHAM, Ed - s Mrs. Sina Latham (3/17/05)

LATHAM, Mrs. Ed - dt Bernard McDonald (dec); d recently in Columbus, OH, bur Marion IOOF Cem (2/3/05; 3/17/05)

LATHAM, Nettie (Maddy) - f of Fmt., now of Muncie; dt J. Maddy; sues f husband Joel D. Latham for $500 (12/2/04)

LATHAM, Sina M. (Duling) - of Fmt.; dt Edmund and Mary Duling (2/18/01); sold the Latham Blk. (a 2-story brick bldg.) and lot to F.O. Gephart (3/18/02); mbr, Fmt. M.P. Ch. (11/4/02); mbr Fmt. WCTU; recently dec (3/25/02)

LAY, Oliver - d 21 Mar 1902 while a prisoner at Jeffersonville Reformatory, bur Jonesboro Cem (3/25/02)

LEACH, Charles E. - a Director, Fowlerton Land & Gas Co. (4/1/01); on his farm SE of Fmt. is a new oil well producing 100 barrels of oil daily (7/4/02)

LEACH, Ed S. - Asst. Supt., Fmt. Mining Co. (9/5/01; 1/16/02)

LEACH, Edmund C. - and George W., Benjamin F., Wilson T., Reuben J., Mary E. Leach, and Nancy J. Leach are children of Esom and Lucinda (Corn) Leach (8/8/02)

LEACH, Edna - dt M/M Esom O. Leach of Fmt.; is amateur actress (2/10/02; 3/28/02)

LEACH, Elgie W. - 1902-03 Lake Sch tchr (8/29/02); 1903-04 tchr, Fowlerton Sch (9/4/03); brother of Jake Leach of Mill Grove (1/26/04)

LEACH, Esom O. - recently sold his restaurant to W.E. Mackay (2/29/02); is Fmt. Marshal (3/28/02); manages his son Noah's cotton plantation in Mississippi (5/26/05)

LEACH, Mrs. J.M. - of Kokomo; dt Mrs. James Phillips (dec) (2/3/02)

LEACH, Jacob - of Fowlerton; 29 Sep 1903 m Blanch Duling, dt Mrs. Caroline Duling of near Fowlerton (10/2/03)

LEACH, Jessie - sister of Noah Leach of Matthews (1/15/04); employee of Miller & Haas Dry Goods Store (2/2/04); - see Robert BROWN

LEACH, Lucinda (Corn) - b KY 15 Dec 1823; dt Joseph and Nancy Corn; 24 Aug 1834 m Esom Leach (dec ca 1892, was s William Leach); lives in Fowlerton (8/8/02)

LEACH, Lula - 1901 Fmt. Twp. Dist. # 5 Sch grad (5/30/01); - see Claud MITTANK

LEACH, Noah - s Esom O. and Susan Leach; m; owns cotton plantation in Mississippi (5/26/05)

LEACH, Perry - is att Adrian Coll, MI (9/19/05)

LEACH, Simon B. - s Esom and Lucinda (Corn) Leach (8/8/02); 75 barrel per day oil well was brought in on his farm near Fowlerton 23 Aug 1902 (8/26/02)

LEACH, Susan (Brown) - dt William A. and Margaret A. Brown; of Fmt. (5/27/02); files for divorce from Esom O. Leach (7/19/04); is granted a divorce from Esom O. Leach (10/7/04)

LEACH, William J. - a Director in Fowlerton Land & Gas Co. (4/1/01); s Esom and Lucinda (Corn) Leach (8/8/02)

LEASE, Bert - prop. of a Main St. Cigar Store; is accused by Lenora McCombs of assault (6/14/04); he denies assaulting her, is released on his own recognizance (6/17/04); is fined $100 for assault of Lenora McCombs (9/27/04)

LEASE, Lucille - 4 Mar 1905 is her 8th birthday (3/7/05)

LECKENBY, Emeline (Hammond) - b Chattergues Co., NY 29 May 1842; m Eliphelet Leckenby 5 Apr 1865; mbr Baptists; d 13 Oct 1902, bur Park Cem (10/24/02)

LEE, Mrs. William - of 4 mi. SW of Fmt.; age 61; d 9 Dec 1903 (12/11/03)

LEER, Mrs. Lud - of 7 mi. S of Fmt.; dt John Wells (dec) (1/17/05)

LEER, Will - serv with US Army in Philippines; FFA grad 1903; 1903-05 att Earlham Coll (1/26/04; 12/16/04)

LELAND, Ralph - s M/M E.D. Leland; is att Howe Military Sch (6/6/01)

LEMON/LEMONS, Ike - has re-purchased the Big Four Restaurant (11/21/02)

LEMONS, Leslie - and wife 17 Mar 1904 att wedding anniv. dinner for M/M James Kirkpatrick (3/22/04)

LEMON, Marion - f of Fmt.; d Larwill 25 Jan 1905, bur Larwill cem (1/27/05)

LEWIS, __ - b recently; dt M/M Clyde Lewis (2/25/02)

LEWIS, __ - b 10 Nov 1904; dt M/M Will Lewis of SE of Fmt. (11/11/04)

LEWIS, __ - b 10 Jul 1905; dt M/M Clyde Lewis (7/14/05)

LEWIS, Clyde - 23 May 1901 m Emma, dt J.W. Parrill (5/27/01)

LEWIS, Mrs. David - dt Mrs. Lucinda Ward (1/29/04)

LEWIS, Ed - 7 Jul 1904 is his 47th birthday (7/12/04)

LEWIS, Ida (Rau) - see Ida RAU

LEWIS, Isabelle (Ward) - of near Fmt.; dt Elijah and Elizabeth Ward (4/18/02)

LEWIS, John S.D. - dec; serv Pvt., Co. H, 12th Ind. Inf. during CW (5/26/05)

LEWIS, Josephine - 1905-06 Liberty Twp. Sch tchr (7/28/05)

LEWIS, Oliver - lives 1.5 mi. NW of Fowlerton, 4 mi. E of Fmt. (12/4/03)

LEWIS, Rachel - is granted a divorce from Leander L. Lewis (10/31/01); mbr Fmt. Baptist Ch. (5/23/02); dt Mrs. Celia Wright (8/29/05)

LEWIS, William G. - of 1.5 mi. SE of Fmt. came to Grant Co. 18 Nov 1834 (11/22/04); age 79; is related to the famous Davy Crockett (7/18/05)

LIBERTY TOWNSHIP - Dennis Haisley is retiring Trustee; Frank McCabe of Hackleman is new Trustee (12/23/04; 12/27/04)

LIBERTY TOWNSHIP SCHOOLS - O.J. Hockett is 1903-04 Principal, Twp. Schs (12/8/03); 1904 grads: George Hasty, Grace Winslow, Valerie Jenkins, Wilson Haisley, Mossia Moon, Pearle Pearson, Everett Martin, Myrtle Davis, Donnie Howell, Charles Cox, Murven Haisley, Vernie Wright, Otis Johnson (4/19/04); 1904-05 tchrs: Elwood H. Garner (Bethel Sch), Amiel Stewart, John Burden, Tom Jenkins, Mamie Ellis, Stella Buller, H. Sophia Johnson (Oak Ridge Sch), Oliver Hockett, Oren Dickey, Carlos Kirk, S.M. Phillips, William Ware, Wiley Hosier, Dora Bogue (12/27/04); 1905-06 tchrs: Oliver B. Hockett, Chester Carter, Stella Buller, Carlos Kirk, Aimuel Stewart, John W. Burden, B. Pinkerman, S.M. Phillips, Lake Florea, Harvey Wright, Addie Wright, Josephine Lewis (7/28/05) DISTRICT #1 (BETHEL) - 1903-04 tchr is H. Sophia Johnson (9/11/03); 1904-05 tchr, Elwood H. Garner (12/27/04); E.H.

Garner resigns to tch in Mill Twp.; Edna Ballenger becomes Bethel tchr (3/3/05)

DIST. #2 (OAK RIDGE) - 1904-05 tchr, H. Sophia Johnson (12/27/04)

DIST. #3 - 1903-04 tchr is John W. Burden (9/11/03)

DIST. #4 - 1903-04 tchr is W.H. Young (9/11/03)

DIST. #5 - 1903-04 tchr is Miss Stella Buller (9/11/03)

DIST. #6 - 1903-04 tchr is E.H. Garner (9/11/03)

DIST. #7 (CENTER) - 1901-02 tchr, Will Young (9/5/01); 1903-04 tchr, O.J. Hockett (9/11/03)

DIST. #8 (ANTIOCH) - 1903-04 tchr, Clayton Johnson (9/11/03)

DIST. #9 - 1903-04 tchr is Tom Jenkins (9/11/03)

DIST. #11 - tchr, Prof. __ Garner (2/25/02); 1903-04 tchr, Carlos Kirk (9/11/03)

DIST. #12 (LITTLE RIDGE) - 1903-04 tchrs are W.W. Ware and Miss Edna Ballenger (9/11/03)

DIST. #14 - 1901 grad is Chester Carter (5/30/01); 1903-04 tchr, Wiley Hosier (9/11/03)

LIFE, Glennis - dt M/M J.F. Life; soph., FHS (6/13/05); 2 Jul 1905 given party for her 17th birthday (7/4/05)

LIGHTFOOT, Eli B. - dec; serv Pvt., Co. G, 26th Ind. Inf. during CW (5/27/04; 5/26/05)

LIGHTLE, Albert - dec; serv Pvt., Co. C, 89th Ind. Inf. during CW (5/26/05)

LIGHTLE, Enoch - Pvt., Co. H, 12th Ind. Inf. during CW (5/26/05)

LIGHTLE, Henry - dec; serv Pvt., Co. H, 8th Ind. Inf. during CW (5/26/05)

LIGHTLE, Newton - dec; serv Pvt., Co. H, 8th Ind. Inf. during CW (5/26/05)

LIGHTLE, Stanton - dec; serv Co. C, 89th Ind. Inf. during CW (5/26/05)

LIGHTNER, Will - of Hartford City; s M/M Joseph Lightner; 1 Jul 1905 m Opha Swaim; will live in Hartford City (7/4/05)

LILLIBRIDGE, Charles A. - of Marion; f of Fmt.; d 16 Aug 1903, bur Marion IOOF Cem (8/18/03; 8/21/03)

LILLIBRIDGE, John - dec; serv Pvt., Co. F, 113th Ohio Inf. during CW (5/27/04; 5/26/05)

LINDLEY, Florence - att Earlham Coll 1904-05 (12/16/04)

LINDLEY, Gurney - 3 Apr 1902 m Alice Young of Neoga, IL; will live near Fmt. at his home, 'Woodside' (4/4/02)

LINDLEY, Mary O. - of Fmt.; is Earlham Coll 1901 grad (5/27/01); - see Harry D. WOOD

LINDSEY, Alex - is suing Union Traction Co. for $10,000 for injuries while working for them in Fmt. (11/4/01)

LINDSEY, William - ran his milling and lumber business for ca 20 yrs.; is selling his business to A.C. Kies of Jonesboro (8/15/01), for $17,000 (8/22/01); purchases an interest in Fmt. Machine Works from J.O. Fink (12/4/03); his sawmill burned in 1900 (1/17/05); s Mrs. Nancy Lindsey (age 78) (3/28/05)

LINDSEY, Mrs. William - her mother, Mrs. Crouch, d in Fmt. 26 Dec 1901 (12/30/01)

LITTLE, __ - b last wk.; s M/M Leonard Little (12/13/04)

LITTLE, __ - see Mrs. Winfield CRISCO; Mrs. George HILL

LITTLE, Alex - s Nathan Little (7/22/02); serv Pvt., Co. H, 12th Ind. Inf. and Pvt., Co. B, 7th Ind. Cav. during CW (5/27/04; 5/26/05); is living in State Soldier's Home, Lafayette (10/20/05)

LITTLE, Almeda (Butler) - dt George and Martha Butler; m Ruff Little (killed in hunting accident several yrs. ago); d 28 Nov 1904, bur Park Cem (11/29/04)

LITTLE, Azel - dec; serv Pvt., Co. H, Ind. Inf. and 24th Ind. Battery during CW (5/26/05)

LITTLE, Effie (Davis) - age 26; dt M/M Robert Davis of W of Fmt.; m John R. Little; d 14 Sep 1905, funeral in Back Creek Friends MH, bur Back Creek Friends Cem (9/15/05; 9/19/05)

LITTLE, John, Sr. - lives in Leach (8/22/01)

LITTLE, John R. - s M/M Thomas Little; 1903-06 tchr, Fmt. Twp. Dist. # 3 (Grant Sch) (9/4/03; 8/30/04; 8/15/05)

LITTLE, Joseph - Pvt., Co. C, 89th Ind. Inf. during CW (5/26/05)

LITTLE, Lawrence - age 2; s M/M Sanford Little; d 19 Feb 1904, bur Park Cem (2/26/04)

LITTLE, Leonard - 25 Aug 1903 m Leona Hockett of 1 mi. W of Jonesboro (8/28/03); 1903-04 tchr, Fmt. Twp. Leachburg Sch (9/4/03); 1904-05 Lake Sch tchr (7/26/04); FFA grad; transfers from Lake Sch to be Principal, Fowlerton Sch (1/24/05); Leachburg Sch tchr 1905-06 (8/15/05)

LITTLE, Louisa - see Mrs. Louisa CRAWFORD

LITTLE, Mary - see Mary (Little) BULLER

LITTLE, Minnie - see Earl PRICE

LITTLE, Nathan - age 87 (7/8/02); d 22 Jul 1902; bur Back Creek Friends Cem (7/22/02); had a tan yard near center of Fmt. at an early date (1/13/05)

LITTLE, Ralph - of Matthews; s Ruff and Almeda (Butler) Little (11/29/04)

LITTLE, Thomas - dec; serv Pvt., Co. H, 84th Ind. Inf. and Pvt., Co. B, 7th Ind. Cav. during CW (5/27/04; 5/26/05)

LITTLE, Zimri - dec; serv Pvt., Co. C, 89th Ind. Inf. during CW (5/27/04; 5/26/05)

LIVELY, Mariah Jane (Ward) - b near Mocksville, NC 20 Jul 1832; dt Elijah and Elizabeth Ward; 1836 came to Grant Co.; 10 Feb 1870 m Abner D. Eaton (d 19 Feb 1878); Aug 1894 m James H. Lively; mbr M.P. Ch.; d 11 Apr 1902, bur Park Cem (4/15/02; 4/18/02)

LLOYD, __ - b 13 Jan 1905; dt M/M Charles Lloyd (1/17/05)

LLOYD, Mrs. Charles - adopted dt of Calvin and Elizabeth (Winslow) Rush (11/29/04)

LOCKNER, Sidney J. - 1901-02 FFA science tchr (8/19/01)

LOER, __ - b 10 Apr 1904; s M/M O.H. Loer (4/12/04)

LOER, Harvey - of Fmt.; s Z.T. Loer (9/15/03)

LOER, O.H. - of Fmt.; during CW serv in 160th Ind. Inf. (8/21/03)

LOER/LOWER, Z.T. - 1st sch tcher in Grant Co.; is visiting in Fmt. (3/14/01); of Lebanon, OH; 1865-71 taught schs in Green Twp. and in Liberty Twp. (9/15/03)

LOMAN, Dr. J.O. - 27 Dec 1888 m Allie Wilson at New Castle (12/15/05)

LONG, Mrs. J.C. - dt Mrs. Laura Foust (dec) (4/28/05)

LONG, Miss Lizzie - sister of Mrs. Minnie Wilson of near Deer Creek; recently dec; bur Oak Ridge Cem (12/9/04)

LOVE, Blanche - 1 Oct 1904 is her 20th birthday (10/7/04)

LOVE, Byram - serv Pvt., Co. D, 34th Ind. Inf. during CW (5/27/04; 5/26/05), was captured in southern Louisiana, spent Nov and Dec 1863 in a prisoner-of-war camp (1/10/05)

LOVE, Henry - b Delaware Co. 8 Aug 1829; s Isaiah and Margaret; m 1st 1 Jul 1852 Elizabeth S. Johnson (dec 1871); moved to Fmt. 1867; m 2nd 9 Jul 1872 Mary Ann Creek (dec 17 Mar 1881); m 3rd Martha A. Cecil 25 May 1882; f mbr New Light Ch.; mbr Fmt. Friends; d 5 Jul 1901, bur Walker Cem near Summitville (7/8/01; 7/11/01)

LOVE, Marion - has purchased Big Four Barber Shop (8/26/01)

LOVE, Nathan O. - s M/M Byram Love; 21 Oct 1905 m Leatha, dt Luther Brookshire (10/24/05)

LOWRY, Rev. Oscar - 1 Sep 1901 to resume Fmt. Congregational Ch. pastorate (6/13/01); Chairman/mbr, Finance & Bldg. Committee raising money to build tabernacle for Billy Sunday revival to start 20 Mar 1902 (1/30/02); m; resigns pastorate, will be full-time evangelist (9/23/02)

LOY, __ - b recently; child of M/M Oscar Loy (6/20/02)

LUCAS, D. Carl - Acting Secretary, Fmt. Fair (7/15/01)

LUCAS, David - age 75; lived in Jonesboro 40 yrs.; d there recently (7/28/05)

LUCAS, Dr. Karl D. - grad Ind. Dental Coll 1902 (4/11/02); sets up dental practice in Indianapolis (6/13/02); s T.J. Lucas (8/14/03)

LUCAS, Mabel - transfers from Earlham Coll to Conservatory of Music, Marion (1/15/04)

LUCAS, Newton - and wife 17 Mar 1904 att wedding anniv. dinner for M/M James Kirkpatrick (3/22/04)

LUCAS, Preston - Lake Sch tchr 1905-06 (8/15/05); FFA grad (9/15/05); 17 Dec 1905 m Fay Hopkins of Matthews (12/26/05)

LUCAS, T.J. - b Jefferson Twp. 1849; moved to Fmt. ca 1891; Pres., Fmt. Fair Assoc. (8/14/03)

LUCAS, Mrs. T.J. - dt Mrs. Mary Dunn of Matthews (7/14/05)

LUCAS, Dr. Wilbur - Asst. Surgeon, Northwestern RR at Chicago (3/21/02); s T.J. Lucas; M.D. degree from Northwestern Univ., Chicago; has medical practice in Pueblo, CO (8/14/03)

LUCE/LUSE, Elmira C. - mbr, Fmt. WCTU (9/16/02)

LUSE, Ora D. - see Ora D. (Luse) OSBORN; see Eli J. COX

LUCE/LUSE, Walter S. - operates the Wheeler Mill (7/25/01)

LUSE, Mrs. Walter S. - dt N.D. Coffin of Westland (3/28/05)

LUNG, Lucy (Beals) - f of Fmt.; is granted a divorce from Edison Lung (10/4/04)

LUTHER, __ - see Mrs. Elias BUNDY; Mrs. Alvin SCOTT

LUTHER, Dorothy - 1881, Fmt. Twp. Sch grad (7/4/05); dt Ivy and Sarah Luther (8/18/05)

LUTHER, Ivy - and wife will celebrate 50th wedding anniv 28 Aug 1905 (8/15/05); age 72; m Sarah (age 72) in Randolph Co., NC; came to Fmt. ca 1872 (9/1/05)

LUTHER, James - Secretary, National Drain Tile Co. (9/16/02); of Terre Haute; s Ivy and Sarah Luther (8/18/05)

LYNCH, __ - infant of James Lynch; d 20 Oct 1905, bur Musick Cem (10/24/05)

LYNCH, Ruth - age 3; dt M/M Herbert Lynch (1/15/04)

LYONS, Arthur - of Van Buren; s Mrs. Lydia Lyons (10/24/05)

LYONS, C.C. - a Director, Hoosier Mining Co. (7/4/01); s Charles Lyons (dec) (1/27/02); is daily selling out his merchandise in the Hotel Blk. (6/24/02)

LYONS, Charles C. - b Baltimore, MD 22 Apr 1839; m Lydia E. Woolweaver of Gallipollis, OH 29 Dec 1859; M.E. minister; d 26 Jan 1902, bur Park Cem (1/27/02; 1/30/02)

LYONS, Robert - age 10; s M/M C.C. Lyons (10/17/05)

MacKAY, W.E. - of Danville; buys E.O. Leach Restaurant (2/28/02)

McCABE, Frank - of Hackleman; Liberty Twp. Trustee (12/23/04)

McCANDLESS, __ - see Mrs. W.M. WARNER

McCANDLESS, Richard - f of Fmt.; lives in Soldier's Home, Marion (12/12/05)

McCASHLIN, J.C. - Chairman, election committee, Bethel M.P. Ch. (11/11/01)

McCLEARY, Mrs. S.M. - of Parker City; dt M/M Jacob Briles (12/8/05)

McCOMBS, __ - b 20 Nov 1903; s M/M John McCombs (11/24/03)

McCOMBS, John - of Hackleman; Dec 1890, killed 45 quail with 3 shots (12/15/05)

McCOMBS, Mrs. John - of Liberty Twp.; dt Luther Brookshire (dec) (2/19/04)

McCOMBS, Lenora - of Fmt. is recently given party for her 14th birthday (9/9/02); age 15; dt M/M Alonzo McCombs; accuses Bert Lease of assaulting her (6/4/04)

McCONN, William - of Fmt.; d 28 Aug 1902 (8/29/02)

McCORKLE, __ - age 18 mon.; child of M/M John McCorkle; d recently, bur Back Creek Friends Cem (2/10/05)

McCOY, Achsah T. [(Arnett)] - granted divorce from Nathan H. McCoy recently (7/1/02)

McCOY, Anna A. - see Anna A. (McCoy) MILLER

McCOY, Elizabeth - [dt William Henry and Ann (Moon) McCoy] - see George F. KINCH

McCOY, Frank - s Nathan H. McCoy, farmer of W of Fmt. (5/13/02)

McCOY, Jacob - dec; Co. D, 33rd Ind. Inf. during CW (5/26/05)

McCOY, Nathan H. - pleads guilty to rape of his dts (5/16/02); taken to State Prison to begin 2-14 yr. sentence (5/30/02)

McCOY, Thurza - dt Nate McCoy (8/26/01)

McCOY, Willis - 10 Aug 1904 m Mrs. Ella Allred (10/18/04)

McDONALD, __ - see Mrs. Ed LATHAM

McDONALD/McDONNELL, Bernard - of Fmt.; age 94 (5/23/02); b Dublin, Ireland; came to USA in 1828, to Grant Co. in 1852 (8/14/03); b 12 Jul 1812; s Lawrence (dec in Ireland) and Nellie McDonald; ca 1842 m Elizabeth Heavenridge (dec 1885 or earlier) in Liberty, IN; mbr Friends; d 28 Oct 1903, bur Park Cem (10/30/03; 11/10/03)

McDONALD, E. Lawrence - s Bernard McDonnell of Fmt.; widower; d at his home in Muskegon, MI 20 Apr 1902 (4/22/02); age 51; willed $40,000 to establish home for indigent old women in Fmt. (4/25/02); was b in Fmt.; will is defective, his father Bernard McDonald will get the entire estate of $65,000 (5/23/02)

McDONALD/McDONNELL, Mrs. E. Lawrence - b Fmt. 18 Sep 1854; dt M/M L.L. Fankboner; m 1875; mbr M.E. Ch.; d Muskegon, MI 12 Apr 1901 (4/22/01)

McDONALD, Elizabeth 'Lizzie' - of Fmt.; dt Bernard McDonald (5/23/02; 5/25/02); - see W.B. THOMAS

McDONALD, John - of Marion; s Bernard (4/25/02)

McDONALD, T.B. - of Lovila, IA; s Bernard McDonald (5/23/02; 8/7/03); tchr, log Back Creek Friends Sch; moved to IA ca 1870 (2/14/05)

McFADDEN, Mabel - age 17; wife of Leon McFadden; d 11 Jul 1905, bur Park Cem (7/14/05)

McGRATH, John - employee of Fmt. Glass Works (6/13/02)

McHATTON, LeRoy - of Fmt.; s Milton McHatton (dec recently) (4/26/04); is given party 17 Jun 1904 for his 43rd birthday (6/21/04); m; s Lydia McHatton (recently dec) (6/16/05)

McHATTON, Lydia - of Amboy; d recently (6/16/05)

McMASTERS, __ - see Adelbert BRILES

McMASTERS, Lawrence W. - b 5 mi. W of Fmt. 10 Oct 1878; s J.C. and Nancy (dec); d Fmt. 17 Nov 1901 (11/21/01)

McMASTERS, Neal - age ca 27; d 30 Jul 1901, bur Back Creek Friends Cem (8/1/01)

McNAUGHTON, Rev. Robert - pastor, Fmt. Congregational Ch. (10/17/02); resigns pastorate; will soon m Helen Reid Duncan of Stanley, Scotland; will live in New Zealand (2/24/05)

McPHERSON, Lydia - see Benjamin F. MORRIS

McQUOID, __ - see Mrs. Robert DARE

McQUOID, Caleb - age 63; m; ca 1892 came to Fmt.; d 11 Sep 1904, bur Malta Bend, MO cem (9/13/04)

MADDOX, James - colored; age 28; d Fmt. 14 Aug 1903, bur Glascow, KY (8/18/03)

MADDY, Nettie - see Nettie (Maddy) LATHAM

MAHONEY, Joseph - 27 Dec 1903 d near Fmt., bur Park Cem (12/29/03; 1/1/04); serv Pvt., Co. F, 147th Ind. Inf. during CW (5/27/04; 5/26/05)

MAIN, Ed - f Fmt. printer; is in Denver, CO for health (6/3/02); son-in-law of Alex Little; d 13 Oct 1902 in Greentown; bur Fmt. cem (10/14/02)

MALONEY, Nettie - 1904-05 Fmt. Sch tchr (9/2/04); - see Paul LaRUE

MALOTT, Robert - of Marion; age 74; was 1st white child b in Grant Co.; had Columbia Hotel here with his son Nate several yrs. ago (7/18/01)

MANG, Martin L. - now lives in Pleasant Twp.; father of Tacie Mang (murdered a few yrs. ago); may be mentally ill (4/1/01)

MANN, Andrew - dec; serv Pvt., Co. E, 101st Ind. Inf. during CW (5/27/04; 5/26/05)

MANN, Buck - buys M. West's cigar & sundry store (9/26/01)

MANNING, John - serv Co. G, 34th Ind. Inf. during CW (5/27/04; 5/26/05)

MARINE, __ - young dt Jack Marine of Jonesboro; d recently (12/18/03)

MARK, M. - Apr 1887, investor in Fmt. Mining Co. (1/17/05)

MARKS, Robert - given dinner 27 Mar 1904 for his 80th birthday (3/29/04); b 27 Mar 1824 (8/12/04); age 81 (8/15/05)

MARSHALL, Mrs. James - dt Mrs. Daniel Fowler (7/4/02)

MART, __ - b recently; dt M/M Frank Mart (10/6/03)

MART, Benjamin Frank - Liberty Twp. farmer; owns 80 acres (8/12/02)

MART, Charles - s Oscar Mart (7/29/04)

MART, Ella (Ink) - mbr Fmt. Congregational Ch. (9/5/01)

MART, Elma Leona (Templeton) - b 3 Aug 1872 near Cadiz, Henry Co.; dt Charles and Jennie Templeton; moved to near Fmt. 1873; m Benjamin Frank Mart 23 Feb 1888; mbr Back Creek W.M. Ch.; d 5 Jan 1904 (1/8/04)

MART, Miss Grace - of Fmt.; lives with her grandmother Rachel Scott (8/28/03); - see Asa J. GASKILL

MART, Mrs. Mary - widow of Joseph Mart of Liberty Twp.; d recently in her home in Jonesboro, bur Park Cem (9/15/05)

MART, Mrs. Nancy - see Jonathan HARVEY

MART, Samuel - bought W.A. Dolman's Lunch Room (12/30/01)

MARTIN, Everett - grad, Liberty Twp. Sch 1904 (4/19/04)

MARTIN, John - age 44; 20 Feb 1905 m Mrs. Ellen Brewer (age 37); live in Fmt. (2/24/05)

MARYLAND, came from - see Susan Frances COAHRAN; Charles C. LYONS

MASON, Anna (Coleman) - dt Thomas Coleman (8/26/01); 17 Mar att wedding anniv. dinner for M/M James Kirkpatrick (3/22/04)

MASON, Charles - 17 Mar 1904 att wedding anniv. dinner for M/M James Kirkpatrick (3/22/04)

MASON, F. - stockholder, Fmt. Banking Co. (11/18/02)

MASON, Florence - 17 Mar 1904 att wedding anniv. dinner for M/M James Kirkpatrick (3/22/04)

MASON, Miss Flossie - of near Gas City is mentioned (8/29/05)

MASON, Fred - age 62; southern Grant Co. farmer; d 25 Jul 1905, bur Mt. Zion Cem (7/28/05)

MASON, Frederick - serv Pvt., Co. G, 140th Ind. Inf. during CW (5/27/04; 5/26/05)

MASON, Ida - see Ida [(Mason)] DeHOFF

MASON, John - and wife 17 Mar 1904 att wedding anniv. dinner for M/M James Kirkpatrick (3/22/04)

MASON, William - and wife [of Glencoe Farm] 17 Mar 1904 att wedding anniv. dinner for M/M James Kirkpatrick (3/22/04)

MATHIS, Mabel - grad, Fmt. HS 1904 (4/22/04)

MATTHEWS, Town of - A new bridge over Mississinewa River to be built on Massachusetts Ave. (7/25/01); new M.E. Ch. to be built soon (8/1/02); town has 15 saloons and one church (9/2/02)
DREW HOTEL - a dance is held here (11/24/03)
FARMER'S TELEPHONE LINE - is now organized with R.C. Nottingham, Pres.; Michael Cory, Sect.; J.W. Richards, Treas.; has 14 mbrs (3/14/01); exchange to be working by June 1st (5/20/01)

FRENCH HOTEL - burned 7 Mar 1902 (3/7/02)

FURR HOTEL - new 2-story hotel owned by L.A. Furr; he intends to raffle it off by selling 4,000 raffle tickets at $1.00 per ticket (9/5/01)

MATTHEWS STEEL PLANT - Hort Ribble is bookkeeper (9/4/03)

OPERA HOUSE - 'Tony, the Convict' to be offered April 5th (3/25/02)

VanCAMP WINDOW GLASS CO. - Ted Middlehurst of Fmt. is an employee (9/8/03); Adolph Wuchner is Manager (10/13/03)

WINSLOW GLASS FACTORY - Will Rudicil is a shipping clerk (10/31/01); Harvey Smith is a shipping clerk (12/16/01); Ralph Brown, employee (2/17/02); manager is D.A. Baldwin (8/7/03); owner Palmer Winslow moves factory to Louisville, KY (4/15/04)

MATTHEWS GUN CLUB - 1,200-1,500 live pigeons will be shot during a Shoot next Sat. (9/2/02)

MAXEY, Alice - see Will HUNTER

MAXEY, Eva - dt M/M Albert Maxey; d 5 May 1904; colored (5/6/04)

MAXEY, Fanny - age 8; dt M/M Albert Maxey; d 7 Jun 1904, bur Park Cem; colored (6/10/04)

MAXEY, Fred - age 10; s M/M Albert Maxey; d 8 Dec 1903, bur Park Cem; colored (12/11/03)

MAXEY, Ira - age 5 mo.; s M/M Albert Maxey; d 7 May 1904, bur Park Cem; colored (5/10/04)

MAXEY, Margaret - age 23; dt Mrs. Eliza Maxey; d 17 Dec 1904, bur Park Cem; colored (12/20/04)

MAXEY, Thomas - age 34; d 12 Oct 1905, bur Park Cem (10/17/05)

MAYER, Lucien - is a Director, Industrial Window Glass Co. of Fowlerton (10/14/01)

MEEK/MEEKS, Emily - of Jonesboro; recently shot/wounded her husband, William, when she found him consorting with colored girls at a saloon near the river; she was arrested (1/17/01)

MEEKS, Isaac - 1867, 1st pastor, Fmt. W.M. Ch. (1/24/05)

MEEK, Dr. J.R. - of Jonesboro; age ca 81; d 11 Jul 1901 (7/15/01)

MENDENHALL, Clementina - see Cuthbert HIATT

MENDENHALL, George - Secretary, Bates Oil Co. Board of Directors (7/11/01)

MENDENHALL, W.K. - and wife of 1 mi. W of Jonesboro celebrated their 25th wedding anniv 30 Mar 1901 (4/1/01)

MESSLER, [Allie] - see [Allie] (Messler) PASCHAL

METZGER, __ - b 10 Sep 1905; s M/M Carl Metzger (9/12/05)

MICHAELS, Erny - d last wk., bur Park Cem (2/6/02)

MICHAELS, Mary - see Mark CRISCO

MICHIGAN, came from - see Bell (Story) WRIGHT

MICHIGAN, gone to - see Thomas J. CARTER; E. Lawrence McDONALD; H.A. SCOTT

MIDDLEHURST, Ted - of Fmt. is employee of VanCamp Window Glass Co., Matthews (9/8/03)

MILHOLLAND, Thomas - serv Pvt., Co. B, 52nd Ind. Inf. during CW (5/27/04; 5/26/05)

MILIKAN, Bernice - 28 Apr 1901 is her 8th birthday (4/29/01)

MILLER, __ - infant of M/M Charles Miller of Fowlerton; d 30 Jul 1905, bur Harmony Cem (8/1/05)

MILLER, Mrs. Adam - of Jonesboro; age 74 yr., 5 m, 19 da; d 25 Jul 1901, bur Jonesboro cem (7/29/01)

MILLER, Anna A. (McCoy) - b 2 Jun 1875; dt Willis E. and Mary E. McCoy; 16 Feb 1902 m Samuel Miller; d 14 Mar 1902, bur Park Cem (3/18/02; 3/21/02; 3/25/02)

MILLER, Mrs. Belle - see Addison SCOTT

MILLER, Mrs. D.K. - age 25; m; d 27 Jun 1904, bur Park Cem (6/28/04)

MILLER, Elwood - elected Director, Fmt. YMCA (12/18/03)

MILLER, Emma - see Richard A. WILEY

MILLER, Mrs. Ephraim - dt Mrs. Ellen Sheets (8/22/01)

MILLER, Fred - s Joe X. Miller; age 20; employee of Bell Window Glass Factory; is in Marion jail after shooting dead Will Stibbs 30 Apr 1901 in Fmt. Fair Grounds (5/2/01); indicted for 1st degree murder (5/6/01); is found guilty of manslaughter (6/10/01); is taken to Jeffersonville Prison (6/13/01)

MILLER, H.O. - Supt./Mgr., Fmt. Telephone Co. (3/7/02; 4/1/04)

MILLER, Minnie (Gibson) - of Hackleman; sister of Miss Pearl Gibson (9/16/01)

MILLER, William - and Martin Rutherford saved [David] F. Highley's wife from drowning in Pipe Creek; Highley is appealing judgement against him for $1,000; case is in Wabash Circuit Court (4/15/01); court rules that he and Rutherford must be paid the $1,000 (10/24/01); finally gets half of $450 in settlement of Highley case (12/12/01)

MILLIKAN, Mrs. Joe - of Coffeyville, KS; sister of Henry Rittenhouse (5/2/05)

MILLS, A.E. - candidate for Fmt. Marshal (4/1/01)

MILLS, Gertrude C. - 1901-02 FFA tchr of literature and language (8/19/01); is studying music in Berlin, Germany (12/22/03)

MILNER, Jesse - dec; Co. F, 139th Ind. Inf. during CW (5/26/05)

MINNICK, Floyd - age 15; s M/M Frank Minnick; d 14 Dec 1905 (12/19/05)

MINNICK, Mabel - dt Mrs. W.H. Minnick (10/23/03)

MIRIOR, Alfred - is a Director, Industrial Window Glass Co. of Fowlerton (10/14/01)

MISSISSINEWA RIVER - new bridge is being constructed between Gas City and Jonesboro (6/17/01); new bridge to be built in Matthews on Massachusetts Ave. (7/25/01); 4 Nov 1901 old wooden bridge between Jonesboro and Gas City burned (11/4/01); foot bridge is between Jonesboro and Gas City (11/7/01); work is hastened on new bridge being built between Jonesboro and Gas City (11/21/01); Union Traction Co. to build its Jonesboro bridge over the river using the abutments and piers of the old wooden bridge that burned 4 Nov 1901; to pay Grant County $100 per yr. for site use (1/1/02); foot bridge recently constructed between Jonesboro and Gas City is washed out 13 Dec 1901 by heavy rains (12/16/01); Union Traction Co. bridge between Jonesboro and Gas City is now completed as is the wagon and foot bridge [at 10th St., Jonesboro] (2/3/02)

MISSISSIPPI, came from - see James BOYD

MISSISSIPPI, gone to - Noah LEACH

MISSOURI, came from - see Phoebe LaRUE

MITTANK, Claud - 26 Nov 1902 m Lula Leach (11/28/02)

MITTANK, Michael - serv Pvt., 32nd Ind. Inf. during CW (5/27/04; 5/26/05)

MITTANK, Vida - see John E. MORRISH

MODLIN, George - dec; serv Pvt., Co. C, 89th Ind. Inf. during CW (5/26/05)

MOLES, Orley - see Mada HASTING

MONAHAN, __ - b 7 Dec 1903; s M/M William Monahan (12/8/03)

MONAHAN, Edward - Principal, Fmt. HS fall 1896 until Jan 1899 when he dec (12/19/05)

MONAHAN, James - serv Pvt., Co. K, 33rd New Jersey Inf. during CW (5/27/04; 5/26/05)

MONAHAN, John - s M/M Thomas Monahan (8/12/04)

MONAHAN, William - of E of Fmt.; age 73 (8/25/05)

MONROE TOWNSHIP - DISTRICT # 7 SCHOOL - 1905-06 tchr is Miss Nellie Simons (9/5/05)

MONTGOMERY, John - a winner in recent Fmt. Gun Club Shoot (4/1/01); and wife are mbrs Fmt. Congregational Ch. (9/5/01); dec; serv 101st Ind. Inf. during CW (5/26/05)

MONTGOMERY, Solomon - dec; serv 101st Ind. Inf. during CW (5/26/05)

MOON, __ - b 2 Mar 1904; dt M/M Lon Moon (3/4/04)

MOON, A.R. - f of Fmt.; is Escondido, CA jeweler (6/27/05)

MOON, Caleb - s Isaiah Moon (dec) (3/1/04); serv Corp., Co. K, 130th Ind. Inf. during CW (5/26/05)

MOON, Glenn - 1904-05 Fmt. Sch tchr (9/2/04)

MOON, Ida E. - see Calvin B. COOK

MOON, Isaiah - age 84; came to Grant Co. 1855; d 26 Feb 1904, bur Little Ridge Friends Cem (3/1/04)

MOON, Mrs. Jennie - lives in Hackleman (10/3/01)

MOON, Lewis - elected Chaplain, Beeson GAR Post 386 (1/24/02); serv Pvt., Co. C, 79th Ohio Inf. and Capt., Co. G, 118th Kentucky Inf. during CW (5/27/04; 5/26/05)

MOON, Maggie Belle - see Maggie Belle (Moon) MORGAN

MOON, Mossia - of Hackleman; her 13th birthday is 19 Oct 1901 (10/24/01); grad, Liberty Twp. Sch 1904 (4/19/04)

MOON, W.G. - is selling settings of Buff Leghorn eggs (4/8/02); can be hired to plow gardens in Fmt. (4/29/02); his poultry farm is 0.5 mi. W of Fmt. (4/5/04)

MOORE, __ - b 20 Jan 1904; s M/M James C. Moore (1/22/04)

MOORE, Hazel - dt M/M Charles Moore (4/18/05)

MOORE, Thomas W. - a Director, Fmt. Fair Assoc. (1/12/04)

MORELAND, Mrs. Mattie - d Fmt. 12 Nov 1902 (11/14/02)

MORGAN, E.A. - 1900, established Fairmount Daily Journal (1/24/05)

MORGAN, Maggie Belle (Moon) - of Converse; dt Caleb Moon; d 12 Feb 1904 (2/16/04)

MORGAN, Mark - 5 Jan 1905 is his 14th birthday (1/10/05)

MORLEY, Mary - see Mary (Morley) FLANAGAN

MORRIS, A.J. - and Claud Dillon own the Cottage Laundry (5/30/01)

MORRIS, Abbie - dt Mrs. Maria Morris; att Friends Training Sch, Cleveland, OH 1905-06 (11/17/05)

MORRIS, Aaron - stockholder/Pres., Fmt. Banking Co. (11/18/02)

MORRIS, Andy - of Summitville; ca Dec 1880, rents old M.E. Ch. bldg. on corner of Main & 2nd St. as a pool hall (12/15/05)

MORRIS, Benjamin F. - b Dublin, Wayne Co. 11 Jun 1834; s William and Elizabeth Morris; Marion, IN m 1st Nov 1851 Ruth Thomas (dec 1867); m 2nd Sep 1879 Lydia McPherson of New Lexington, OH; recorded Friends Minister 1864; Upland Friends Pastor 1898-1900; serv as pastor for Oak Ridge Friends, Bethel Friends, and Back Creek Friends 1900-1902; d 8 Oct 1902 (10/10/02; 10/14/02)

MORRIS, Della - mbr Back Creek [Friends] WCTU (5/16/02); - see William KIRKPATRICK

MORRIS, Earl - sch tchr near Muncie (10/27/05)

MORRIS, Exum - recently d in North Branch, KS (7/29/01)

MORRIS, John T. - age 82; walked from Fmt. to Franklin Coll in 1845 with John Ratliff, Nelson Turner and Joseph Jay; all att Franklin Coll 1845-46 (2/12/04); b 22 Nov 1821 (8/12/04); 19 Oct 1904 m Mrs. __ Hill of Spiceland; will live in Spiceland (10/21/04)

MORRIS, Luther - a Director, Fmt. Fair Assoc. (1/12/04); s John T. Morris (10/21/04)

MORRIS, R.A. - stockholder and Cashier, Fmt. Banking Co. (11/18/02); Fmt. YMCA Board mbr (8/28/03)

MORRIS, W.F. - of Pendleton; stockholder, Fmt. Banking Co. (11/18/02)

MORRISH, Henry - mbr, Fmt. Twp. Advisory Bd. (3/25/04)

MORRISH, John E. - 1901 Fmt. Twp. Dist. # 4 Sch grad (5/30/01); s Henry Morrish of E of Fmt.; 14 Sep 1905 m Vida, dt M/M Lewis Mittank (9/19/05)

MORRISON, Moses - grad Fmt. HS 1900 (12/19/05)

MOTT, Albert P. - dec; serv Corp., Co. H, 12th Ind. Inf. during CW (5/26/05)

MULL, J.H. - Dec 1886, is prop., New Central Hotel (12/15/05)

MULLEN, Jean - 18 Sep 1903 is his 36th birthday (9/22/03)

MUSICK CEMETERY - infant of James Lynch is bur (10/24/05)

MYERS, Alex - Pres., Fmt. Mining Co. (1/16/02)

NATIONAL DRAIN TILE CO. - of Terre Haute; S.C. Cowgill, Pres.; J.M. Powell, Vice Pres.; James Luther, Sect.; L.R. Whitney, Treas. (9/16/02); Fred Oakley is an employee (11/6/03)

NAVE, __ - b 10 Nov 1903; dt M/M Frank Nave (11/13/03)

NEAL, Elam H. - is re-appointed Jonesboro postmaster (2/10/02)

NEAL, Hershel - grad Pike Sch 1905 (5/12/05); 25 Aug 1905 is given party for his 16th birthday (8/29/05)

NEAL, Maria - mbr, Back Creek W.M. Ch. (11/4/02)

NEAL, William - layed out first plat of Fmt. (6/27/05)

NEAL, Winslow - and wife are only living witnesses of 13 Dec 1854 wedding of M/M Lindsey Wilson (12/16/04)

NEBRASKA, gone to - see Wilson WINSLOW

NEELY, Ira L. - is building an automobile (8/5/01); completed his auto with help of Will Gossett; a public demonstration of auto was successful (9/12/01); has purchased a new auto (4/18/02); will drive in auto race at State Fair grounds in class of less than 1,000 lb. autos (5/30/02); purchased a new Oldsmobile (7/25/02); and wife are hosting Rev. W.A. Sunday, in Fmt. for a 28 Jul 1902 lecture (which was rained out); owns the first motor bicycle ever to be in Fmt. (7/29/02); Director, Roaring Gimlet Gold Mining Syndicate (9/26/02); owned 1st auto in Fmt. (1/20/05); now lives in Muncie (9/8/05)

NELSON, Chester - att Purdue Univ 1902-03 (9/12/02)

NELSON, Elizabeth Jane (George) - b Randolph Co., NC 19 Mar 1823; m 8 Dec 1844 John M. Nelson (dec 10 Jul 1881); mbr Fmt.

Congregational Ch.; d 1 Aug 1901, bur Anderson cem (8/1/01; 8/5/01)

NELSON, Erasmus - 1881, Principal, Fmt. Schs (4/4/05)

NELSON, Merimon H. - s John M. and Elizabeth J. (George) Nelson (8/5/01)

NELSON, Sarah F. - see Sarah F. (Nelson) INK

NEVADA, gone to - see Thomas J. NIXON

NEW YORK, came from - see Emeline (Hammond) LECKENBY

NEWBY, Aaron - Supt., Citizens Telephone Co. (1/3/05)

NEWBY, Harmon T. - b Fmt. Twp.; grandson of Thomas W. Newby; employee of Fmt. Glass Works (11/7/05)

NEWBY, Mrs. Nancy - of Whittier, CA; sister of Mrs. Louisa Rush; d recently (12/29/03)

NEWBY, Mrs. Sally - age 80 (8/15/05)

NEWBY, Thomas - d 7 Dec 1903, bur Back Creek Friends Cem (12/11/03)

NEWBY, William - dec; serv Pvt., Co. C, 89th Ind. Inf. during CW (5/26/05)

NICHOLSON, Daniel - serv Pvt., Co. G, 69th Ind. Inf. during CW (5/27/04; 5/26/05)

NICHOLSON, Josiah 'Cy' - was initiated into IOOF Lodge 11 Sep 1901 (9/12/01); 8 Oct 1905 is his 57th birthday (10/10/05)

NICHOLSON, Pearl - see Eli A. WILSON

NICKLE, Alta Loretta - see Verling W. DAVIS

NICKLES, Rev. J.M. - pastor, Fmt. A.M.E. Ch. (8/14/03; 1/24/05)

NIXON, Mrs. Alice - see Samuel C. COWGILL

NIXON, Inez - att Earlham Coll 1901-02 (8/26/01); dt M/M Thomas J. Nixon; is studying music in Chicago (6/7/04)

NIXON, Mollie - see Roger PIERCE

NIXON, Thomas J. - 1881, has a Fmt. warehouse (1/13/1881 as reprinted 3/29/04); 26 Dec 1893 disappeared; his wife, thinking him dead, has remarried; he now writes from a small Nevada town (6/7/04); his mother d ca 1899 (7/8/04); Apr 1887, investor in Fmt. Mining Co. (1/17/05); 15 Feb 1879, sold his interest in the flax mill to J.P. Winslow (12/15/05)

NOLAN, Clarence - age 16; is accidentally shot/wounded (8/12/02)

NOLDER, __ - baby of M/M Layton Nolder d 8 Sep 1902 (9/9/02)

NOLDER, __ - b 12 Nov 1902; dt M/M L.E. Nolder (11/14/02)

NOLDER, Dea - dt Mrs. Rachel A. Nolder (1/21/01); 1904-05 Fmt. Sch tchr (9/2/04)

NOLDER, Layton E. - s Mrs. Rachel A. Nolder (1/21/01)

NOLDER, Rachel A. (Ellis) - grew up 2 mi. W of Jonesboro; dt M/M James Ellis; d 19 Jan 1901, bur Park Cem (1/21/01); dec mbr, Shakespeare Club (3/7/05)

NOLDER, Dr. S.M. - lives in Paragould, Ark. (2/13/02)

NORRIS, Mattie - see John LANGSDON

NORTH CAROLINA, came from - see Daniel BALDWIN; Mrs. Elizabeth BRILES; Jacob BRILES; Mary (Little) BULLER; Elizabeth (Wilson) COX; William COX; Cuthbert HIATT; Mariah Jane (Ward) LIVELY; Ivy LUTHER; Susan RUSH; Mrs. Jane STALKER; Henry WINSLOW; Jane (Henley) WINSLOW

NORTON, A.F. - serv Pvt., Co. C, 118th Ind. Inf. and Pvt., Co. D, 33rd Ind. Inf. during CW (5/27/04; 5/26/05)

NORTON, Mrs. Ania - mbr Fmt. Congregational Ch. (9/5/01)

NORTON, Arthur - of Marion; aged; d 8 Aug 1901 (8/12/01)

NORTON, Fred - f of Fmt.; d Anderson 15 Apr 1904, bur Gas City cem (4/19/04)

NORTON, George - dec; serv Pvt., Co. H, 8th Ind. Inf. during CW (5/27/04; 5/26/05)

NORTON, Harry - dec; serv Pvt., Co. H, 8th Ind. Inf. during CW (5/27/04; 5/26/05)

NORTON, James - dec; serv Pvt., Co. D, 33rd Ind. Inf. during CW (5/27/04; 5/26/05)

NOSE, Emma (Douglass) - sister of John Douglass (9/15/05)

NOTTINGHAM, George - s Mary Nottingham; recently dec (4/12/04)

NOTTINGHAM, R.C. - President, Farmer's Telephone Line of Matthews (3/14/01)

OAK RIDGE FRIENDS CEMETERY - Miss Lizzie Long bur (12/9/04)

OAKLEY, Miss Bernice - cashier, Norton Grocery (2/3/02)

OAKLEY, Charles - employee, Bell Window Glass factory; s Mrs. Sallie Oakley (7/26/04)

OAKLEY, Fred D. - employed in office of American Window Glass Co. (8/29/01); Secretary, Fmt. YMCA Board of Directors (6/3/02; 6/6/02); moves family to Terre Haute where he is employed by National Drain & Tile Co. (11/6/03)

OAKLEY, John - s Sarah J. Oakley (11/24/05)

O'BRIEN, Pat T. - contractor of Elwood; will brick portions of Main St. and Henley Ave. (2/11/01)

O'BRIEN, Thomas - d recently (10/31/01)

ODELL, Henry - serv Pvt., Co. K, 35th Ohio Inf. during CW (5/27/04; 5/26/05)

OHIO, came from - see Elizabeth (COLEMAN) BALDWIN; Charles Arthur BEWLEY; Phebe A. (Pence)DOWNS; Edmund DULING; L.L. FANKBONER; Mathias S. FRIEND; Amy (Wright) HARVEY; Mahlon HARVEY; Joseph HOCKETT; John Burgess HOLLINGSWORTH; Rev. John HUBERT; May JAY; Henry D. KEPLER; Rachel (Pearson) PIERCE; Susan (Jay) RATLIFF; William H.H. TRASTERS

OHIO, gone to - see David A. BALDWIN; H.I. WHEELER

OIL & GAS WELLS - a well producing 100 barrels of oil per day is on the Charles Leach farm SE of Fmt. (7/4/02); 75 barrel per day well was brought in 23 Aug 1902 on farm of S.B. Leach near Fowlerton (8/26/02); a new well producing gas and oil is on the Marcus Gaddis farm W of Fmt., Lafayette Gas Co. drilled and shot it (10/21/02); well on William Bell farm 1 mi. W of Fmt. is producing 75 barrels of oil per day (11/11/02); oil well was brought in on Alvin Scott farm SE of Fmt. (12/2/02)

OKLAHOMA, gone to - see W.S. COYLE; Charles PAYNE

O'NEAL, Mrs. James - of Findley, OH; dt William Coyle (dec) (4/19/04)

OREGON, came from - see Rachel (Elliott) FOWLER

OREGON, gone to - see Mrs. Charles CUNNINGHAM; Nathan D. ELLIOTT; William SMALL

OSBORN, __ - baby of M/M John Osborn; d 23 Aug 1901 (8/26/01)

OSBORN, __ - young dt of M/M Alfred Osborn; recently dec (8/1/02)

OSBORN, __ - b 27 Jul 1904; s M/M Will Osborn of E of Fmt. (7/26/04)

OSBORN, Jesse L. - b near Fmt. 30 Jan 1864; s Samuel (dec) and Mary (now Mary Rich) Osborn; Jan 1896 m Ora D. Luse, dt Walter

S. and Elmina Luse of Fmt.; farmed NW of Fmt. until health failed; d 11 Feb 1902 (2/13/02; 2/20/02)

OSBORN, Lawrence - of Fmt.; mbr Fmt. IOOF Lodge; d 19 Jun 1901, bur Park Cem (6/20/01; 6/24/01; 7/8/01)

OSBORN, Mrs. Mary - see Mary RICH

OSBORN, Nancy J. (Ice) - is being sued by Eva Hasty for tearing down a house in Fmt. that Osborn bought at a tax sale (9/23/01); case dismissed (10/17/01); dt Ransom and Sarah Ice (10/24/05)

OSBORN, Ora. D. (Luse) - dt Walter S. and Elmina Luse; Jan 1896 m Jesse L. Osborn (dec); mbr Fmt. WCTU (2/20/02; 2/25/02); sister of A.W. Luse of Westland (4/12/04); see E.J. COX

OVERMAN, __ - see Mrs. Fred DAVIS; see Mrs. S.E. HAISLEY

OVERMAN, C.D. - is re-appointed Fmt. postmaster (2/10/02); investor, Roaring Gimlet Gold Mining Syndicate (9/26/02)

OVERMAN, Edna - voted prettiest girl present at the FFA Athletic Association basket supper held in Back Creek Sch (2/17/02)

OVERMAN, J.C. - plant Supt., Fmt. Mining Co. (8/26/01; 1/16/02); resigns as Supt., has a fruit farm near Knightstown (9/19/02)

OVERMAN, Joel - of Marion; age ca 80; d 19 Oct 1901 (10/21/01)

OVERMAN, Louise - 4 Jun 1902 was her 10th birthday (6/6/02)

OVERMAN, R.E. - had a music store in Fmt. for several yrs.; 25 Jul 1905 d in Anderson (7/28/05)

OXLEY, Rev. __ - pastor of Fmt. U.B. Ch. (1/28/01)

PARK CEMETERY - Lot Owner's Assn. Pres. is Denny Winslow (6/10/02)

PARKER, Allen - is promoted to 1st Lieut., 25th Inf. in Philippines (6/6/01); assigned to 26th Inf. (6/13/01); stationed Ft. Leavenworth, KS as student in military sch (9/1/03); 1st Lieut., 26th Inf., Ft. Brown, TX (9/9/04); last summer, m Pearl Siddons (2/10/05)

PARKER, Charles T. - his law office is in Borrey Blk. (2/11/01); a winner in recent Fmt. Gun Club Shoot (4/1/01); m; is Fmt. Town Attorney (6/24/02)

PARKER, Chauncey - s M/M Charles Parker (8/26/04)

PARKER, Creola - infant of M/M Everett Parker; d 14 Jan 1904, bur Park Cem (1/19/04)

PARKER, Chester - s M/M Charles T. Parker; d this wk. (5/2/02)

PARKER, Everett - m; s Mrs. Frank Parker of Middlebury (1/19/04)

PARKER, Harry Noel - b Fmt. 28 Oct 1898; s Mark and Lizzie Parker; d 14 Feb 1902 (2/13/02; 2/17/02)

PARKER, J.H. - is Fmt. hardware dealer (10/21/01); during CW serv Pvt., Co. G, 153rd Ind. Inf. (8/7/03), and Pvt., Co. K, 16th US Inf. (5/27/04; 5/26/05); 1881, dealer in hardware & groceries (1/13/1881 as reprinted 3/29/04); 1 Jan 1887, Vice Pres., Fmt. Fair Assn. stockholder; Dec 1892, his Parker Opera House Blk. is being built (12/15/05)

PARKER, Mark - Fmt. Gun Club Shoot winner (4/1/01); and wife given dinner 30 Apr 1905 for their 10th wedding anniv (5/2/05)

PARKS, Hazel - [and brother] Pearly 17 Mar 1904 att wedding anniv. dinner for M/M James Kirkpatrick (3/22/04)

PARRILL, __ - infant of M/M Will Parrill; d recently (11/4/04)

PARRILL, Emma - dt J.W. Parrill (5/27/01); grad Fmt. HS 1900 (12/19/05); - see Clyde LEWIS

PARRILL, Lucia - 1904-05 Fmt. Sch tchr (9/2/04)

PARRILL, William - s J.W. Parrill (10/23/03)

PARRILL, Mrs. William - 12 Nov 1903 is given party for her 20th birthday (11/17/03)

PARSONS, Grace - dt James L. Parsons (9/23/01)

PARSONS, Harper - serv Pvt., Co. I, 147th Ind. Inf. during CW (5/27/04; 5/26/05)

PARSONS, James L. - b Rigdon 31 Jan 1862; m; d 15 Sep 1901 (9/16/01; 9/23/01)

PARSONS, Nellie - dt James L. Parsons (9/23/01)

PARTRIDGE, Mrs. M.F. - of Fowlerton; d 29 Dec 1903 (1/1/04)

PASCHAL, [Allie] (Messler) - b 17 Apr 1861; m Jesse L. Paschal 24 May 1885; mbr M.E. Ch.; d 4 Nov 1901 (11/11/01)

PATTERSON, Mrs. D.P. - is mbr Fmt. Congregational Ch. (1/1/02)

PATTERSON, Hannah Adeline - see Hannah Adeline Winslow

PATTERSON, Dr. J.W. - s Dr. Philip and Mary Patterson (3/18/04); a Trustee, Fmt. Schs (6/10/04)

PATTERSON, Joe - injured while at work for Crystal Ice Co. (8/26/01)

PATTERSON, Kitty - dt Dr./M J.W. Patterson (9/29/03)

PAYNE, __ - b 13 Jun 1902; dt M/M Dick Payne (6/13/02)

PAYNE, __ - b recently; s M/M Mack Payne (11/21/02)

PAYNE, __ - b 5 Mar 1905; dt M/M George Payne of S of Fmt. (3/7/05)

PAYNE, Mrs. Ann - widow of Ephraim L. Payne (serv CW); is granted pension of $8 per month (10/4/04)

PAYNE, B.S. - serv Pvt., Co. K, 130th Ind. Inf. during CW (5/27/04; 5/26/05)

PAYNE, Blanch - and Dick are sons of James Payne (dec) (12/1/03)

PAYNE, Charles - returned from army serv in Philippines; now has a beard (3/21/01); is on way from Oklahoma City, OK to the Wichita Mts., OK walking 150 mi. with a wheel barrow of gold hunter equipment (8/26/01)

PAYNE, Capt. David L. - 28 Nov 1884 d Wellington, KS (12/2/04); CW vet (6/6/05)

PAYNE, Ephraim L. - CW vet; d 4 Oct 1902, bur Fankboner Cem (10/7/02; 10/10/02); serv Pvt., Co. H, 12th Ind. Inf. and 1st Serg., Co. K, 130th Ind. Inf. during CW (5/27/04; 5/26/05)

PAYNE, Fern - dt M/M Zim Payne; 8th grader, Fmt. Sch (6/13/05)

PAYNE, June - dt Dick Payne (12/8/03)

PAYNE, James - is a squirrel hunter (6/24/02); age 56; m; Fmt. Marshal; murdered 26 Nov 1903 by Harry Hooper; bur Park Cem (11/27/03; 12/1/03); serv Pvt., Co. C, 140th Ind. Inf. during CW (5/27/04; 5/26/05)

PAYNE, John M. - dec; serv Co. C, 89th Ind. Inf. during CW (5/27/04; 5/26/05)

PAYNE, Lewis - dec; serv Co. C, 89th Ind. Inf. during CW (5/27/04; 5/26/05)

PAYNE, Mrs. Lida/Lide - mbr Pike United Brethren Ch. (11/4/02); is living in State Soldier's Home, Lafayette (12/15/05)

PAYNE, Mack - is a gas well shooter, uses nitro-glycerine to start flow in gas wells (5/16/01)

PAYNE, Thomas - dec; serv Pvt., Co. G, 140th Ind. Inf. during CW (5/27/04; 5/26/05)

PAYNE, Tony - 1904 Fmt. HS grad (4/19/04)

PAYNE, W.R. - of Fmt.; serv as Corp., US Army in P.I. (7/8/01)

PAYNE, Wesley - dec; serv Pvt., Co. H, 12th Ind. Inf. during CW (5/26/05)

PEACOCK, ___ - b 26 Jun 1904; dt M/M Carlton Peacock (6/28/04)

PEACOCK, Edward - s Mrs. Ruth Peacock (12/30/01); age 7; s M/M John Peacock of 1 mi. E of Fmt.; d 6 Mar 1904, bur Park Cem (3/8/04)

PEACOCK, Joseph - now of Kokomo; 1849, built 1st house in Fmt. for Joseph Baldwin at site of present Borrey Blk. (6/20/05)

PEACOCK, Mary P. - see Mary P. (Peacock) FARLOW

PEACOCK, Myron - s M/M John Peacock (12/30/01; 12/11/03)

PEARCE [PIERCE], Samuel H. - of near Back Creek Sch N of Fmt.; d 30 Mar 1902, bur Back Creek Friends Cem (4/1/02)

PEARSON, ___ - b 20 Jan 1905; s M/M Ernest Pearson (1/24/05)

PEARSON, Mrs. Charles - age 48; m; came to Fmt. ca 1900; d 4 May 1904, bur Park Cem (5/6/04)

PEARSON, Ernest - 1903 FFA grad; 18 May 1904 m Muriel Cox (5/20/04)

PEARSON, Miss Ethel - is in nurse's training in Richmond (1/31/01); mbr, Fmt. WCTU (6/3/02)

PEARSON, Fred - s Christopher Pearson; works in Ulrey Mill; 19 Dec 1903 m Ella Harvey, dt Jonathan Harvey; will live in Fmt. (12/22/03)

PEARSON, Glenn - 1904 Fmt. HS grad (4/19/04)

PEARSON, Lemuel - President, Bates Oil Co. Board of Directors (7/11/01); serv Pvt., Co. K, 118th Ind. Inf. during CW (5/27/04; 5/26/05); 1881, Trustee of Fmt. Twp. (7/4/05)

PEARSON, Miss Mary E. - 1903-06 tchr, Fowlerton Sch (8/28/03; 8/30/04; 8/15/05)

PEARSON, Pearle - 1904 Liberty Twp. Sch grad (4/19/04)

PEARSON, Rachel - see Rachel (Pearson) PIERCE

PEARSON, S.Y. - photographer in Cottage Photography Gallery (10/21/01)

PEARSON, Sim - Bell Window Glass factory employee (3/29/04)

PELL, Rev. Millard - Fmt. M.E. Ch. pastor (1/17/01); leaves Fmt. to be Lapel M.E. Ch. pastor (4/18/01)

PEMBERTON, Cyrus - is on way home from Philippines where he serv in US Army (4/29/01); is home; out of the Army (5/20/01)

PEMBERTON, Elihu - of Mill Twp. is Co. Commissioner (4/11/02)

PEMBERTON, Lemuel - of near Roseburg is brother of Cyrus (2/20/02)

PENNINGTON, Benjamin - is a patient in the Richmond Hospital for the Insane (2/11/01)

PENNINGTON, Mary - see Mary (Pennington) DICKS

PENNSYLVANIA, came from - see Malinda KIRK; Armada J. (Howe) REED

PENNSYLVANIA, gone to - see Will DeSHON

PERMAR, Mrs. Winnie - age 31; mbr RC Ch.; d 28 Jan 1901 (1/31/01)

PERRY, H.L. - buys blacksmith shop from Will Gossett (7/29/04)

PETTIFORD, __ - infant of Grace Pettiford; d 5 Jan 1902 (1/6/02)

PHILLIPS, Emma - a Friends missionary in Cuba (2/7/01); Oct 1903 m Juan F. Martinez (10/23/03)

PHILLIPS, James - serv Pvt., Co. A, 120th Ind. Inf. during CW (5/26/05)

PHILLIPS, Mrs. James - d 31 Jan 1902 (2/3/02)

PHILLIPS, S.M. - tchr, Liberty Twp. Sch 1904-06 (12/27/04; 7/28/05)

PICKARD, Alex - dec; serv Pvt., Co. K, 16th Ind. Inf. during CW (5/27/04; 5/26/05)

PICKARD, Bowman - Director, Bates Oil Co. (7/11/01)

PICKARD, Mrs. Bowman - dt William Hasting (dec) (2/7/05)

PICKARD, John - age 5; s Otto Pickard; d 24 Sep 1903 (9/25/03)

PICKARD, John - mail carrier, Marion; 12 Sep 1904 m Caroline Hoyt (9/16/04); b and grew up in Fmt.; is arrested for stealing mail (12/8/05)

PICKARD, Mrs. John - b Fmt.; dt Zimri and Martha Richardson; d 11 Nov 1903 in Marion (11/13/03)

PICKARD, Lucy - see John H. ENGLISH

PICKARD, Otto - hangs wallpaper; has wallpaper store on N. Main St. (3/29/04)

PIERCE, Eliza [(Carey)] - m Thomas J. Pierce; d ca 1883 (1/6/02)

PIERCE, Elvira - mbr Back Creek [Friends] WCTU (5/16/02)

PIERCE, Fred - age 8; s M/M Will Pierce; d recently, funeral in Back Creek Friends MH (4/7/05)

PIERCE, Grace - see Grace Pierce CRILLEY

PIERCE, Rachel (Pearson) - b Miami Co., OH 31 Mar 1830; dt Benjamin and Dorcas Pearson; m 1st OH 24 Mar 1853 Isaiah Pemberton (d 2 Mar 1874); m 2nd OH 10 Apr 1878 William Pierce (d 17 Oct 1895); came to Grant Co. ca 1879; mbr Friends; mbr WCTU; killed by train at Wilson crossing 2 mi. N of Fmt. 12 Apr 1901 (4/15/01; 5/2/01)

PIERCE, Roger - 16 Jul 1904 m Mollie, dt M/M Mordica Nixon (7/19/04)

PIERCE, Samuel - step-son of Rachel Pierce (4/15/01)

PIERCE, T.J. - is laying bricks for new Back Creek W.M. Ch. (10/25/04)

PINKERMAN, B. - 1905-06 Liberty Twp. Sch tchr (7/28/05)

PLASTER, Rebecca - age 74; mother-in-law of John Underwood (11/17/05)

PLASTERER, Mrs. Ralph - of Marion; f of Fmt.; 23 May 1905 d, bur Mt. Etna Cem (5/26/05)

PLASTERS, John - dec; serv Pvt., Co. I, 1st Ind. Inf. during Mexican War (5/27/04; 5/26/05)

PLASTERS, Mrs. William - dt M/M Elias Vancannon (10/28/04)

POGUE, Lee - electrician working in Indianapolis; s M/M Robert T. Pogue of Fmt. (5/13/02)

POGUE, Mrs. Robert T. - sister of Thomas Powell of Wells Co. (1/26/04)

POOLE, Florence - see Charles HOSKINS

POOLE, Minnie - dt Felix Pool (8/12/01)

POWELL, __ - see Mrs. Robert T. POGUE

POWELL, Burr F. - 6 Jul 1902 m Cora E. Smith (7/8/02)

POWELL, J.M. - Vice Pres., National Drain Tile Co. (9/16/02)

POWELL, Sallie (Cox) - sister of Nathan, John W. and Tilman Cox (9/26/05)

POWELL, Thomas - an early Fmt. area settler (1/13/05)

PRATT, Minnie - files for divorce from Ora E. Pratt of Matthews (12/26/05)

PRESNALL, Alfred M. - b Henry Co. 8 Oct 1847; s James and Anna; 27 Jan 1870 m Phebe J. Brandon of Windfall; f mbr Friends; mbr Fmt. M.E. Ch.; d 30 Dec 1900 (1/3/01)

PRESNALL, Dempsey W. - of IA; serv CW in 36th Ind. Inf.; f mbr Fmt. Friends Ch.; lived in Henry and Grant Co.'s until going to IA ca 1882; d recently (4/5/04); widow is Eliza (11/21/05)

PRESNALL, Frank - 1881, Fmt. Twp. Sch grad (7/4/05)

PRESNALL, Harvey F. - of Fmt.; s James and Anna (1/3/01); 2 Apr 1901 m Lydia Edwards of Middletown; will live in Fmt. (4/4/01); retires from firm of Hill & Co. (12/16/04)

PRESNALL, Lutie - Fmt. HS Freshman; given party for her 16th birthday last wk. (3/18/01); 1904 Fmt. HS grad (4/19/04); dt M/M Harvey Presnall (6/10/04); see Frank STEWART

PRESNALL, Lydia (Edwards) - wife of Harvey F. Presnall; dt Mrs. Susan Edwards of Waynesville, OH (8/22/05)

PRESNALL, Mrs. Phoebe - see Joseph A. SHAWHAN

PRETLOW, Dr. Clotilde L. - and Elizabeth Pretlow are children of Robert S. and Isabella H. (Cook) Pretlow (9/26/02)

PRETLOW, Elizabeth - dt Dr. Clotilde Pretlow; f employee, Citizens Telephone Exchange (11/4/04); - see Cyrus BALDWIN

PRETLOW, Isabella H. (Cook) - b VA 8 Dec 1824; dt Joel and Deborah H. Cook; 6 Aug 1845 m Robert S. Pretlow (dec 21 Feb 1885); mbr Friends; d 23 Sep 1902 (9/26/02; 10/3/02)

PRICE, Earl - of East Branch; 20 Feb 1905 m Minnie Little of near Gas City (2/24/05)

PRICKETT, Laura - see Laura (Prickett) WINSLOW

PROHIBITION ALLIANCE - to meet in Parker's Hall (2/28/02)

PUGH, Dr. __ - of Upland; d recently (1/3/01)

QUINET, Leon - of Matthews; is a Director, Industrial Window Glass Co. of Fowlerton (10/14/01)

RADER, Simeon - of Fmt.; m; serv Pvt., Co. B, 84th Ind. Regmt. during CW (11/28/01; 5/27/04; 5/26/05)

RAILROADS & INTERURBANS -
BIG FOUR - passenger train wrecked at Alexandria in Jan 1901 with John Bates of Fmt. as fireman; Bates was permanently injured (10/14/01); depot clerk is Clarence Kimes (6/13/02); Frank Buck is flagman at Washington St. RR crossing (4/29/04); Fred Kimes is a brakeman (10/10/05)
C.C.&L. - is the former C.R.&M. (8/7/03)
CHICAGO, INDIANA & EASTERN (C.I.&E.) - to construct large, new depot at Fowlerton (11/11/01); John S. Baker, Construction Supt., completes the Fowlerton depot (1/30/02); old Fowlerton passenger depot hauled recently to Fmt. on a flat car, to be a freight house (8/19/02); Adams Express Co. has office in station (1/20/05)
CINCINNATI, RICHMOND & MUNCIE (C.R. & M.) - is grading line from Jonesboro to Muncie (5/9/01); is building overpass over 10th St., Jonesboro (7/18/01); has franchise to pass through Marion (7/25/01); is constructed as far N as Gaston (7/29/01); 30 Jul 1901 is completed to Leach where it crossed the C.I.&E. today (8/1/01); about 200 feet of a swamp E of Fmt. is too soft to build track over, will try to fill swamp (8/5/01); a length of 300 feet over swamp continues to sink even though much dirt has been dumped in it; a nearby tract of timber was purchased and trees will be placed in the hole (8/22/01); overpass completed over 10th St., Jonesboro (8/22/01); grading crew is at 38th St., Marion; tracks are laid to 1 mi. NW of Fowlerton (8/29/01); track is now laid to Jonesboro (9/23/01); Jonesboro passenger depot almost completed and is in use, T.H. Sewall, agent (10/21/01); crossing of Union Traction Line in Jonesboro complete (10/28/01); laying track between Jonesboro and Marion this wk. (10/31/01); construction train was wrecked 2 mi. E of Peru with 2 deaths and many injuries (12/12/01); track is now completed to Peru (12/30/01); - see C.C.&L.
CINCINNATI, WABASH & MICHIGAN (C.W.&M.) - fall 1875 is constructed through Fmt.; 1888, American Express Co. had office in depot; later purchased by Big Four RR (1/20/05)

EASTERN INDIANA TRACTION CO. - line from Upland to Marion will be in operation by 1 Jun 1902 (4/8/02)
OIL BELT TRACTION LINE - to be electric interurban from Hartford City-New Cumberland-Matthews-Fowlerton-Fmt. (11/7/02)
UNION TRACTION CO. - ties for use on S. Main St., Fmt. are now here (9/19/01); steel track for S. Main St. is here (9/30/01); sued for $10,000 by Alex Lindsey for injuries while working for them in Fmt. (11/4/01); its tracks in Jonesboro are now crossed by the C.R.&M. tracks (10/28/01); to build its Jonesboro bridge over the Mississinewa River using the abutments and piers of wooden bridge that recently burned; to pay Grant County $100 per yr. for bridge site (1/1/02); new bridge is completed between Jonesboro and Gas City (2/3/02); has 50-yr. lease on Indianapolis Northern Traction Co. (7/22/02); 1899, constructed through Fmt. (1/24/05)

RATLIFF, __ - b recently; s M/M Charles M. Ratliff (11/4/01)

RATLIFF, __ - b 19 Nov 1901; dt Dr/M W.N. Ratliff (11/21/01)

RATLIFF, Mrs. Ancil - of near Little Ridge is dt Mahlon Harvey (7/1/04; 8/22/05)

RATLIFF, Charles M. - an attorney living 2.5 mi. SW of Fmt.; his buggy and harness were vandalized during night of 15 Jun 1901; John Buller is arrested and charged with the crime (6/17/01); he represented Buller's wife in her successful suit for divorce from John in March 1901; John is found guilty of malicious trespass (10/10/01); is farming after nearly abandoning the practice of law (6/7/04)

RATLIFF, Hix -s Levi and Belle Ratliff (7/8/04)

RATLIFF, Miss Ina - FFA grad; is substitute tchr, Leach Sch (1/17/05); att Earlham Coll 1905-06 (12/5/05)

RATLIFF, John - walked from Fmt. to Franklin Coll in 1845 with John Morris, Nelson Turner and Joseph Jay; all att Franklin Coll 1845-46 (2/12/04)

RATLIFF, John - s Levi and Belle Ratliff; d 4 Jul 1904 (7/8/04)

RATLIFF, Levi - recently divorced from his wife, Belle (7/8/04)

RATLIFF, Dr. M.E. - Fmt. dentist with office over Citizens Exchange Bank; has 7 yrs. dental experience (8/25/03); sells dental office to Dr. Will N. Ratliff; is now Supt., Fmt. Tile Co. (9/23/04)

RATLIFF, Martha - 11 May 1905 is her 5th birthday (5/12/05)

RATLIFF, Prof. Russell - tchr, Ft. Peck Indian Reservation Sch, Poplar, Montana; s George and Susan (Jay) Ratliff (3/25/04; 3/29/04; 4/12/04)

RATLIFF, Ruth (Harvey) - mbr, Hadley WCTU (10/24/02); dt Mahlon and Zilpha (Hadley) Harvey (8/25/05)

RATLIFF, Prof. Ryland - of Danville Normal Coll; s George and Susan (Jay) Ratliff (3/25/04)

RATLIFF, Susan (Jay) - 1830 b Miami Co., OH; dt Denny and Mary Jay; 1855 m George Ratliff (dec); she was a Friends Minister; d 22 Mar 1904, bur beside her husband in Marion IOOF Cem (3/25/04)

RATLIFF, Dr. Will N. - and family move to CA (10/20/03); has dental practice in Whittier, CA (12/11/03); sets up his dental practice in Fmt. (9/23/04)

RAU, Carl P. - mbr, Finance & Bldg. Committee raising money to build tabernacle for Billy Sunday revival (1/30/02); Director, Fmt. WCTU (6/6/02); a Director, Fmt. Fair Assoc. (1/12/04)

RAU, Charles - resigns as Supt., Fmt. Glass Works (6/21/04); and his brother, Daniel Rau, is building glass factory in New Albany (10/7/04)

RAU, Emma - see Clayton JOHNSON

RAU, Ida - dt M/M Dan Rau; engaged to Dr. M.J. Lewis of Marion (8/28/03); m Dr. Lewis 21 Oct 1903 (10/27/03)

RAU, John, Jr. - 1904 Fmt. HS grad (4/19/04); att Ind. Univ 1904-05 (11/18/04)

RAU, John - came to Fmt. ca 1890, worked in Winslow Glass Factory, became a partner with W.C. Winslow, then bought the factory; he and his brothers Carl P., Fred, Charles, Daniel, now control 4 glass factories here (10/7/04)

RAU, Louise - dt M/M Carl P. Rau (7/11/02)

RAU, Lucille (James) - b Louisville, KY 24 Oct 1864; dt Robert and Margaret James; m Carl P. Rau ca 1892; mbr Fmt. M.E. Ch.; d Winona Lake 21 Aug 1902, bur Cave Hill Cem, Louisville, KY (8/22/02; 8/26/02); was mbr Fmt. Ladies Shakespeare Club (9/12/02)

RAY, Asbury W. - dec; serv Pvt., Co. D, 79th Ind. Inf. during CW (5/27/04; 5/26/05)

RAY, Charles W. - b Fmt. 21 May 1881; s Asbury W. (dec 22 May 1896) and Jane Ray; d 19 May 1901 (5/20/01; 5/23/01)

RAY, Will A. - s Mrs. A.J. Ray of Fmt.; Summitville Marshal; 16 May 1902 accidentally shot/wounded himself in Fmt. with his own revolver (5/20/02)

REASONER, Clem - s Richard Reasoner of Upland; age 45; widower; killed 29 Nov 1901 in gas well accident 0.75 mi. SW of Upland (12/2/01)

REBEKAH LODGE - 21 Jun 1901 in Parker's Opera House will give "Society Ministrels in Black Faces called the Honolulu Belles" (6/13/01)

REECE, Joel - 1877, established 1st newspaper here, <u>Fairmount News</u> (1/24/05), 1st issue was 22 Dec 1877 (12/19/05)

REED, A.L. - s Mrs. Mary Reed of McKeesport, PA; Mgr., American Window Glass Factory # 27 (7/25/01); Supt., Big Four Window Glass Factory (7/18/02); Director, Roaring Gimlet Gold Mining Syndicate (9/26/02); moves to Anderson (11/14/02); partner of 1st owners of Big Four Window Glass Factory (4/18/05)

REED, Armada J. (Howe) - b Butler Co., PA 26 Mar 1867; dt Mrs. J.B. White of New Castle, PA; grad New Castle, PA HS 1884; m A.L. Reed 12 May 1886; worked in office of American Window Glass Co.

Factory # 27 with her husband; d Fmt. 19 Jul 1901, bur Park Cem (7/22/01; 7/25/01); dec mbr, Shakespeare Club (3/7/05)

REEDER, Asenath - see Cuthbert HIATT

REESE, Joel - founded Fairmount News in 1877; recently d in the West (12/5/01); Editor, Fairmount News in 1878 (9/28/1878 as reprinted 2/26/04)

REEVE, Maude - 1905 Fowlerton Sch grad (5/12/05)

REEVE, Miss Myrtle - 1904-06 Fowlerton Sch tchr (8/30/04; 8/15/05)

REEVES, Joe - dec; Pvt., Co. C, 89th Ind. Inf. during CW (5/26/05)

RELFE, Mary Ruby - b 29 Mar 1900; dt Frank and Tressie Relfe; d 27 Feb 1902 (3/7/02)

RENBARGER, Alva - employee of Hoosier Mining Co. (3/7/02)

REYNOLDS, Louis - of Liberty Twp.; f tchr; CW vet; is Grant Co. Truant Officer (5/26/05)

RIBBLE, Charles - s William Ribble of Muncie (3/1/04)

RIBBLE, Hort - Dale Hardware employee (7/18/01); bookkeeper, Matthews Steel Plant (9/4/03); and brother Lafe are tailors in Masonic Temple, Fmt. (8/22/05)

RICE, Charlotte (Scott) - sister of Alvin Scott; m William Humphrey Rice; lives in Boston, MA (11/8/04)

RICH, __ - b 9 Feb 1904; s M/M Allie Rich (2/12/04)

RICH, Birchie M. - see Birchie M. (Rich) BULLER

RICH, Mary - m 1st Samuel Osborn (dec); m 2nd __ Rich (2/20/02)

RICH, Rosa - see Perry SEALE

RICHARDS, __ - b 16 Nov 1903; s Prof./M Lewis E. Richards (11/17/03)

RICHARDS, Daniel - serv 32nd Ind. Inf. during CW (5/26/05)

RICHARDS, J.W. - Treasurer, Farmer's Telephone Line of Matthews (3/14/01)

RICHARDS, Lewis E. - of near Matthews; grad DePauw Univ 1902 (6/10/02); 1902-03 will teach science at FFA (6/24/02)

RICHARDSON, __ - see Mrs. John PICKARD

RICHARDSON, Eva - see Clarence COX

RICHEY, Rev. J.W. - pastor, Pt. Isabel M.E. Ch. (9/25/03)

RICKS, Lewis - CW vet (6/6/05)

RIDDLE, Maggie - 24 Oct 1905 is granted divorce fron Joshua Riddle (10/27/05)

RIGDON, __ - of SW Grant Co.; widow of Dr. Price/Pierce Rigdon; d 25 Aug 1901 (8/29/01)

RIGDON, B.T. - 1881, is Fmt. grocer (1/13/1881 as reprinted 3/29/04)

RILEY, Rev. G.P. 'Father Riley' - 24 Jul 1901 brought 50 boys from his Marion 'Boys Brigade' to Fmt. Fair Grounds for a picnic (7/25/01); and a boy preacher will hold sevice at 3 PM next Sunday in the Bethel M.P. Ch. (6/27/02)

RITTENHOUSE, __ - see Mrs. Joe MILLIKAN

RITTENHOUSE, Bernard - s Henry Rittenhouse (5/2/05)

RITTENHOUSE, Henry - age 46; adopted son of Lewis and Susannah Hockett; m; d 30 Apr 1905, bur Park Cem (5/2/05)

RITTENHOUSE, Mrs. Henry - of Fmt. is sister of E.B. Scott of Sims (1/15/04)

RITTENHOUSE, Olive - dt Henry Rittenhouse; employee, Bee Hive Cash Store (4/11/05); - see Oz B. WILSON

ROADS - County Line Road is being graveled by 50 teams hauling gravel from Joseph Ware farm (9/12/02)

ROARING GIMLET GOLD MINING SYNDICATE - of Jackson Co., OR; Directors are: Isaac Smithson, Pres.; Alpheus Henley, Vice Pres.; William A. Beasley, Sect.-Treas.; Ira L. Neely, A.L. Reed, William T. Cammack, and J. Stivers; other investor/mbrs are A.W. Kelsay, Z.M. Gossett, C.D. Overman, Palmer Ice, and Zeb Rush (9/26/02); is now insolvent; owns and controls several mines (3/17/05)

ROBERTS, __ - b recently; s M/M Charles Roberts (7/29/02)

ROBERTS, Charles - of Fmt.; s John Roberts of New Castle (4/22/02)

ROBERTS, John - serv Pvt., Co. I, 117th Ind. Inf. during CW (5/27/04; 5/26/05)

ROBEY, L.C. - 1904-05 Fmt. HS tchr (9/2/04)

ROBINSON, M.D. - is a gas well shooter (i.e., explodes nitro-glycerine in well to start gas flow) (7/11/01)

ROMAIN, Eugene - a Director, Industrial Window Glass Co. of Fowlerton (10/14/01)

RONEY, __ - see Mrs. Eugene LaRUE

RONEY, Elias M. - b Fayette Co. 11 Jan 1821; s James and Phoebe; 18 Feb 1847 m Lucetta Harvey; serv Pvt., Co. A, 57th Ind. Regmt. 30 Oct 1861-18 Nov 1864; mbr M.E. Ch.; d 24 Feb 1902 (2/25/02; 2/28/02; 5/27/04; 5/26/05)

RONEY, Lucetta (Harvey) - widow of Elias M. Roney; d 14 May 1902 (5/16/02)

ROTHINGHOUSE, Albert - Chief, Gas City Volunteer Fire Dept.; d 4 Mar 1901 as result of injuries received in fighting a Gas City fire (3/7/01)

ROUSH, Mabel - see Charles KURTH

ROYAL, Carrie - see Charles KIMES

RUDICIL, Will - resigns as barber at Acme Barber Shop, Fmt.; is shipping clerk at Winslow Glass Factory, Matthews (10/31/01)

RUSH, __ - see Mrs. Robert CARTER; Mrs. Charles LLOYD

RUSH, Calvin - b near Fmt.; age 71 yr., 4 mon., 15 da.; s Iredell and Elizabeth Rush; 24 Jun 1857 m Elizabeth Winslow; d 28 Nov 1904, bur Park Cem (11/29/04)

RUSH, Calvin - of Rush Hill; grad FFA; is Haverford Coll student (6/10/02); 1903-05 att Univ of Pennsylvania (6/7/04; 12/16/04); s Nixon and Louisa Rush (1/10/05)

RUSH, Charles E. - att Earlham Coll 1904-05 (12/16/04)

RUSH, Clarkson - of Minnesota; s Susan Rush (2/16/04)

RUSH, Dora E. (Rutherford) - sister of Austin Rutherford (12/11/03); dt Hiram Rutherford (dec) of Sims (1/5/04); is filing for divorce from husband, Walter C. Rush (8/18/05); is divorced (10/20/05)

RUSH, Edgar - of Oklahoma; s Susan Rush (2/16/04)

RUSH, Elsie - att Wesleyan Coll, Houghton, NY 1904-05 (9/9/04)

RUSH, Iredel B. - retires as a Columbia City banker (4/29/04); retires with his family to his cottage on Shriner Lake near Columbia City (7/26/04); had 1st velocipede in Fmt. (1/20/05)

RUSH, J.N. - CW vet (6/6/05)

RUSH, Margaret - dt Iredell B. Rush; is engaged to m Will Matchette of Pierceton (8/4/03)

RUSH, Mary (Harvey) - of near Jonesboro; dt William and Ruth (Hadley) Harvey; wife of Elwood Rush (12/15/03; 8/25/05)

RUSH, Millicent - see Millicent (Rush) HAISLEY

RUSH, Myra - 1881, Fmt. Twp. Sch grad (7/4/05)

RUSH, Nixon - Dec 1894, sells land to Wesleyans for Wesleyan Camp Grounds (12/15/05); s Iredell and Elizabeth Rush (11/29/04); wife is Louisa (1/10/05)

RUSH, Olive - has her artist studio in Philadelphia (12/8/03); dt Nixon and Louisa Rush (1/10/05)

RUSH, Susan - age ca 82; came from NC 1866; d 14 Feb 1904, bur Park Cem (2/16/04)

RUSH, T.E. - and wife of 1 mi. SW of Jonesboro m and settled in Liberty Twp. ca 1852 (12/30/04)

RUSH, Walter C. - s Susan Rush (8/11/03); of Fmt. (2/16/04); disappeared last wk. (6/9/05); is being sued for divorce by wife, Dora (8/18/05)

RUSH, Z.F. - of Fmt.; s Susan Rush (2/16/04)

RUSH, Zeb - investor, Roaring Gimlet Gold Mining Syndicate (9/26/02)

'RUSH HILL' - home of Rush family; located at NW edge of Fmt. (6/10/02)

RUTHERFORD, Austin - m; d 12/10/03, bur Park Cem (12/11/03; 12/15/03); s Hiram Rutherford (dec) of Sims (1/5/04)

RUTHERFORD, Dora E. - see Dora E. (Rutherford) RUSH

RUTHERFORD/RETHERFORD, Martin - and William Miller saved [David] F. Highley's wife from drowning; Highley is appealing judgement against him for $1,000; case is in Wabash Circuit Court (4/15/01); court affirms that $1,000 must be paid to him and Wm. Miller (10/24/01); finally gets half of $450 in settlement of Highley case (12/12/01)

SAGE, Ira S. - a tailor with his shop in Borrey Blk. (5/16/01); sells his tailor business (2/3/05)

SANDERS, __ - see Mrs. Walter L. JAY

SANDERS, Miss Bernice - of Matthews is sister of Mrs. Walter Jay (7/5/04)

SANDERS, John - of 7 mi. E of Fmt.; serv Co. B, 84th Ind. Regmt. during CW (11/28/01)

SCHOONOVER, Peter - is fireman on engine that brings dirt 1.5 mi. to Cowgill Tile Mill (10/21/01)

SCHOONOVER, Prof. W.E. - Principal of FFA (4/15/01)

SCOTT, __ - see Mrs Amos BOGUE; see Mrs. Henry RITTENHOUSE

SCOTT, __ - b 7 Sep 1903; s M/M Alvin Scott (9/11/03)

SCOTT, __ - b 16 Feb 1904; dt M/M Walter Scott (2/19/04)

SCOTT, Addison - mail carrier on Fmt. Rural Rte. #19 (8/14/03); 4 Feb 1905 m Mrs. Belle Miller (2/7/05)

SCOTT, Alvin - oil well is brought in on his farm SE of Fmt. (12/2/02)

SCOTT, Mrs. Alvin - dt Ivy and Sarah Luther (8/18/05)

SCOTT, Charles - s Eli Scott; d recently in NM, bur Park Cem (5/30/01)

SCOTT, Charlotte - see Charlotte (Scott) RICE

SCOTT, Clarence - s Lin Scott of near Jonesboro; d 25 Dec 1904 (12/27/04)

SCOTT, Clyde - 12 Jul 1904 m Lillian May Dunbar (7/12/04)

SCOTT, Elenor - wife of Rev. Eli J. Scott; d recently in Indianapolis, bur Park Cem (2/28/01)

SCOTT, Rev. Eli J. - s Stephen Scott, Sr.; m Elenor (dec) (2/28/01)

SCOTT, Rev. Elwood - is new Marion Friends Ch. pastor (8/19/01)

SCOTT, Evaline - age 47; wife of Addison Scott; d 13 Jan 1904, bur Park Cem (1/15/04; 1/19/04)

SCOTT, Frances - see George CLOTHIER

SCOTT, H.A. - sold the Columbia Hotel to __ Thomas of Jonesboro (4/25/01); now lives in St. Joseph, MI (12/15/03)

SCOTT, James - performed m of M/M J.B. Smithson 50 yrs. ago (7/8/02); b Wayne Co. 26 Dec 1814; s John and Rachel; 20 Apr 1839 m Annis Arnett, dt Jesse and Margaret Arnett; and wife settled in Liberty Twp. 2.75 mi. NW of Fmt. in Dec 1842; mbr Fmt. Friends; d 27 Nov 1902 (11/28/02; 12/2/02; 12/5/02)

SCOTT, Levi - and family move from Pasadena, CA to Vallejo, CA (2/21/01); serv Pvt., Co. C, 118th Ind. Inf. during CW (5/27/04; 5/26/05);1881, is a Fmt. dry goods dealer (1/13/1881 as reprinted 3/29/04); Apr 1887, an investor in Fmt. Mining Co. (1/17/05); 1882, established 1st Fmt. bank (1/20/05); is granted pension of $12 per mon. (2/28/05); 1 Jan 1887, Treas., Fmt. Fair Assn. stockholders (12/15/05)

SCOTT, Lin - of near Jonesboro; will sell out and move to OR (11/14/01)

SCOTT, Lindley - 1881, a dry goods dealer with O.R. Scott (1/13/1881 as reprinted 3/29/04)

SCOTT, Linn - s Rachel Scott; employee of Boston Store (8/1/01)

SCOTT, Mary - 29 Sep 1904 is her 6th birthday (9/30/04)

SCOTT, Mary E. (Allen) - sister of Newton Allen; wife of R.E. Scott of Fmt.; d 11 Oct 1903, bur Eaton Cem (10/13/03)

SCOTT, O.R. - 1881, a dry goods dealer with Lindley Scott (1/13/1881 as reprinted 3/29/04)

SCOTT, Rachel (Cloud) - sister of Joseph Cloud of Wayne Co. (6/17/01); 7 Oct 1902 celebrates her 81st birthday (10/7/02); widow of Stephen Scott (dec 1 Nov 1889); f of Oak Ridge, now of Fmt. (8/28/03); b 7 Oct 1821 (8/12/04); age 83 (8/15/05)

SCOTT, Rev. Stephen - is leaving Little Ridge Friends pastorate (2/25/02), to become pastor of a Sheridan church (3/4/02)

SCOTT, William - b Wayne Co. 7 Jan 1844; s Stephen and Mahala; came to Grant Co. ca 1849; m Susannah Carey 17 Oct 1863; mbr Oak Ridge Friends; farmer of W of Fmt.; d 29 Sep 1901, bur Back Creek Friends Cem (9/30/01; 10/3/01)

SEAFORD, [William] - 1879 is tchr, Fmt. Sch; and __ Stout run printing shop where 'Fairmount News' is published (2/15/1879 reprinted in 1/29/04)

SEALE, __ - age 7; dt M/M Perry Seale of 1 mi. W of Fmt.; severely bitten by a sow, recently (6/20/01)

SEALE, __ - infant of M/M Luther Seale of Fowlerton; d recently, bur Park Cem (1/17/05)

SEALE, Alvin - s John Seale; grad of FFA and of Stanford Univ; is collecting birds on Nukuhiva, Marquesas Islands (11/4/02); has been collecting in Marquesas, Paumotu, Society, New Hebrides, Solomon Islands and Bougainille, South Pacific for 2 yrs. for Bishop Museum; is now in Australia (10/20/03); employee, US Fish Commission; is stationed at Stanford Univ, Palo Alto, CA (1/10/05); is serv on a special fish commission for Hawaiian government (9/12/05); introduces 'top minnow' into Hawaii to control mosquitos (10/10/05); working in Washington, DC for US Fish Commission (10/27/05)

SEALE, Arthur Ernest - of Denver, CO; s William P. and Elizabeth (9/23/01); b 8 Aug 1868 at Fmt.; 28 Sep 1898 m N. Ella Kennedy of Fmt.; att FFA 2 yrs; bookkeeper; mbr Friends; moved to Denver, CO Jul 1895 for health; d Denver, CO 6 Nov 1901, bur Fmt. cem (11/7/01; 11/14/01)

SEALE, Arthur Edwin - s Arthur E. and N. Ella (Kennedy) Seale (11/14/01)

SEALE, Bertha - withdrew from Earlham Coll for reasons of health (3/11/01); dt John Seale (11/4/01); - see Virgil TRUEBLOOD

SEALE, Clista - dt M/M John Seale (5/16/05)

SEALE, E.J. - of Liberty Twp.; s John Seale of Liberty Twp. (9/15/03)

SEALE, Mrs. E.J. - sister of Nathan, John W. and Tilman Cox (9/26/05)

SEALE, Edwin - s Mrs. Ella Seale (9/11/03)

SEALE, Mrs. I.N. - mbr, Linwood WCTU (2/5/04)

SEALE, John, Sr. - came from England ca 1854 (7/15/04); 27 Dec 1905 is given party for his 79th birthday (12/29/05)

SEALE, Dr. John Pearl - is taking a course at Johns Hopkins Hospital, Baltimore,MD (7/8/02); s John P. Seale (11/28/02); is in Dr. Henley's office on W. side of S. Main, Fmt. (8/7/03); a Director, Fmt. Fair Assoc. (1/12/04); has office in Borrey Blk. (6/2/05); moves his office to corner of Main & 1st St. (12/8/05)

SEALE, Leland - s E.J. Seale (2/16/04)

SEALE, M. Luther - is stocking his Fowlerton store with furniture and caskets (2/6/02); s William; is Fmt. and Fowlerton embalmer (3/7/05); moves his Fowlerton undertaking business to Summitville (9/15/05)

SEALE, Perry - 24 Dec 1890 m Rosa Rich (12/15/05)

SEALE, Mrs. Rilla - sister-in-law of Arthur E. Seale (dec); d Sep 1898 (11/14/01)

SEALE, Miss Treva - Fowlerton Sch substitute tchr (10/24/05)

SEALE, William - came from England ca 1854 (7/15/04)

SEEKINS, Clayton - young s of Rev./M W.J. Seekins (4/15/02); recently ran away from home (9/13/04)

SEEKINS, Rev. W.J. - his sons, ages 8 and 12, ran away from home, stole a horse and buggy in Tipton, are headed for Noblesville (4/25/01); sons have not been heard from as yet (7/25/01); sons are now home, they were found working for a farmer near Danville, IL (2/6/02); is moving back to Fmt. from LaGro (3/4/04)

SEEKINS, Mrs. W.J. - dt Mrs. Charles Phillips of Liverpool, England (10/20/05)

SEEKINS, Willie - s Rev. W.J. Seekins; is in USN aboard USS Topeka (2/7/05)

SELBY, John - stockholder and Cashier, Citizen's Exchange Bank (3/7/01; 3/18/02); serv Pvt., Co. F, 139th Ind. Inf. during CW (5/27/04; 5/26/05)

SELBY, Victor - s M/M John Selby (6/9/05)

SELBY, William A. - s M/M John Selby (5/30/01); of Durango, CO (9/2/02); age 24; d 30 May 1905, bur Park Cem (6/2/05; 6/9/05)

SEWALL, T.H. - Big Four RR agent, Jonesboro passenger depot (10/21/01)

SHAUGHNESSY, John - employed at Big Four Window Glass Factory since ca 1894, resigns and takes job at Headley Glass Factory (8/29/01)

SHAWHAN, Joseph A. - of Kokomo; 5 Sep 1905 m Mrs. Phoebe Presnall; will live in Kokomo (10/24/05)

SHEETS, Ellen - age 79; mother of Mrs. Ephraim Miller; d 21 Aug 1901 (8/22/01)

SHERRON, Mrs. Roy - of Marion is dt M/M George Crabb of Fmt. (4/15/02)

SHERWIN, Bert - a barber in the Acme Barber Shop (2/7/01)

SHIELDS, Al - recently bought a Star Windmill, sold and erected by Fmt. Buggy Co. (3/25/02); 6 Aug 1904 m Mrs. Lizzie Atkinson of near Summitville (8/9/04)

SHIELDS, Eliza Ann (Cox) - b 14 Jun 1860; dt William and Elizabeth Cox; 11 Apr 1878 m William Shields; mbr Friends; d 16/17 Jul 1902 (7/18/02; 7/22/02)

SHIELDS, Josephine - dt John Shields of Fmt. (7/11/02) - see Josephine (Shields) KELLEY

SHIELDS, Kate (DeShon) - dt Amos and Phoebe DeShon (5/19/05)

SHIELDS, Trenton A. - of Golden, CO; s William and Eliza Ann (Cox) Shields (7/22/02)

SHIMEL, F. - a Director, Fmt. Hunting & Fishing Club (1/1/04)

SHOEMAKER, Clarence - of Muncie; 8 Nov 1905 m Lola, dt M/M Robert Hasting of S of Fmt.; will live in Muncie (11/10/05)

SHUEY, Allen W. - baker for Crescent Bakery (4/18/05)

SHUEY, Ethel Charlotte (Downs) - dt M/M Allen B. and Phebe A. (Pence) Downs; m Allen W. Shuey (1/10/01; 1/14/01); mbr Fmt. Congregational Ch. (9/5/01; 6/24/02)

SHUGART, Mrs. Bennett - mbr Back Creek WCTU (5/16/02)

SHUGART, Miss Edith - 1904-05 tchr, Mill Twp. Dist. # 1 Sch (4/28/05)

SIDDONS, Pearl - see Lieut. Allen PARKER

SIGAFOOSE, Cora Lee - home and office is on Henley Ave.; is Diplomate in Osteopathy (D.O.); husband Prof. John W. Sigafoose is her assistant (4/22/02)

SIMONS, Carrie - 1903-04 Fowlerton Sch tchr (9/4/03); dt Levi Simons (7/1/04); is att Adrian Coll, MI (9/19/05)

SIMONS, Eva - dt Levi Simons (7/1/04)

SIMONS, Harry - s M/M John Simons (10/17/05)

SIMONS, Henry - of 1 mi. E of Fowlerton; age 86; d 31 Mar 1902 (4/1/02)

SIMONS, John - of Fmt.; s Henry Simons (dec) (4/1/02); 17 Nov 1904 was given party for his 50th birthday (11/22/04); 1 Jan 1887, Vice Pres., Fmt. Fair Assn. stockholders (12/15/05)

SIMONS, L.P. - Royal Glass Co. of Fowlerton brought in a dry gas well on his farm recently (1/5/04)

SIMONS, Levi - and wife of Fowlerton 17 Nov 1905 celebrated their silver wedding anniv; he is employee of Fowlerton Canning Factory (11/21/05)

SIMONS, Mary Alice - b 22 Oct 1902; dt John and Ruth Simons; d 8 Feb 1904, bur Park Cem (2/9/04; 2/12/04)

SIMONS, Miss Nellie - 1903-05 tchr, Fmt. Twp. Sch # 4 (9/4/03; 8/30/04); Monroe Twp. Dist. # 7 Sch tchr 1905-06 (9/5/05)

SIMONS, William - Pvt., Co. C, 89th Ind. Inf. during CW (5/26/05)

SINNINGER, Cal - editor of Fowlerton Index (5/23/02)

SKINNER, J.P. - saloon keeper on E. Washington St. (7/21/05)

SLUDER, I.N. - and wife move back to Fmt. from KY (10/7/01)

SMALL, Aaron - aged man; d 4 Jul 1902 (7/8/02)

SMALL, Albert - s Elvira Small (2/7/01); att Earlham Coll 1901-02 (1/1/02); grad Earlham Coll 1902 (5/27/02); grad FFA (7/29/02); att Harvard Univ 1904-05 (12/16/04)

SMALL, Cornelius R. - mbr, Finance & Bldg. Committee raising money to build tabernacle for Billy Sunday revival (1/30/02); agent for Provident Life & Trust Co. (5/30/02); Director, Fmt. YMCA (6/6/02); Asst. Cashier and stockholder, Fmt. Banking Co. (11/18/02); Apr 1887, an investor in Fmt. Mining Co. (1/17/05); and John A. Hunt purchase Fmt. Tile Factory (9/1/05)

SMALL, Effie - see Jasper E. WINSLOW

SMALL, Elihu - b 5 Feb 1823 (8/12/04); age 82 (8/15/05)

SMALL, Mrs. Elvira - d 26 Jan 1901, bur Park Cem (1/28/01); was charter mbr, Fmt. WCTU (2/7/01)

SMALL, Mrs. Rachel - b 26 Apr 1824 (8/12/04; 8/15/05)

SMALL, William - of Corvallis, OR; s Elihu Small (11/7/05)

SMILEY, Dory - 1901 Jefferson Twp. Dist. # 9 Sch grad (5/30/01)

SMITH, __ - see Mrs. Elmer GOSSETT; see Mrs. Charles FRY

SMITH, __ - recently b; s M/M Birney Smith (9/16/02)

SMITH, __ - b 24 Nov 1904; dt M/M Esom Smith (11/25/04)

SMITH, Mrs. Bessie - see Gilbert LaRUE

SMITH, Birney - s Jason B. and Cythia A. Smith (8/12/01)

SMITH, C.D. - brother of Stephen R. Smith; lost court case to keep money from sale of Barren Creek mammoth bones (1/17/05)

SMITH, Cora E. - see Burr F. POWELL

SMITH, Rev. Charles S. - Fmt. W.M. Ch. pastor (1/17/01); now pastor, Pleasant Grove W.M. Ch., Wabash Co. (8/19/04)

SMITH, Charles W. - m; d Coffeyville, KS 17 Jan 1904, bur Park Cem (2/5/04; 5/24/04)

SMITH, Cora E. - see Burr F. POWELL

SMITH, Dodge - age 13 (10/17/05)

SMITH, Elwood - of near Jonesboro; age 76; d 3 Aug 1905, bur Gas City Cem (8/8/05)

SMITH, Ephraim - of Fmt.; settled in Franklin Twp. in 1840; early Grant Co. surveyor; elected Grant Co. Treasurer 1854 (8/28/03); b 5 Mar 1821 (8/12/04); age 84 (8/15/05)

SMITH, Esom - of Fmt.; s Elwood Smith (dec) (8/8/05)

SMITH, Mrs. Esom - dt Mrs. Margaret Grindle (dec) of Gas City (11/24/05)

SMITH, Frank - employed as a blacksmith by St. Clair & Morrison, Fowlerton (5/23/02)

SMITH, Mrs. Frank - mbr Back Creek [Friends] WCTU (5/16/02)

SMITH, Glenn - 1901 Fmt. Twp. Dist. # 7 Sch grad (5/30/01)

SMITH, Rev. Hansen C. - Fmt. M.E. Ch. pastor (5/9/01); is transferred to a pastorate away from Fmt. (4/18/02)

SMITH, Harry - 1904 Fmt. HS grad (4/19/04); att Indianapolis Dental Coll 1904-05 (12/16/04)

SMITH, Harry Dobbins - b Clarksburg 14 Oct 1872; s Jason B. and Cythia A. Smith (f of Fmt.); came to Fmt. 1890; mbr Friends; d 9 Aug 1901, bur Park Cem (8/12/01; 8/15/01)

SMITH, Harvey - is shipping clerk, Winslow Glass Co., Matthews (12/16/01)

SMITH, Mrs. Harvey - of Matthews; dt Mrs. Margaret Dillon of Fmt. (11/6/03)

SMITH, Ichabod - Serg., Co. C, 89th Ind. Inf. during CW (5/26/05)

SMITH, Rev. J. Challen - resigns as pastor of Fmt. Congregational Ch. (3/18/01)

SMITH, Jason B. - serv Pvt., Co. B, 123rd Ind. Inf. during CW (5/27/04; 5/26/05)

SMITH, John - s Caleb Smith, 1st judge of Grant Co. court; m Mary Ann with 1st marriage license sold in Grant Co.; lived 1.5 mi. W of Fmt. (9/18/03); and wife live S of Fmt.; m ca 1830 (10/11/04)

SMITH, John - f of Fmt.; s Leander Smith, f of Fmt.; 13 Sep 1905 killed in Marion RR accident, bur Park Cem (9/15/05; 9/19/05)

SMITH, John L. - age 44; injured in nitro-glycerine explosion on Caskey farm several wks. ago (5/16/05)

SMITH, Leander - serv Pvt., unassigned, 83rd Ind. Inf. during CW (5/27/04; 5/26/05); father of Mrs. El. Gossett (9/15/05)

SMITH, Mayme - see Otto L. WINSLOW

SMITH, Rev. Moses - serv Pvt., Co. G, 4th/6th Ind. Inf. during CW (5/27/04; 5/26/05); of Purdy, MO; and wife visit Fmt.; 1880 moved to Fmt.; 1883 organized Harrisburg Baptist Ch.; 1886 organized Fmt. Baptist Ch.; 1894 moved to Missouri (9/30/04)

SMITH, Roland - elected O.G., Beeson GAR Post 386 (1/24/02); serv Serg., Co. H, 12th Ind. Inf. during CW (5/27/04; 5/26/05); and wife are spending winter in State Soldier's Home, Lafayette (10/20/05; 10/27/05)

SMITH, Stephen R. - and brother, C.D. Smith, lease from Mrs. Dora Gift the Barren Creek farm where the mammoth bones were found (6/17/04); lost court case to keep money from sale of Barren Creek mammoth bones (1/17/05)

SMITH, Sylvester - of near Lake Sch; age 65; brother-in-law of John Selby; d 2 Mar 1901; funeral in Bethel M.P. MH conducted by Rev. Iliff (3/7/01)

SMITH, W.C. 'Heavy' - d 26 Jul 1904 in Marion (7/29/04)

SMITH, William J. - elected O.D., Beeson GAR Post 386 (1/24/02); b 31 Mar 1837 near Jonesboro; s John and Mary Ann Smith; ca 1852 moved with parents to farm 2 mi. S of Fmt.; during CW serv Serg., Co. K, 130th Ind. Inf., was wounded (10/27/03; 5/26/05)

SMITHSON, Isaac - Pres. of Board of Directors, Roaring Gimlet Gold Mining Syndicate (9/26/02); serv color bearer, Co. C, 89th Ind. Inf. during CW (5/26/05)

SMITHSON, Mrs. Isaac - d recently (1/20/05)

SMITHSON, Judiah B. 'Jude' - elected Surgeon, Beeson GAR Post 386 (1/24/02); and wife celebrate their 50th wedding anniv today; James Scott of Fmt. married them (7/8/02); b Wayne Co. 27 Jan 1831; came to Grant Co. 1839; serv in Co. B, 130th Ind. Inf. 12/19/1863-12/2/1865 (10/30/03); 27 Jan 1904 is given a dinner for his 73rd birthday (1/29/04); serv Co. K, 130th Ind. Inf. during CW (5/27/04); serv Pvt., Co. B, 130th Ind. Inf. during CW (5/26/05); and wife are spending winter in State Soldier's Home, Lafayette (11/7/05)

SMITHSON, Schuyler - while in Matthews 25 Mar 1902, saved a small boy from burning to death (3/28/02)

SMITHSON, Mrs. Schuyler - dt John Askran (dec) (12/6/04)

SPANGLER, Richard - of near Weaver; age 47; m; d 31 Jan 1905, bur Park Cem (2/3/05)

SPARKS, Sarah - see Cleave FURNISH

SPENCER, J.A. - resigns as Fmt. Water Works engineer (9/16/01)

SPENCER, Mrs. John - age 28; d 5 Feb 1904, bur Montpelier Cem (2/9/04)

STALKER, Mrs. Jane - lived in NC during CW; husband d of disease in CW; her son was age 17 during CW (5/3/04)

STANFIELD, David - early settler of Fmt. area (1/13/05); 28 Dec 1850 platted town of Fmt. (1/20/05); wife was Elizabeth; f home, at corner of Main & Madison St., burned 20 May 1905 (5/23/05)

STANSBURY, Theodore - serv 1st Serg., Co. K, 2nd Ohio Inf. and 1st Serg., Co. D, 66th Ohio Inf. during CW (5/27/04; 5/26/05)

STARR, Caleb A. - serv Pvt., Co. K, 130th Ind. Inf. during CW (5/27/04; 5/26/05)

STARR, Daisy - see Daisy (Starr) DYSON

STARR, John P. - Seaman, US Navy (1/15/04); serv aboard battleship 'Missouri' (2/12/04); b Madison Co. 6 Jun 1882; s M/M C.A. Starr; grad, FHS 1900; enlisted USN 7 Apr 1903; killed recently in explosion in turret of USS Missouri (4/15/04); grad Fmt. HS 1900 (12/19/05)

STARR, Osha - dt M/M C.A. Starr (6/24/02); mbr, Ladies Shakespeare Club (9/30/02); 1904-05 Fmt. Sch tchr (9/2/04); - see Osha (Starr) YOCUM

STECH, A.D. - owns a grocery store (8/29/05)

STEELMAN, Pearl - age 19; 3 Jul 1905, he d at Fowlerton (7/4/05)

STEPHENS, Sallie (Winslow) - f of Jonesboro; was M.E. missionary in India for many yrs.; while in Madras, India m Harry Stephens, a British army officer; family now retires to USA (3/11/04)

STEPHENS, Veda - age 17; dt Harry and Sallie Stephens (3/11/04); att DePauw Univ 1904-05 (8/30/04)

STEPHENSON, Jennie - mbr, Back Creek WCTU (11/11/04)

STEVENS, Benjamin F. - mbr Fmt. Congregational Ch. (9/5/01); is Justice of Peace, Fmt. Twp. (11/28/02); CW vet; son-in-law of Abraham Covalt of Green Twp. (12/29/03); serv Pvt., Co. I, 60th Ind. Inf. during CW (5/27/04; 5/26/05)

STEVENS, Mrs. C.H. - age 62; m; d 20 Oct 1905, bur IOOF Cem, Greentown (10/24/05)

STEVENS, Clara - see Lew CASKEY

STEVENS, George - age 53; m; d Fmt. 3 Oct 1902, bur Holland, IN (10/7/02)

STEWART, __ - see Mrs. Charles ENGLE

STEWART, Aimuel - tchr, Liberty Twp. Schs 1904-06 (12/27/04; 7/28/05)

STEWART, Elizabeth - 1904-05 Fmt. Schs tchr (9/2/04); tchr, Fmt. Schs for past 3 yrs. (8/1/05); - see J.E. CARTER

STEWART, Frank - s M/M J.E. Stewart; glassblower for Fmt. Glass Works; 8 Jun 1904 m Lutie Presnall, dt M/M Harvey Presnall (6/10/04)

STEWART, Mrs. James - of Fmt.; dt Eli Kimbrough (5/24/04)

STEWART, John H. - serv Pvt., Co. C, 12th Ind. Inf. during CW (5/27/04; 5/26/05); of Fmt. is f Liberty Twp farmer (8/18/05); brother of Samuel and Robert (12/26/05)

STEWART, Miss Leona - and Miss M. Elizabeth Stewart are mbrs Fmt. Congregational Ch. (9/5/01)

STEWART, Robert - of 8 mi. W of Fmt.; brother of John and Samuel; age 60; d 23 Dec 1905, bur Park Cem (12/26/05)

STEWART, Samuel - serv Pvt., Co. G, 153rd Ind. Inf. during CW (5/27/04; 5/26/05); brother of John and Robert (12/26/05)

STEWART, Mrs. Samuel - mbr Fmt. Congregational Ch. (9/5/01); of Fmt.; dt Eli Kimbrough (5/24/04)

STIBBS, Jess - employee of Rau Glass Factory (5/2/01)

STIBBS, Will - age 23; s Jess Stibbs; m dt of Joe Arc[Ark] of Matthews; employee of Rau Glass Factory; 30 Apr 1901 is shot dead in Fmt. Fair Grounds by Fred Miller; bur Park Cem (5/2/01)

STINSON, Louisiana - see Luther BROOKSHIRE

STIVERS, Jackson - Director, Fmt. YMCA (6/6/02); Director, Roaring Gimlet Gold Mining Syndicate (9/26/02); leaves Board of Fmt. YMCA (8/28/03); a Director, Fmt. Fair Assoc. (1/12/04);

and family moves to LaJara, CO; lived in Fmt. 1888-1904 (4/5/04); lives in San Diego, CA (8/1/05)

STIVERS, Mrs. J. - mbr, Fmt. Congregational Ch. (9/12/02)

STONE, Amanda _ 1901 Fmt. Twp. Dist. # 1 Sch grad (5/30/01)

STONER, Thomas R. - is in charge of Machine & Tool Works (10/21/02); sold his interest in Fmt. Machine & Tool Works to James O. Fink (11/27/03)

STORY, Bell - see Bell (Story) WRIGHT

STOUT, __ - see Mrs. Robert YOUNG

STOUT, Charles E. - 1879 has printing office with [William] Seaford (2/15/1879 as reprinted 1/29/04); 1881, and wife, Emma C. Stout are Fairmount News editors (1/13/1881 as reprinted 3/29/04)

STOUT, Dudley - s Sarah J. Stout (age 83) (2/28/01)

STOUT, Edward - s Dudley and Mary Stout (6/27/05)

STOUT, Emma C. - of Columbus, GA; f Assoc. Editor, Fairmount News ca 1884, is visiting in Marion (8/5/04)

STOUT, John - Grant Co. pioneer; d at Upland recently (10/31/02)

STOUT, Mary - dt Dudley and Mary Stout (6/27/05)

STOUT, Mary - age 62; wife of Dudley Stout; d 23 Jun 1905, bur Park Cem (6/27/05)

STOVER, Ed - of Fmt.; serv US Army in P. Islands (7/8/01)

STOVER, Elijah - dec; serv Pvt., Co. D, 34th Ind. Inf. during CW (5/26/05)

STREET, John - Grant Co. pioneer; d in Matthews 7 Sep 1902 (9/9/02)

STUCKEY, John A. - and wife of near Rigdon will celebrate their 50th wedding anniv 1 Nov 1904 (10/21/04)

STURDEVANT, Minnie - see Minnie (Sturdevant) TYLER

SUMMERVILLE, J.B. - 1888, 1st pastor of Fmt. Baptist Ch. (1/24/05)

SUMMITVILLE, Town of -
MODEL GLASS WORKS - stenographer is Grace VanArsdall (9/8/05)
SEALE UNDERTAKING - owned by M. Luther Seale; is moved here from Fowlerton (9/15/05)

SUNDAY, Rev. William A. 'Billy' - to hold revival in Fmt. 20 Mar 1902 (1/9/02; 1/30/02); PHOTO; revival to start 30 Mar 1902 (3/21/02); a chorus of 75 to 100 voices backs up his preaching (4/1/02); standing room only at revival (4/4/02); at least 1,300 in tabernacle with 500 people turned away some nights (4/15/02); PHOTO; wife is with him in Fmt. (4/22/02); to dedicate the Fmt. YMCA Hall when it is completed (7/8/02); guest of M/M Ira Neeley; is in Fmt. to give a lecture 28 Jul 1902 but lecture was rained out (7/29/02); 11 Aug 1902 lectured at Friends Ch. (8/15/02)

SUTTON, R.E. - serv Lieut., Co. B, 72nd New York Inf. during CW (5/27/04; 5/26/05)

SWAIM, __ - b 13 Nov 1905; dt M/M Frank Swaim (11/17/05)

SWAIM, Everett - age 20; d 13 May 1905, bur Barber Mills Cem (5/16/05)

SWAIM, Ida - 8 Aug 1904 was her 10th birthday (8/12/04)

SWAIM, Julian L. - owns Swaim Lumber Co.; is enlarging its bldg. (1/6/02); gas was struck at the nearby well (1/9/02); his burned sawmill is rebuilt and running (8/5/04); is installing counters and other woodwork in new Fowlerton Bank (1/10/05)

SWAIM, Opha - 1904 Fmt. HS grad (4/19/04); mbr, Shakespeare Club (2/28/05); dt M/M J.L. Swaim (7/4/05); - see Will LIGHTNER

SWAIM, Ray - age 21; s Mrs. Nancy Swaim; mbr Modern Woodsmen Lodge; d 8 May 1904, bur Barber Mills Cem, Wells Co. (5/10/04)

SWAIM, Vance - age 27; d 29 May 1905, bur Barber Mills Cem (5/30/05)

SWARTS, __ - b 16 Oct 1905; s M/M Emory Swarts (10/17/05)

SWARTZ, Emma - grad Fowlerton Sch 1905 (5/12/05)

SWEAT, Ben F. - colored; has boarding house on E. 7th St., Fmt. (11/14/02)

TATUM, David - Quaker evangelist of Denver, CO; will lecture in Fmt. Friends MH next Sunday (5/30/01)

TAYLOR, __ - see Mrs. Ed HARVEY

TEMPLETON, Elma Leona - see Elma Leona (Templeton) MART

TEMPLETON, Isa - grad Fowlerton Sch 1905 (5/12/05)

TENNESSEE, came from - see Benjamin BENBOW; Will F. BROWN

TENNESSEE, gone to - see L. Amelia BROWN; Mrs. Emory CARPENTER

THISTLE, John - of Jonesboro; d recently, bur Park Cem (11/21/05)

THOMAS, __ - b 26 Nov 1904; dt M/M Eli Thomas (11/29/04)

THOMAS, __ - b 7 Mar 1905; dt W.A. and Lizzie (McDonald) Thomas of Marion (3/10/05)

THOMAS, __ - b 18 Nov 1905; s M/M Howard Thomas (11/21/05)

THOMAS, Alonzo - Fmt. ice dealer; accidentally burned down his chicken house while trying to kill chicken lice with burning straw (4/11/01); has stored 400 tons of ice for sale to customers (3/4/02); has stored 350 tons of ice cut from pits S of Fmt. (2/10/05); settled in Fmt. in 1876 (11/7/05)

THOMAS, Benjamin - age 36; d Gas City 8 Aug 1901 (8/8/01)

THOMAS, Mrs. Charles - of Fmt.; dt Susan Rush (2/16/04)

THOMAS, Cora - is granted a divorce from her husband, William (1/21/01)

THOMAS, Daniel - age 61; d 2 Nov 1880 (12/15/05)

THOMAS, Mrs. Denny - of Back Creek Friends area; dt Susan Rush (2/16/04)

THOMAS, Eleanor - age ca 78; widow of Daniel Thomas; d at her home 0.5 mi. SW of Fmt. (5/27/02)

THOMAS, Fred - s M/M Eli Thomas (10/21/01)

THOMAS, Mrs. George - is again owner of Columbia Hotel (6/24/04)

THOMAS, H.D. - is again prop., Columbia Hotel (7/5/04)

THOMAS, Isaiah - serv Pvt., Co. F, 34th Ind. Inf. during CW (5/27/04; 5/26/05)

THOMAS, Miss Lydia - age 43; dt Amos Thomas of 3 mi. SW of Fmt.; mbr W.M. Ch.; d 15 Dec 1904, bur Park Cem (12/20/04)

THOMAS, Rose - of Back Creek Friends area; is att Nursing Sch, Crawfordsville (9/22/05)

THOMAS, Ruth - see Benjamin F. MORRIS

THOMAS, Mrs. Shively - of Swayzee; d 12 Apr 1901 (4/15/01)

THOMAS, W.B. - 19 Nov 1902 m Elizabeth McDonald, dt Bernard and Elizabeth (Heavenridge) McDonald (11/21/02; 11/10/03)

THOMAS, Mrs. Will - d 3 Jan 1889 (12/15/05)

THOMPSON, ___ - see Mrs. James LARKINS

THOMPSON, Benjamin - 28 Aug 1904 m Martha Belle, dt M/M M.S. Friend (8/30/04)

THOMPSON, Homer - 1904 Fmt. HS grad (4/19/04); att Ind. Univ 1904-05 (12/16/04)

THOMPSON, Walter L. - pastor, Fmt. W.M. Ch. (9/16/04); pastor, Back Creek W.M. Ch. (1/24/05)

THORN, Chauncy - mail carrier, Fmt. Rural Rte. # 21 (8/8/02; 8/14/03); 15 Apr 1905 m Gertrude Bradford (4/21/05)

THORN, George - serv Lieut., Co. K, 153rd Ind. Inf. during CW (5/27/04; 5/26/05)

THORN, James - CW vet; recently celebrated his 57th birthday (8/12/02); serv Pvt., Co. B, 36th Ind. Inf. and Pvt., Co I, 19th Ind. Inf. during CW (5/27/04; 5/26/05)

THORNBURG, Arthur - age 23; accidentally killed near Jonesboro 27 Dec 1904 (12/30/04)

TIGNER, Charles - and wife are parents of twin dts b 25 Sep 1902 (9/26/02)

TINN, Mrs. Caroline - age 77; d 8 Jun 1902 (6/13/02)

TOMLINSON, __ - b 31 Nov 1903; s M/M Noah Tomlinson (12/4/03)

TOMLINSON, John - employee of Crystal Ice Co. (7/22/01); age 68; d 23 Sep 1902, bur Park Cem (9/26/02)

TOSH, Dan - of Radley; m; came from VA in 1865 (8/7/03)

TRADER, Ada - and dt, Cleo, are mbrs, Fmt. WCTU (6/3/02)

TRADER, Everett - s M/M Luther Trader (9/19/01)

TRADER, Mart - s M/M Harvey Trader;12 Mar 1904 m Jessie, dt M/M Charles Ferree; will live on farm near Wheeling; Mart and Jessie f att FFA (3/15/04)

TRADER, Oscar H. - sells and erects Star Windmills (8/12/01); his horse/buggy were stolen from Wesleyan Camp Ground (7/21/05)

TRADER, Robert - raises/sells vegetables (8/26/01)

TRASK, Dr. Harrison J. - of Matthews; was assaulted/robbed 3 Aug 1901 (8/5/01); was taken to his home in state of NY, he may not recover (8/22/01); a piece of his skull was removed by surgery at Buffalo, NY General Hospital (9/16/01); is in Matthews preparing to move to CA; is partially paralyzed on one side (10/17/01)

TRASK, Town of - post office will cease 31 May 1901; Miss Myrtle Hamilton is Post Mistress (5/13/01)

TRASTER(S), Byron - s William H.H. and Elsie (Cooper); age 8 (1/6/02)

TRASTER(S), Helen - dt William H.H. and Elsie (Cooper) Trasters; age 10 (1/6/02)

TRASTERS, William H.H. - b Cedar Valley, OH 31 Jul 1857; s Daniel and Maria; grad medical sch, Columbus, OH 1889; m 17 Jul 1890 Elsie Cooper (dt Rev. J.M. Cooper, M.E. minister); sch tchr; d 30 Dec 1901 (12/30/01; 1/6/02)

TREON, Charles - m Nettie Harvey 27 Jan 1901 (2/4/01)

TREON, Mrs. John - age 32; m; d 8 Mar 1905, bur Park Cem (3/10/05)

TROY, ___ - age 16 days; baby of M/M John Troy; d 11 Jan 1904 (1/12/04)

TROY, Mrs. John - of Fmt.; is mbr St. Cecilia's RC Ch. (6/20/02)

TRUEBLOOD, Virgil - 30 Jun 1904 m Bertha Seale; both are of Whittier, CA (7/15/04)

TUCKER, Elon - Editor, <u>Jonesboro Herald</u> (12/18/03)

TURNER, Elizabeth - see Emmet BASTAIN

TURNER, Nelson - Grant Co. pioneer; d 12 Jul 1902 in Washington Twp. (7/15/02); walked from Fmt. to Franklin Coll in 1845 with John Morris, John Ratliff and Joseph Jay; all att Franklin Coll 1845-46 (2/12/04)

TYLER, Prof. Leon L. - of Grand Ledge, MI; is new FFA Principal (8/1/01);m; 1903-04 FFA Principal (9/4/03)

TYLER, Minnie (Sturdevant) - wife of Leon L. Tyler; 1901-02 FFA history and English tchr (8/19/01); dt Mrs. Cynthia Sturdevant (6/24/02)

ULREY, A.A. - stockholder in Citizen's Exchange Bank (3/18/02)

ULRICH, Mrs. Anton - mbr, St. Cecilia RC Ch. (10/20/03)

UNDERWOOD, __ - child of Al. Underwood; d 18 Mar 1904, bur Back Creek Friends Cem (3/22/04)

UNDERWOOD, __ - age 6 mon.; dt M/M Ben Underwood of 3 mi. SE of Fmt.; d recently, bur Park Cem (2/17/05)

UNDERWOOD, Earl - 17 Oct 1903 m Clysta Addison; lives SE of Fmt. (10/20/03)

UNDERWOOD, Frank - grad Pike Sch 1905 (5/12/05)

UNDERWOOD, John - son-in-law of Rebecca Plaster (11/17/05)

VALENTINE, James Bester - 5 Jul 1902 m Julia Conliff (7/8/02)

VanARSDALL, Chester - resigns as local agent for Fmt. American Express office (3/25/04)

VanARSDALL, Glenn - s M/M W.P. VanArsdall; 9 Jun 1902 m Florence Anderson; will live in Fmt. (6/27/02)

VanARSDALL, Miss Grace - stenographer for Model Glass Works, Summitville (9/8/05)

VanARSDALL, Russel [May] - see Lee BROWN

VanCANNON, __ - see Mrs. William PLASTERS

VanCANNON, Elias - of E of Fmt.; m; target of attempted robbery (8/22/01); serv Pvt., Co. B, 33rd Ind. Inf. during CW (5/27/04; 5/26/05); 22 Oct 1904 is given a dinner for his 78th birthday (10/25/04); his house burns down (10/28/04)

VanCANNON, Mrs. Elias - 21 Oct 1903 celebrated her 76th birthday (10/27/03)

VanDYNE, Neal - is serv Troop L, 1st US Cav. in Philippines (9/5/01); is home from army serv in P.I. (3/14/02)

VanDYNE, Percy - recently enlisted in US Army (7/18/01)

VAUGHN, Frank - recently discharged from military serv (8/8/02)

VAUGHN, George - a winner in Fmt. Gun Club Shoot (4/1/01); serv Pvt., Co. C, 7th Michigan Inf. during CW (5/27/04; 5/26/05)

VENIS, Mrs. Sarah - of E of Fmt.; d 28 Mar 1902 (3/28/02)

VENITZ, John - age ca 46; m; prop., Klondyke Saloon in Fmt.; d 5 Sep 1903, bur Park Cem (9/8/03)

VETOR, John - b 22 Nov 1817 Cohasen, Germany; came to USA in 1831; serv 1 yr. under General Zachary Taylor in Border Ruffian War; serv Co. C, 1st Michigan Inf. during Mexican War; came to Fmt. ca 1868 (10/16/03); serv Pvt., 3rd Michigan Inf. during Mexican War (5/27/04; 5/26/05); age 87 (8/15/05)

VIGUS, __ - b 24 Dec 1903; s Dr./M C.B. Vigus (12/29/03)

VIGUS, Dr. C.B. - and wife live in Rigdon (9/19/01); moves with family to Mississippi (1/22/04)

VIGUS, Mrs. C.B. - of Rigdon; dt Mrs. S.M. Latham of Fmt. (6/24/02)

VINSON, Ezra - has organ and sewing machine shop in Winslow's Livery Stable (9/23/01); is traveling through Arkansas repairing sewing machines and organs (3/17/05)

VINSON, Mrs. Lucinda - of Fmt.; d recently (6/6/01)

VINSON, Nathan - dec early settler of Fmt. area (1/13/05)

VINSON, William - 5 Apr 1902 m Mrs. Eva Barry (4/4/02)

VIRGIN, Allen - new Fowlerton Postmaster (10/9/03)

VIRGINIA, came from - see Isabella H. (Cook) PRETLOW; Dan TOSH

VIRGINIA, gone to - see Mrs. Samuel C. ALE

WAGGY, Phillip - dec; serv Co. H, 12th Ind. Inf. during CW (5/27/04; 5/26/05)

WAITE, Sullivan T. - of Trask is s Mrs. Margaret Waite (age 80+; of Gilead, Miami Co.) (11/4/01)

WALDON, Alfred - dec; serv Pvt., Co. K, 130th Ind. Inf. during CW (5/26/05)

WALL, Violet - grad Fowlerton Sch 1905 (5/12/05)

WALTERS, Elsie - 18 May 1904 is her 10th birthday (5/20/04)

WARD, Miss Alta L. - Fmt. telephone exchange operator (5/30/01); - see Nelson E. DUCKWALL

WARD, Isabelle - see Isabelle (Ward) LEWIS

WARD, Mrs. Jessie - sister of Lucinda (Eastes) Ward (1/29/04)

WARD, Lucinda (Eastes) - age 63; d 28 Jan 1904, bur Park Cem (1/29/04; 2/2/04)

WARD, Mariah Jane - see Mariah Jane (Ward) LIVELY

WARE, Joseph - his farm is source of gravel being used on County Line Road (9/12/02)

WARE, Mrs. Nettie - mbr, Fmt. WCTU (6/3/02); Pres., Fowlerton WCTU (7/29/04); wife of William Ware (8/30/04)

WARE, William W. - 1900-01 Fowlerton Sch tchr (3/28/01); new mbr FFA Board of Trustees (12/23/01); tchr in Fmt. Twp. for 14 yrs.; tchr, 1903-04, Liberty Twp. Sch # 12 (9/11/03; 9/15/03); tchr, Liberty Twp. Sch 1904-05 (12/27/04)

WARNER, Merville - 29 Aug 1905 is his 7th birthday (9/1/05)

WARNER, Dr. W.M. - has a multi-nebulizer in his office for treatment of chronic bronchitis (4/4/02); appointed Fmt. Health Officer (9/23/04); grad Pulte Medical Coll, Cincinnati, OH (10/25/04)

WARNER, Mrs. W.M. - sister of Homer McCandless of Indianapolis (12/12/05)

WATKINS, __ - infant of Elmer and Emma Watkins; d 28 Nov 1905, bur Park Cem; colored (12/1/05)

WATKINS, Mrs. Elmer - d 24 Mar 1904, bur Park Cem; colored (3/25/04)

WEAVER CEMETERY - William Bass is bur (9/2/01)

WEAVER, Mrs. Eunice - b Mar 1824 (8/12/04; 8/15/05)

WEAVER, Henry - colored pioneer of Liberty Twp.; d last Sun (8/15/02)

WEBSTER, Arthur - age 28; s Daniel Webster of 1 mi. S of Summitville; d 11 Nov 1902 (11/11/02)

WEEKLY, Mrs. Nancy - b17 Nov 1820 (8/12/04; 11/22/04); age 84 (8/15/05)

WEEKS, Charles - of Palo Alto, CA; FFA grad (1/10/05); 9 Mar 1905 m Mary Alice, dt M/M Barclay Johnson; will live in Mountain View, CA (3/21/05)

WEIRAUCH, Mrs. William - age 35; m; d 27 Oct 1904, bur Park Cem (11/1/04)

WELCH, Hosea - of Jonesboro; 8 Nov 1902 m Mamie Brown, dt James Brown (11/18/02)

WELLS, __ - see Mrs. Lud LEER

WELLS, James A. - serv Co. H, 84th Ind. Inf. during CW (5/27/04; 5/26/05)

WELLS, John B. - b 1 Jun 1822 Fayette Co.; 1855 came to Grant Co.; serv 2nd Lieut., Co. C, 89th Ind. Inf. 1862-24 Aug 1864; lived 6 mi. W of Fmt. in Liberty Twp; d recently (4/18/01); CW serv noted (5/27/04; 5/26/05)

WELLS, Newton J. - serv Co. C, 89th Ind. Inf. during CW (5/27/04; 5/26/05)

WELLS, Mrs. Newton - dt Mrs. James Flanagan (dec) (4/15/01)

WELLS, Sarah B. - widow of John B. Wells; d at her Liberty Twp. home 27 Mar 1902 (3/28/02)

WELLS, Sophia - see Sophia WENCE

WELSH, __ - infant of M/M Hosea Welsh; d 3 Mar 1905 (3/3/05)

WENCE, Sophia (Wells) - age 35; dt John Wells (dec); 11 Jan 1905 d at her home in Farmersburg, bur Park Cem (1/17/05)

WESLEYAN CAMP GROUNDS - now has 7 arc lights installed by Will Bowers, Fmt. Electric Light Plant electrician (8/26/01)

WEST, M. - sold his cigar & sundry store to Buck Mann (9/26/01)

WEST, Walter - grad Back Creek Friends Sch 1905 (5/12/05)

WEST VIRGINIA, came from - see William A. FRAZIER

WESTON, Mrs. Elizabeth - age 92 (8/12/04)

WESTON, Elizabeth (Coulter) - b Franklin Co. 11 Jan 1844; dt Samuel and Helen Coulter; 12 Jan 1875 m Capt. Hugh Weston; came to Fmt. 1892; mbr Fmt. M.E. Ch.; d 13 Mar 1904, bur Park Cem (3/15/04; 3/25/04)

WESTON, Helen - of Fmt.; grad DePauw Univ 1902 (6/10/02)

WESTON, Hugh - his mother, Mrs. __ Weston, is age 97 4/29/04); serv Pvt., Co. F, 7th Ind. Inf. and Capt., Co. A, 123rd Ind. Inf. during CW (5/27/04; 5/26/05)

WESTON, Nellie - grad DePauw Univ 1902 (6/10/02); dt Hugh and Elizabeth (Coulter) Weston (3/15/04)

WHARTON, William - age 85; d Matthews 20 Jul 1901 (7/25/01)

WHEELER, H.I. - f clerk, Beasley Drug Store; now is farmer near Zanesville, OH (1/13/05)

WHEELER, Leota - age 24; dt John Wheeler; d 6 May 1904, bur Back Creek Friends Cem (5/10/04)

WHINNERY, Mrs. Elsworth - of Marshall Co., IA; adopted dt of Calvin and Elizabeth (Winslow) Rush (11/29/04)

WHITE, Rev. T.J. - pastor, Fmt. A.M.E. Ch (11/24/05)

WHITE RIVER - will be dredged and made navigible for steamboats for the 80 mi. between Muncie and Indianapolis (9/26/01)

WHITELY, Mrs. Dora - mbr, Hadley WCTU (6/13/05)

WHITNEY, Harry Orville - b Franklin Co. 21 Mar 1870; s George G. and Eliza A.; grad Indianapolis Business Univ 1891; m Luzena T. Cowgill 2 Jul 1896; bookkeeper/partner, Cowgill Tile Co.; d 27 Oct 1901 Canon City, CO, bur Park Cem, Fmt. (10/28/01; 11/4/01)

WHITNEY, Mrs. Harry - dec mbr, Shakespeare Club (3/7/05)

WHITNEY, L.R.(?) - Treas., National Drain Tile Co. (9/16/02)

WHITSON, Dr. E.M. - of Jonesboro; age 63; d 7 Nov 1905 (11/10/05)

WHYBREW, __ - b 1 Dec 1904; dt M/M Clinton Whybrew of W of Fmt. (12/2/04)

WHYBREW, Joseph - CW vet; bur Back Creek Cem (6/6/05)

WIEDENHOEFT, Rev. William - 1888 is 1st pastor of Fmt. Congregational Ch. (1/24/05)

WILBURN, Ottis - 4 Nov 1903 m Catherine Brown of Fmt. (11/6/03)

WILDLIFE & PESTS -
QUAIL - Dec 1890, John McCombs of Hackleman killed 45 with 3 shots (12/15/05)
RATS - Sunday, men and boys with clubs, revolvers, and dogs killed 221 rats on the farm of C.R. Kimes 4 mi. E of Fmt. (4/4/01)
RABBITS - S.B. Hill bagged 12 while hunting on Thanksgiving Day (12/5/05)

WILEY, Debbie A. - see Debbie A. BROWN

WILEY, Hol - of Jonesboro; s Mrs. Debbie A. Brown (4/18/02)

WILEY, Richard A. - of Driggs, Wright & Wiley Hardware; 7 Jun 1905 m Emma Miller of near Muncie (6/9/05)

WILEY, Mrs. Will H. - of Marion; dt Mrs. Elizabeth Bogue of Fmt. (7/29/02; 4/8/04)

WILEY, Zoe - grad, Fmt. HS 1904 (4/22/04)

WILLIAMS, Clara - dt Mrs. John Williams (5/23/02)

WILLIAMS, Mrs. John - age ca 30; m; d Fmt. 23 Sep 1902, bur Findley, OH (9/26/02)

WILSON, __ - b 30 Sep 1904; s M/M Charles Wilson (10/4/04)

WILSON, Rev. __ - pastor, Center Christian Ch. (2/3/02)

WILSON, Allie - see Dr. J.O. LOMAN

WILSON, Alvin - to be Fmt. Twp. Trustee 1 Jan 1905 (11/29/04)

WILSON, Amanda (Dean) - m Paxton Wilson; d ca 1899 (8/7/03)

WILSON, Dr. C.M. - moved his dental office into new Fmt. Blk. (11/7/01)

WILSON, Mrs. C.M. - dt Daniel W. Simpson (CW vet) of Howard Co. (3/10/05)

WILSON, Chester - s Alvin Wilson; is working in Colon, Panama (10/18/04); f worked on Panama Canal; is engineering construction of a smelter in DuPue, IL (11/10/05)

WILSON, Mrs. Clement - d recently, bur Oak Ridge Cem (5/23/01)

WILSON, Daniel - of Wabash Co.; f of Grant Co.; age ca 61; s M/M Jesse Wilson; m 1st Lavina Jones; m 2nd ca 1892 Miss Deborah Weesner; d 26 May 1904 (5/31/04)

WILSON, Deborah - see Deborah (Wilson) ELLIOTT

WILSON, Dorinda E. - mbr Back Creek [Friends WCTU] (11/11/04)

WILSON, Effie - wife of Lindsey Wilson; mbr Back Creek [Friends] WCTU (5/16/02; 11/11/04)

WILSON, Eli A. - of Hackleman; 27 Sep 1905 m Pearl, dt M/M Cy Nicholson; will live in Fmt. (9/29/05)

WILSON, Elizabeth - see Elizabeth (Wilson) COX

WILSON, Eunice P. - PHOTO; Pres., Indiana WCTU (4/8/01); step-dt of Rachel Pierce (dec) (4/18/01); mbr Back Creek WCTU, still Pres., Indiana WCTU (5/16/02; 12/2/02); of 2 mi. N of Fmt.; wife of Robert; 9 Jul 1905 is her 57th birthday (7/11/05)

WILSON, Frances - dt John H. Wilson of Fmt. (1/30/02); - see E.L. BAKER

WILSON, Mrs. J. - mbr Fmt. Congregational Ch. (9/5/01)

WILSON, John - dec early settler of Fmt. area (1/13/05)

WILSON, John H. - 11 Jan 1883, is 1st person to telephone from Fmt. to Indianapolis (12/15/05)

WILSON, Jep - Secretary, Fmt. Fair Assoc. (1/12/04); s M/M Samuel C. Wilson; Deputy Postmaster, Fmt. (1/10/05)

WILSON, Lindsey - and wife are given party for their 10th wedding anniv 6 Dec 1904 (12/9/04); s M/M Samuel C. Wilson (1/10/05); 6 Dec 1894 m Effie Davis (12/15/05)

WILSON, Lindsay - s John and Mary Wilson (6/17/01); Supt., Fmt. Fair Assoc. (1/12/04); Pvt., unassigned, 33rd Ind. Inf. during CW (5/27/04; 5/26/05); and wife will celebrate 50th wedding anniv 1 Dec 1904 (11/25/04); age 72; m 13 Dec 1854 __ Davis (age 68), dt M/M Harvey Davis of 2.5 mi. SW of Fmt. (12/16/04)

WILSON, Lulu - see George BANNISTER

WILSON, Mrs. Mary - b 11 Dec 1822 (8/12/04; 8/15/05)

WILSON, Micajah - s John and Mary Wilson (6/17/01); Fmt. area early settler (1/13/05); age 80 (8/15/05); and wife were m April 1846 (10/20/05)

WILSON, Minnie (Long) - sister of Lizzie Long (dec); of near Deer Creek (12/9/04)

WILSON, N.A. - 3 Jan 1889 m Hattie Bixbey at Wabash (12/15/05); and wife celebrate 16th wedding anniv 1 Jan 1905 (12/30/04)

WILSON, Nancy - see Nancy (Wilson)DAUGHERTY

WILSON, Nathan D. - wife is Mary (11/20/03)

WILSON, Dr. Olive - of Paragould, AR is sister of Dr. Etta Charles of Summitville (11/3/05)

WILSON, Oz B. - 2 Nov 1905 m Olive, dt Mrs. Thurza Rittenhouse (11/7/05)

WILSON, Paxton - has not recovered his horse that was stolen Sat. (7/25/01); of N of Fmt.; 21 Nov 1903 m Mrs. Malinda Bradford (11/27/03)

WILSON, Russell Dean - b 13 Sep 1898; s Paxton and Amanda (Dean) Wilson; d 2 Aug 1903, funeral Back Creek Friends MH (8/4/03; 8/7/03)

WILSON, Saloma (Brown) - dt William A. and Margaret A. Brown; m [John H.] Wilson; dec (5/27/02)

WILSON, Samuel C. - s John and Mary Wilson (6/17/01); serv 1 term in Ind. State Legislature; and wife celebrate 38th wedding anniv 10 Jan 1905 (1/10/05); and wife are given party 9 Nov 1905 when each has a birthday (11/14/05)

WILSON, Sarah - see Cyrus BALDWIN

WILSON, Tom - dec; serv Pvt., Co. C, 89th Ind. Inf. during CW (5/26/05)

WILSON, Warren F. - mail carrier, Fmt. Rural Rte. #19 (8/8/02)

WILSON, Miss Zola - sister of Frances (Wilson) Baker (2/3/02); of Fmt.; grad Mershon Sch of Music, Marion 1902 (6/24/02); cashier, Bee Hive Cash Store (10/13/05)

WILTSEE, Beatrice - dt C.A. Wiltsee (7/26/04)

WILTSEE, Mrs. C.A. - dt Mrs. Elvira Small (1/28/01)

WILTSEE, Cassie E. - see Guy H. KELSAY

WILTSIE, Charles A. - 13 Jul 1902, his 12th birthday (7/15/02)

WILTSIE, Gertrude - mbr Fmt. WCTU (8/8/02); 1904 Earlham Coll grad (4/22/04); 11 Jun 1904, her 19th birthday (6/14/04)

WILTSIE/WILTSEE, Mrs. Martin - dt M/M Alex Burnworth of Huntington Co. (10/17/05)

WIMMER, Herman - 1901-02 tchr at Puckett Sch (Center Twp.#4) (1/9/02); 1903-05 tchr, Fmt. Twp. Sch #1 (9/4/03; 8/30/04); is att Terre Haute State Normal (3/25/04); 1904-05 Back Creek Sch tchr (8/30/04); resigns to become Principal, Mier Sch (10/11/04)

WIMPEY, Mollie (Rush) - of NC; dt Susan Rush (2/16/04)

WINANS, __ - b 13 Sep 1903; dt M/M Harry Winans (9/15/03)

WINANS, Myrtle A. - see William D. FRIEND

WINSLOW, __ - b this wk.; s M/M Kiah Winslow (6/13/02)

WINSLOW, __ - b 19 Sep 1904; dt M/M Jabe Winslow (9/23/04)

WINSLOW, Abigail (Cox) - of Hartford City; sister of Nathan, John W. and Tilman Cox (9/26/05)

WINSLOW, Albert 'Allie' - s Henry and Mary J. (Dillon); is serv US Army in Philippines (3/25/01; 6/27/01); is home from Army and P.I. (7/4/01)

WINSLOW, Alice - see Frank ELLIS

WINSLOW, Ancil - contracted Nathan Davidson to build a new 10-room house on his farm 2 mi. N of Fmt. (4/8/04); house framework is up and has a large 'porte cochere' on the north; a Weir Hot Air Furnace has been purchased from A.D. Bryan (5/31/04); and family will move into their new house 1 Sep 1904 (8/12/04)

WINSLOW, Mrs. Annie - mbr Radley WCTU (7/29/02)

WINSLOW, Mrs. Clint - of Fmt.; dt M/M James Ellis (1/21/01)

WINSLOW, Cynthia (Jay) - mbr Fmt. Friends (11/4/02); sister of Susan (Jay) Ratliff (3/25/04); Nixon Winslow's wife (10/21/04)

WINSLOW, Cyrus - serv Pvt., Co. D, 33rd Ind. Inf during CW (5/27/04; 5/26/05); and wife are spending winter in State Soldier's Home, Lafayette (10/24/05)

WINSLOW, Mrs. David - of Jonesboro; dt John Harris (dec) (4/22/04)

WINSLOW, Denny - Pres., Park Cemetery Lot Owner's Assn. (6/10/02)

WINSLOW, Donald - s Joe Winslow of N of Fmt. (1/31/05)

WINSLOW, Dottie - att Tudor Hall Coll 1904-05 (12/16/04)

WINSLOW, Ed L. - is a Fmt. sign painter (7/25/01)

WINSLOW, Edgar - mail carrier, Fmt. Rural Rte. #23 (8/8/02)

WINSLOW, Edna - mbr Fmt. WCTU (8/8/02); dt M/M Webster Winslow (10/14/04); sister of Mrs. Will Jones of W of Fmt. (4/18/05); att Earlham Coll 1905-06 (12/5/05)

WINSLOW, Elizabeth - see Calvin RUSH

WINSLOW, Ernest - of Dayton, OH; s M/M Ithamer Winslow (9/19/05)

WINSLOW, Evelyn - dt M/M Clinton Winslow; given party 25 Aug 1905 for her 9th birthday (8/29/05)

WINSLOW, Miss Gertrude - cashier, Flanagan Double Store (2/20/02)

WINSLOW, Grace - grad, Liberty Twp. Sch 1904 (4/19/04)

WINSLOW, Hannah Adeline - b Fmt. 2 Feb 1854; dt Dr. Philip and Mary Patterson; 12 Dec 1875 m William C. Winslow (dec 10 Feb 1895); mbr Fmt. M.E. Ch.; d 15 Mar 1904, bur Park Cem (3/18/04; 3/22/04)

WINSLOW, Harriett 'Hattie' - see Benjamin FRAZIER

WINSLOW, Henry - b NC 26 Jan 1829; s John and Elizabeth; 1840 came to IN; m Mary J. Dillon in 1854; d 18 Mar 1901, bur Park Cem (3/18/01; 3/21/01; 3/25/01); serv Pvt., unassigned, 32nd Ind. Inf. during CW (5/27/04; 5/26/05)

WINSLOW, Henry, Jr. 'Tobe' - CW vet (6/6/05)

WINSLOW, Hugh Walker - drove stage coach on the one-day trip between Anderson and Marion before local RR was built; he started the stage line in 1861 and ran it for 14 yrs.; used 'Governor Morton' type of coach; kept 8 horses for stage, using 4 at a time during winter; sometimes had to change horses in Alexandria; coach was built for 12 people but often carried 16 to 20; US government paid him $300 per yr. to carry mail (kept under driver's seat); final stage driving run was between Fmt. and Marion (11/28/01); 1879 has a livery stable (2/15/1879 as reprinted in 1/29/04); serv Pvt., 79th Ind. Inf. during CW (5/27/04; 5/26/05)

WINSLOW, Mrs. Ida - wife of Ancil; mbr Back Creek WCTU (5/16/02; 11/11/04)

WINSLOW, Irvin - grad Fmt. HS 1900 (12/19/05)

WINSLOW, Irwin - mail carrier, Fmt. Rural Rte. #23 (8/14/03)

WINSLOW, Ithamer - of Fmt.; brother of John M. Winslow of Fmt. and of O.H./H.O. Winslow of New York City (9/22/03)

WINSLOW, Jane (Henley) - b Randolph Co., NC; age 80; of Fmt.; 1860 came to Grant Co. (8/14/03); b 12 May 1823 (8/12/04); age 82 (8/15/05)

WINSLOW, Jasper E. - of Kansas City, MO; 24 Aug 1904 will m Effie, dt M/M C.R. Small; will live in Greenville, NC (8/23/04)

WINSLOW, Jesse - Dec 1890, died (12/15/05)

WINSLOW, John - 6 Dec 1894 is Asst. Cashier, Citizen's Bank (12/15/05)

WINSLOW, Jonathan P. - Feb 1879, bought T.J. Nixon's interest in flaxmill (12/15/05); Apr 1887 is an investor in Fmt. Mining Co. (1/17/05)

WINSLOW, Joseph, Jr. - age 15 (1/13/05); s Joe Winslow of N of Fmt. (1/31/05)

WINSLOW, Joseph - dec early settler of Fmt. area (1/13/05)

WINSLOW, Mrs. Joseph - of Jonesboro; age 55; d 23 Jul 1901 (7/25/01)

WINSLOW, Laura (Prickett) - ca Jun 1905 m Clinton Winslow, f of Fmt.; d 19 Dec 1905 (12/26/05)

WINSLOW, Leslie - age 14; s Jabe Winslow; his oil paintings are displayed at the Fmt. Fair (8/10/05)

WINSLOW, Levi - 1879 has a boarding house (2/15/1879 as reprinted 1/29/04)

WINSLOW, Lizzie - see Lizzy (Winslow) WRIGHT

WINSLOW, Lucy - mbr Fmt. WCTU (8/8/02); - see Will JONES

WINSLOW, Mary - age 85; widow of Milton Winslow (8/14/03); b 15 Jul 1818 (8/12/04); age 87 (8/15/05)

WINSLOW, Mary - att Tudor Hall Coll 1904-05 (12/16/04); 12 Dec 1905 is given party for her birthday (12/15/05)

WINSLOW, Milton - m Mary; author of Poems for Everybody; dec (8/14/03)

WINSLOW, Nixon - Treas., Fmt. Mining Co. (1/16/02); stockholder in Citizen's Exchange Bank (3/18/02); and wife (PHOTO) were m 25 Oct 1854 in Back Creek Friends MH (10/21/04; 10/28/04)

WINSLOW, Oliver - of Grand Rapids, MI; s M/M H. Walker Winslow (4/29/04)

WINSLOW, Ora E. (Winslow) - of Fmt.; dt Mrs. Jane (Henley) Winslow (8/14/03); Presiding Clerk, Fmt. Quarterly Meeting of Friends (9/2/04); 1881, grad Fmt. Twp. Sch (7/4/05)

WINSLOW, Otto L. - of Jonesboro; s M/M Robert Winslow of Elkhart; recently m Mayme Smith, dt M/M W.M. Smith of Wabash; will live in Jonesboro (1/5/04)

WINSLOW, Palmer - starts a glass factory in Columbus, OH (10/31/02); is moving his glass factory from Matthews to Louisville, KY (4/15/04)

WINSLOW, Mrs. Palmer - is sister of Miss Orpha Holding of Carthage (11/14/05)

WINSLOW, Philip - brother of Palmer Winslow (7/18/02); att Culver Military Acad 1904-05 (12/16/04)

WINSLOW, Robert - s M/M Hugh Walker Winslow; an engineer, Lake Shore RR (3/25/04)

WINSLOW, Ruth - dt Mrs. E.L. Winslow (8/19/02)

WINSLOW, Sallie - see Sallie (Winslow) STEPHENS

WINSLOW, Seth - dec early settler of Fmt. area (1/13/05)

WINSLOW, Susie J. - see Susie J. (Winslow) CASSELL

WINSLOW, Will - 1879 has nicest house in Fmt. (2/15/1879 as reprinted 1/29/04)

WINSLOW, Wilson - of Nebr.; s Mrs. Mary Winslow (10/11/04)

WINSLOW, Wint - of South Bend; s M/M H. Walker Winslow (7/29/04)

WINTERS, Hermenia - recently dec (12/26/01)

WISE, Henry - Fmt. Buggy Co. is erecting 2 Star Windmills on his farm E of Gas City (8/22/01)

WOMEN'S CHRISTIAN TEMPERANCE UNION (WCTU) -
BACK CREEK [FRIENDS] UNION - mbrs include Della Morris, Mrs. Bennett Shugart, Mrs. Eunice P. Wilson, Mrs. Frank Smith, Elvira Pierce, Mrs. Ancil Winslow, Ora Bogue, Mrs. Lin Wilson (5/16/02), Ida Winslow, Dorinda E. Wilson, Mattie C. Gibson, Effie Wilson, Della Kirkpatrick, Clara Knight, Jennie Stephenson (11/11/04); 20th anniv meeting of this union was held recently (11/25/04); 7 Nov 1905, 21st anniv meeting is held (11/7/05)
DEER CREEK [FRIENDS] UNION - was established 4 Feb 1891 (1/30/02)
FAIRMOUNT UNION - Elvira Small (dec), charter mbr (2/7/01); Ora D. (Luse) Osborn, mbr (2/25/02); Sina Latham, recently dec,

mbr (3/25/02); mbrs include Mrs. Enos Harvey, Ada Trader, Mary Harvey, Mary Carter, Ethel Pearson, Mary Bogue, Nettie Ware, Cleo Trader (6/3/02); Leora Bogue, Edna Winslow, Hattie Finney Carey, Lucy Winslow, Gertrude Wiltsie (8/8/02); Elmira C. Luce, Sallie Edgerton, Mary Dicks (9/16/02), Arletta Harshbarger (3/1/04)
FOWLERTON UNION - Mrs. Nettie Ware, President (7/29/04)
HADLEY (LITTLE RIDGE) UNION - mbrs include Belle Wright (dec), Sadie B. Harvey, Ruth H. Ratliff (10/31/02), Dora Kimes (dec) (4/29/04), Mrs. Dora Whitely (6/13/05)
INDIANA WCTU - Eunice P. Wilson, Pres. (4/8/01; 2/13/02; 5/16/02); Mattie Cammack-Gibson, Recording Sect. (4/8/01)
RADLEY/LINWOOD UNION - mbrs include Mrs. Sadie B. Harvey (5/13/02), Mrs. Annie Winslow, Mrs. Alice Ballenger (7/29/02), Mrs. I.N. Seale (2/5/04), Mrs. Hiram Harvey (8/23/04)

WOOD, __ - b 26 Oct 1903; s M/M Harry Wood (10/27/03)

WOOD, __ - b 9 Jul 1905; s M/M Harry Wood (7/11/05)

WOOD, __ - b 14 Jul 1905; dt M/M Glenn Wood (7/18/05)

WOOD, Elizabeth - of Liberty Twp.; age 72; often drives her horse and buggy to Fmt. (11/17/05)

WOOD, Harry D. - Director, Fmt. YMCA (6/6/02); prop., Model Grocery Store on E. Washington St.; 21 Aug 1902 m Mary O. Lindley (8/15/02; 8/22/02)

WOOD, Marion - Pvt., Co. K, 8th Ind. Inf. and Sergt., Co. K, 153rd Ind. Inf. (5/27/04; 5/26/05); settled in Fmt. ca 1865 (11/7/05)

WOOD, Mrs. Perry - dt Simon Clarke, dec (8/28/03)

'WOODSIDE' - near Fmt.; home of Gurney and Alice (Young) Lindley (4/4/02)

WOOLEN, Murton - 1901-02 East Branch Sch tchr (8/19/01); organized basket supper held last night in [Friends] Back Creek Sch for FFA Athletic Association (2/17/02); of Cincinnati, OH; s M/M Ed Woolen (6/24/04); 1904-05 att Cincinnati, OH Sch of Veterinary Surgeons (9/13/04)

WOOLEN, William - b 5 Sep 1818 (8/12/04); 5 Sep 1904 given party for his 86th birthday (9/9/04); age 86 (8/15/05)

WOOLWEAVER, Lydia E. - see Charles C. LYONS

WOOTEN, Rev. A.S. - new pastor, Fmt. M.E. Ch. (4/18/02); is new pastor, Angola M.E. Ch. (4/15/04)

WOOTEN, Florence - and Georgina are dts Rev. A.S. Wooten (7/18/02)

WOOTEN, Isaac - is a brick mason (3/18/02); is laying bricks for Odd Fellows Hall (10/24/02); 26 Nov 1903 m Mrs. Elsie D. Wright (12/1/03); 17 Feb 1904 is his 56th birthday (2/19/04)

WOOTEN, Mrs. Isaac - d 2 Aug 1901, bur Park Cem (8/5/01)

WRIGHT TILE FACTORY - of 3 mi. SW of Fmt.; owned by Asa K. Wright; factory destroyed by fire 27 Aug 1901 (8/29/01); will be rebuilt (9/2/01); filed for incorporation as A.K. Wright Tile Co. (10/21/01)

WRIGHT, __ - b recently; s M/M Loraine Wright (10/2/03)

WRIGHT, Miss Addie - substitute tchr, Grant Sch (4/18/05); 1905-06 Liberty Twp. Sch tchr (7/28/05)

WRIGHT, Amy - see Amy (Wright) HARVEY

WRIGHT, Asa K. - contracted to re-ditch and clean out Bell Creek in NW Liberty Twp (2/14/01); will rebuild his burned tile factory (9/2/01)

WRIGHT, Bell (Story) - of Wright's Station, 2 mi. W of Fmt.; b Cass Co., MI 13 Nov 1854; dt Chauncy and Louisa Story (both dec); m Asa K. Wright 3 Mar 1875; mbr Hadley WCTU; d 12 Oct 1902 (10/14/02; 10/21/02; 10/31/02)

WRIGHT, Cerena - see Roy JAY

WRIGHT, Mrs. Clayton - of near Little Ridge; dt Mahlon Harvey (8/22/05)

WRIGHT, David - f Fmt. restaurant owner; 7 Jul 1901 d in Summitville (7/8/01)

WRIGHT, E. Leona - 1901-02 FFA music tchr (8/19/01); 11 Dec 1903 is given birthday party (12/15/03)

WRIGHT, Mrs. Elsie - see Isaac WOOTEN

WRIGHT, Grace Merrie - dt Elwood and Rose Wright; d Aug 1895 (1/13/02)

WRIGHT, Harvey - 1905-06 Liberty Twp. Sch tchr (7/28/05)

WRIGHT, Joseph - serv Pvt., Co. I, 63rd Ind. Inf. during CW (5/27/04; 5/26/05)

WRIGHT, Julian - serv Co. K, 130th Ind. Inf. during CW (5/27/04; 5/26/05)

WRIGHT, Lizzie (Winslow) - of Neosha Falls, KS; dt H. Walker Winslow (5/30/01)

WRIGHT, Mary (Harvey) - wife of Clayton Wright of near Little Ridge; dt Mahlon and Zilpha (Hadley) Harvey (8/22/05; 8/25/05)

WRIGHT, Rev. Milton - is building new house on his farm near Fowlerton (5/6/04)

WRIGHT, Mrs. Norman - of North Grove; sister of Mrs. Harry Stephens of Poonah, India (7/5/04)

WRIGHT, Orville - b 10 Sep 1893; s Elwood and Rose; d 7 Jan 1902 (1/13/02)

WRIGHT, Vernie - grad, Liberty Twp. Sch 1904 (4/19/04)

WUCHNER, Adolph - manager, VanCamp Window Glass Factory, Matthews (10/13/03)

WYCHOFF, Arthur - 1903-04 Grant Sch student (1/5/04)

YERKY, Blanche - employee, Citizens Telephone Exchange (11/29/04)

YOCUM, Osha (Starr) - dt M/M C.A. Starr; 14 Jun 1905 m Harry Yocum of Brazil, IN; will live in Brazil, IN (6/16/05)

YOUNG, Alice - see Gurney LINDLEY

YOUNG, Charles - 20 Jul 1905 m Ethel, dt M/M Tom Hasty (7/21/05); s M/M Ellison Young of W of Summitville (7/25/05)

YOUNG, Mrs. Robert - dt Dudley and Mary Stout (6/27/05)

YOUNG, Will H. - of Marion; 1901-02 Liberty Twp. Dist. #7 (Center) Sch tchr (9/5/01); moves to Radley (11/19/01); 1903-04 tchr, Liberty Twp. Sch #4 (9/11/03)

ZEEK, Cora - see Elmer KIRKWOOD

ZEIGLER, Clyde - and family move to Marion (12/18/03)

ZEIGLER, F.B. - a Director, Hoosier Mining Co. (7/4/01); and family to move to OK (11/21/01), and are moved to OK (12/5/01); one of 1st owners of f Big Four Window Glass Factory (4/18/05)

Other Heritage Books by Ralph D. Kirkpatrick, Ph.D.

Back Creek Friends Cemetery Burial Records
Revised Edition

Burial Records of Four Grant County, Indiana
Quaker Cemeteries

Local History and Genealogy Abstracts from
Fairmount News, *Fairmount, Indiana, 1888–1900*

Local History and Genealogy Abstracts from
Fairmount News, *Fairmount, Indiana, 1901–1905*

Local History and Genealogical Abstracts from
Jonesboro and Gas City, Indiana Newspapers, 1889–1920

Local History and Genealogy Abstracts from
Marion, Indiana Newspapers, 1865–1870

Local History and Genealogy Abstracts from
Marion, Indiana Newspapers, 1871–1875

Local History and Genealogy Abstracts from
Marion, Indiana Newspapers, 1876–1880

Local History and Genealogy Abstracts from
Marion, Indiana Newspapers, 1881–1885

Local History and Genealogical Abstracts from
Upland, Indiana Newspapers, 1891–1901

www.ingramcontent.com/pod-product-compliance
Lightning Source LLC
Chambersburg PA
CBHW050809160426
43192CB00010B/1689